W9-BYB-932

The Reckoning

Canadian Prisoners of War in the Great War

Nathan M. Greenfield

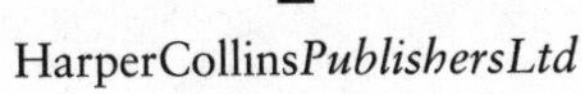

HarperCollins*PublishersLtd*

Also by Nathan M. Greenfield

The Forgotten

The Damned

Baptism of Fire

The Battle of the St. Lawrence

To Micheline,
who is always there to make me smile and my ideal reader.

And to my parents, Anita and Irving,
who taught me that no Sunday breakfast could
be complete without the words "Look it up" and
the subsequent rush to the dictionary or encyclopedia.

The Reckoning

Published by HarperCollins Publishers Ltd

First edition

Map on p. 41 by Dawn Huck.

HarperCollins books may be purchased for educational, business, or sales promotional use through our Special Markets Department.

HarperCollins Publishers Ltd
2 Bloor Street East, 20th Floor
Toronto, Ontario, Canada
M4W 1A8

www.harpercollins.ca

Library and Archives Canada Cataloguing in Publication information is available upon request.

ISBN 978-1-44343-262-7

Printed and bound in the United States
RRD 9 8 7 6 5 4 3 2 1

In the beginning was the Act.

—*Faust* (Goethe)

CONTENTS

A Note to the Reader

A decade ago, in my book *Baptism of Fire*, which tells the story of the Canadians' desperate battle in the days following the first gas attack at Ypres on 22 April 1915, I briefly wrote about how Private Nathan Rice and Private John Finnimore and Major Peter Anderson were captured. And then, like the generals who speak of "closing down" a battle, I ended that book with the end of the Canadians' involvement at Ypres.

My next book, *The Damned*, was different. Every one of the men I interviewed about the battle they fought in between 8 and 25 December 1941 in Hong Kong had been a prisoner of war for more than three and a half years. Men such as Company Sergeant Major George Macdonell and Private Jean-Paul Daillan taught me that although the shooting may have stopped on this or that patch of earth, for prisoners of war, the battle continued for long years. This lesson was underscored by bomb aimer Ian MacDonald, who was shot down in France in April 1942, and the dozens of other men I interviewed (and whose memoirs I read) for *The Forgotten: Canadian POWs, Evaders and Escapers in Europe, 1939–1945*;

some of these men were imprisoned in the same camps discussed here. The book now in your hands picks up Rice's, Finnimore's, and Anderson's stories and those of almost four thousand other Canadians who raised their hands in surrender but remained men at war.

In order to follow the warp and woof of these men's lives behind the barbed wire—and often beyond it on the run—I have again chosen to tell this story chronologically. The uniforms the captured men wore in the years after Ypres may have remained the same, but the army they served in changed radically in the structure, armaments and tactics it used and in its professionalism. To show what sort of news from the front recently captured men whispered to their comrades, I have sketched some of these changes. Similarly, since the letters that came into the camps could not contain any political news from Canada, I sketch what sort of news recently captured men would have known about their Dominion across the sea.

* * *

THE CANADIANS (and the British army they served under) and the Germans reckoned distance and gun calibre differently. I follow each army's usage. Thus, the Canadians speak in terms of yards, miles and pounds (as in a fifteen-pound gun, so named because of the weight of the shell), while the Germans speak of metres and classified shells by millimetres.

In quotations, the spelling of German terms and place names has been standardized.

To provide an idea of the value of monetary figures, at times I have indicated today's equivalents in parentheses: $20 ($211).

Prologue

26–28 April 1915

On the morning of 26 April 1915, a wireless station on Long Island, New York, relayed a communiqué from Berlin to the Associated Press in Manhattan, from where it was sent on to Canadian newswires. A few hours later, the editor of the *Winnipeg Evening Tribune*, Robert L. Richardson, reacted to the cable by penning a headline quite different from the one he had written two days earlier. Then he had extolled the martial prowess of the Canadians in saving Ypres on the 22nd after the first poison gas attack in history had broken the French on the Canadians' left. This second headline, which reported that a thousand Canadians had been taken prisoner, sat uncomfortably close to rotogravure pictures of the "Heroes of Langemarck" (Ypres), which Richardson had originally intended to dominate that afternoon's front page.

In the days after the gas attack, communiqué writers in London and editors in Canada misunderstood what had happened at Ypres. On 24 April, within hours of the Germans' unleashing a gas attack aimed squarely at the Canadians on Gravenstafel Ridge, a few miles northwest of Ypres, the *Manitoba Free Press* published a communiqué referring to the first gas attack. It began with "French soldiers forced to retire before fumes of asphyxiating gas" before stating, "No grave consequences from gas."[1] These latter words were pure spin. The army knew that hundreds of French colonial troops had died of asphyxiation; that the unlucky Canadians died gasping for breath, their faces the colour of mahogany; and that some had survived by breathing through urine-soaked handkerchiefs.

On the 28th the *Globe* published stories referencing both the first attack and the one on the 24th, headed by the words "Asphyxiating gas" and "Thousands of Canadians killed and wounded." Ottawa, however, the paper reported, counselled patience until official casualty lists arrived. At the same time, the paper poured cold water on the story by noting that official despatches from London made no mention of "such a large capture."[2] The names of some of the captured men were, however, already known. That same afternoon the *Winnipeg Evening Tribune* reprinted a cable sent by Colonel G. N. Cory, then serving with the Headquarters of the 3rd British Division, that arrived at his parents' house in Toronto: "Bob prisoner." Of the almost 1,400 who had been in German hands for days, Major Robert Cory (15th Battalion), Colonel Cory's brother, was the first to be publicly named.

Introduction

Names changed, none more quickly than that of Serbia, the pre-war "Servia" being too close to *servile* to be the name of a British ally. In May 1916, a referendum would change the name of Berlin, Ontario, to Kitchener. The British (and effectively Canadian) secretary of state for war, Lord Herbert Kitchener, drowned a month later, and is best remembered for a poster on which Lord Kitchener's disembodied stern face and strongly pointing right hand sit atop the words "Your Country Needs You." A year later, the royal house of Queen Victoria—who, though dead for more than a decade, still seemed to reign, not least on schoolroom maps that showed the world girdled in British Empire pink—had been restyled from Saxe-Coburg and Gotha to the House of Windsor.

And names were mispronounced. The Marne, where Paris was saved from invasion in September 1914, was easy. So was Mons, where the British had stymied the Germans a month earlier. Dunkirk, the last port in Belgium still in Allied hands after the so-called "race to the sea" (which ended with trenches running six hundred miles from the North Sea to Switzerland), was spelled Dunkerque on the French Canadian sides of the Ottawa and Red rivers. Neither side of Canada's linguistic divide could get their tongues around Ploegsteert or Ieper. In October 1914, the flower of the British army was destroyed at Ieper while stopping the Germans. Among the survivors of the battle that Germans called the *Kindermord*, meaning massacre of the innocents (that is, young soldiers, many recruits from universities), was a despatch runner named Adolf Hitler. In April 1915 the Canadians would fight their first battle just outside this town, known in French as Ypres. "Wipers," as many Canadians following the British called it, was where in late April 1915 poison gas was first used on the battlefield, and where more than 2,000 Canadians fell and 1,383 were taken prisoner. Letters home from English-speaking Canadians testify to the orthographic challenges posed by Gravenstafel Ridge, Flers-Courcelette and Passchendaele, which also taxed newspaper compositors; mercifully, Vimy did not.

The languid summer of 1914 was not quite the holiday from history remembered by such men and women as novelist Ralph Connor (Rev. Charles Gordon) and Ottawa socialite Ethel Chadwick. Both recalled gorgeous weather up at lakes near Kenora and the Gatineau Hills, respectively. The British and Europeans, too, enjoyed what many recalled as the perfect summer.

Sepia memories aside, in the months before Gordon himself and tens of thousands of other men signed their Attestation Papers, the daily papers were filled with news, little of it good. The assassination of the heir to the Austro-Hungarian throne, Archduke Franz Ferdinand, seized attention for a few days around Dominion Day (1 July) 1914 and holds our attention still. In the first half of 1914, however, the Irish Home Rule debate roiling in London threatened to split Prime Minister Herbert Asquith's governing Liberals, and to some portended the despatch of an expeditionary force to Ulster in Northern Ireland. Closer to home, the fledgling Royal Canadian Navy had gone into action in May—against the *Komagata Maru*, which entered Burrard Inlet with nothing more dangerous than 376 Indians from the subcontinent. Like all British subjects, under the law of the day, they were legally free to move about the Empire. The RCN's success in preventing all but twenty-four of the passengers from landing in Canada warmed the heart of the suffragette Emily Murphy, who also campaigned against the Yellow Menace and drugs such as "marihuana."

In Winnipeg, the city that just a few years earlier had been the fastest growing in the British Empire, was on its heels, no matter what civic boosters said.[1] Words were cold comfort to the thousands of railway and other workers who lost their jobs because grain could now be shipped more cheaply via the recently completed Panama Canal. The blue skies under which novelist and social activist Nellie McClung's family splashed in the waters of Lake Winnipeg meant drought on the prairies, further depressing the economy of the city that had viewed itself as the next St. Louis.

For years, Militia Minister Sam Hughes had fairly delighted in predicting war with Germany. Others disagreed. In 1898, a Russian-Polish financier named Ivan S. Bloch wrote a book entitled *Is War Now Impossible?*, to which he answered yes. Bloch noted that such new implements of war as machine guns would make manoeuvring impossible, resulting in a stalemate, the cost of which in both financial and human terms could not be sustained; he was half right. A decade later, the British writer Norman Angell argued in *The Grand Illusion* that Europe's economies were so integrated that war between the major powers was impossible. Angell's economic arguments were no more predictive than Bloch's. Given the thousands attending the Peace Year exhibition in Toronto, it is hardly surprising that Canadian editorialists quoted from these books to argue that what diplomats called a General European War was not in the offing, even as the political temperature in Europe heightened after the assassination.

True, there had been two wars in the Balkans in the past two years. For almost eight months in 1912, Servia, Greece, Bulgaria and Montenegro allied against the Ottoman Turks. A year later, Bulgaria attacked Servia and Greece, while Montenegro, Turkey and Romania attacked Bulgaria. Great power diplomacy succeeded in keeping these wars in the Balkans, where, as Connor harrumphed in his autobiography (in British imperial fashion), killing one another was the "chief outdoor sport of the semi-civilized peoples of those Central European countries."[2] In 1905 and again in 1911, Britain and Germany had appeared to gird for war over issues pertaining to Morocco but stepped back each time. Indeed, though these crises were in part due to Kaiser Wilhelm's desire for Germany to have its place under the imperial sun, one of the names on the list being considered for the 1914 Nobel Peace Prize was Friedrich Wilhelm Viktor Albrecht von Preußen of the House of Hohenzollern. He had just celebrated his twenty-fifth anniversary on the German throne without having ever drawn his sword, save for when German troops were sent along with French and British to put down the Boxer Rebellion in China in 1900.

* * *

One of the reasons people recalled the war's breaking as a natural disaster, likened by one French newspaper to a "bolt of lightning," is that Europe seemed so normal.[3] The Kaiser had left for his annual Baltic cruise on schedule. For their part, Parisians were enthralled by the murder trial of Madame Henriette Cailleux. Though she had pulled the trigger, Cailleux was acquitted of killing Gaston Calmette, the publisher of *Le Figaro*. He left behind letters showing that Cailleux's husband, Joseph, the French minister of finance, whom Calmette opposed, had had an affair with Henriette while still married to his first wife.

Behind the scenes, however, the international temperature was rising. Rightly convinced that the assassins were linked to the government in Belgrade, Vienna demanded that Servia allow Austro-Hungarian investigators to operate on its territory. Bolstered by the famous "blank cheque" received from Berlin, the hawks in Emperor Franz Joseph's cabinet (who saw Servian independence as a threat to the empire's Slavic lands) finally carried the day. After Austrian ships began bombarding Belgrade on 28 July, Russia made good on its promise to defend the south Slavs. Russian war plans, however, involved mobilizing against not just Austria but also its ally, Germany. This caused Germany to mobilize against Russia, which in turn caused Russia's ally, France, to mobilize against Germany.

Even as Rosa Luxemburg, one of the leaders of Germany's Socialist Party, and Canadian papers considered the Kaiser a force for peace, his war minister, Helmuth von Moltke, set the Schlieffen plan in motion. To avoid the nightmare of an extended two-front war, the plan called for a holding action in the east against Russia while Germany attacked France, though not through the belt of forts around Verdun. Rather, German armies were to sweep east through neutral Belgium before turning south to envelop Paris, as had been done in just over a month in 1871 during the Franco-Prussian War.

As the guns roared, on 31 July the *Manitoba Free Press* said with confidence that "Britain will not be involved." Prime Minister Sir Robert Borden and his cabinet were of the same mind, which explains why he remained on holiday in the Muskokas. Even Asquith stated that Britain could remain aloof. He was only vaguely aware that as France edged closer to war with Germany, Britain was moving closer too, for under the *Entente Cordiale* signed in 1904, French war plans called for a British Expeditionary Force (BEF) to fill out the French lines toward Belgium.

Then Germany invaded Belgium, prompting Rudyard Kipling to write in his diary, "Incidentally, Armageddon begins."[4]

Along with crass jingoism, cant about manliness and war and the need to smash Prussian autocracy (all of which make for difficult reading today), Canadian papers provided a surprisingly legalistic explanation for why Britain had to go to war and for Canada's participation in it.[5] Both of these arguments are present in the memoirs of POWs and other soldiers. By invading Belgium, Germany violated the Treaty of London, negotiated a quarter-century before Confederation, in which Prussia (and hence, its successor state the German Reich), France and Britain recognized the independence and guaranteed the neutrality of Belgium. No one in Canada knew, of course, that some in the British cabinet had been hoping for just such an invasion because it would provide the *casus belli* that put

Britain on the moral high ground. Editors across Canada quickly seized this point, arguing that Britain and Canada had gone to war to protect the rights of weaker nations. Canada had negligible ties to Belgium. But it was at war without even a vote from the Parliament in Ottawa because Britain controlled the Empire's foreign and military policies.[6] As then prime minister Sir Wilfrid Laurier explained during the 1910 debate about the establishment of the Royal Canadian Navy, in wartime the RCN would operate under the Royal Navy because, "When Britain is at war, Canada is at war. There is no distinction."[7]

As the clock ticked down to midnight in London on August 3, when Britain's ultimatum to Germany to withdraw from Belgium was to expire (and, thus, to war), Sam Hughes growled to Brigadier-General Charles F. Winter that "England was going to skunk it" (betray Belgium). He ordered Winter to pull the Union Jack down from the flagpole at 28–20 Slater Street in Ottawa, but Winter tactfully ignored the order until he could talk Sir Sam down from high dudgeon. A few hours after Britain's ultimatum expired, the Winnipeg Rifles paraded through their namesake city. A few days later, Winnipeg's city council donated several hundred tons of flour to Britain. Later, during the Conscription Crisis of 1917, few English Canadians would remember that in Montreal and St. Boniface, Manitoba, French Canadian crowds sang "La Marseillaise" and "God Save the King." After barely escaping from Alsace—where he had gone to study the survival of the French language in what had been part of France until the Franco-Prussian War—the fiery nationalist Henri Bourassa, who had broken from Laurier over the establishment of the RCN, supported the war. This was a position he would soon reverse.[8]

The crowds—in Paris, Berlin, London, Montreal and, for that matter, small-town Canada—were not completely spontaneous.[9] People had been conditioned to come to newspaper offices for news, so the pictures of crowds splashed across the newspapers of the day have something of the air of being sent from central casting. In Canada, support for the war was strongest in the cities and weakest in villages, where the traditional fear of sons being torn from the family farm ran high. Because most French Quebecers still lived in small towns and villages, the economy of which was largely agrarian, French Quebecers were less primed than English Canadians to troop to the colours.[10] A further reason for French Quebecers' reticence, of course, was their emotional disconnect from the British Empire.

Immigrants to Western Canada, especially German and Austro-Hungarian, were noticeably cool to the war. Four days before the burning of the great library at Louvain, Belgium, *Der Nordwestern*, published in Winnipeg, praised the humanity of German soldiers.[11] The Ukrainian archbishop in Canada called for the faithful belonging to the Ukrainian Catholic Church to support Austria-Hungary (Ukraine being a rather unwilling part of the Austro-Hungarian Empire aside). However, the internment of 5,441 Ruthenians, as Ukrainians were then called, under the War Measures Act as enemy aliens was a vast overreaction. As well, 3,138 Germans and Austrians who either lived in Canada or crewed German ships that were in Canadian ports when the war broke out were interned. Among the Germans who managed to escape to the neutral United States was an Ottawa wine dealer named Joachim von Ribbentrop, who later became Hitler's foreign minister.

Not every man who joined up was moved entirely by patriotism, as Private Harry Howland was when he took the King's shilling in

Victoria, B.C. "Love of adventure, and a desire to see the world" and not patriotism were the reasons Private Mervyn Simmons, a carpenter, gave for signing his Attestation Papers.[12] Lance Corporal Jack O'Brien, a surveyor in Fernie, B.C., joined up after telling his friend Steve, "Oh hell! If you're going I'm going too"; his friend had worked in Germany and disliked the Germans intensely.[13] Private Arthur Gibbons echoed his friend's lie that he had served two years in the Bedfordshire Yeomanry. The recruiting sergeant was more than willing to overlook the fact that the diminutive clerk for the Toronto Electric Light Company had a chest that did not quite meet the measurements decreed by Sir Sam Hughes. Howland, Simmons and Gibbons were all captured at Second Ypres, while O'Brien was captured on the Somme in 1916.

* * *

Canada's pledge of three Dreadnought battleships would have been more helpful had Canada actually had any of these cutting-edge ships of the day to lend Britain. HMCS *Rainbow* and HMCS *Niobe*, two over-aged cruisers now placed under Royal Navy command, were welcome, but they hardly changed the balance of power in the North Pacific. Nor did the two submarines that Sir Richard MacBride, British Columbia's premier, bought without Ottawa's approval and had spirited out of Washington State. Neither submarine saw action. No doubt to suffragette Emily Murphy's chagrin, Canada's west coast was policed by Britain's Asian ally, Japan.

What really mattered to Britain was men. Canada promised 30,000, a division, almost immediately. Sam Hughes was as fond of overblown rhetoric as the Kaiser: both compared recruitment to trooping across the land with a fiery cross as in days of old. Later, Hughes would promise another 50,000 and another 50,000; ultimately, more than 600,000 men would serve in the Canadian Expeditionary Force (CEF).

Many in the First Canadian Contingent had military experience, and some Canadian officers had earned Victoria Crosses and other awards during the Boer War. But, save for the gunners praised by British general Sir John French, in 1910, no one could claim that Canada was prepared for war; French commanded the British Expeditionary Force that the Canadians joined in France in 1915. Hughes considered Canada's tiny army "bar room loafers" and quickly volunteered them to do garrison duty in Jamaica.[14] Sir Sam interfered with training at Valcartier, Quebec, itself a manifestation of the "Mad mullah of Canada," as one officer called Hughes in a letter home.[15] The base was seemingly conjured out of nowhere (by the wood-baron-like Price family) when Hughes decided that the existing plans to gather the troops at Petawawa, Ontario, would not do. The minister revelled in climbing down from his horse and showing "his boys" how to use a bayonet. He promoted and demoted with abandon; on one particular day the 2nd Battalion had five commanding officers. One noted historian has argued, however, that given the underdeveloped Canadian military, it is not clear that anyone could have done any better.[16]

During the winter of 1914/15, the Canadians were billeted on England's Salisbury Plain, where frequent rain played havoc with the training schedule. One storm blew down the paymaster's tent, scattering five-shilling notes, with which the men later bought beer in local taverns or wet canteens.

Despite the mud that dissolved the men's boots (dubbed "Sham shoes" in honour of Sam Hughes), the rain that leaked through their bell tents and the Oliver webbing that cut into the men's armpits (which was replaced by webbing of British design), at least some battalions received training in up-to-date tactics. Pamphlets such as *Some Notes on the Minor Tactics of Trench Warfare* underscored how out of place was Hughes's notion that all a soldier needed to be successful was the ability to "pink the enemy every time."[17] Dreams of glorious cavalry or bayonet charges were equally out of place; what mattered was close cooperation between infantry and engineers in a war that resembled a medieval siege stretching across half the continent. The men of the 4th Battalion had the added advantage of being able to ask the author of *Rapid Training of Company for War* how to square the seemingly endless series of route marches, set battle formations and musketry training with the admonition that "the soldier is now taught to use his brains and to take advantage of cover" and that a key role of the officers was "to foster initiative among the junior ranks."[18] The pamphlet's author, Lieutenant-Colonel Arthur Percival Birchall (on loan from the British army), commanded the battalion.

* * *

WHEN THE WAR BEGAN, Canada possessed neither an armaments industry capable of supporting a field army nor the social welfare infrastructure necessary to care for soldiers' families and wounded, returned soldiers or to send succour to prisoners of war. Each required money and expertise. Within days of the outbreak of the war, Hughes appointed a number of industrialists (and some

Conservative party cronies) to the Shell Committee. Despite having done some good work, the committee was unable to organize production of shells in the massive quantities needed. In November 1915, Borden appointed J. W. Flavelle to head the Imperial Munitions Board, which answered to London, and reorganized Canadian military production. By the end of 1915, Canada had shipped only 5.3 million shells; in 1916, that number would rise to 19.9 million and in 1917, to 23.7 million.[19]

The war thoroughly changed the country's finances. The 1914 budget called for the government in Ottawa to spend a total of $185 million ($4 billion), with $11.1 million ($235 million) to be spent on the militia. By early October 1915, the war was costing approximately one million dollars a day. The government's revenue of $163 million ($3.5 billion)—chiefly customs, excise taxes, railway fees and postage on the almost three-quarters of a billion letters and packages sent—was not enough. Because of its own needs, Britain, Canada's traditional source of capital, could no longer supply capital to the Dominion.

On 7 October 1915, Finance Minister Sir Thomas White told the Toronto Board of Trade that because of Canada's improving economy (due largely to British orders for food and war material), the country would be able to finance its own war effort. A month later, the government's first war loan, of $50 million ($1 billion), was so oversubscribed that the government netted $100 million; White assigned the extra $50 million to the Imperial Munitions Board.

In 1916, to pay for munitions, field an army of 500,000 men and pay each Canadian POW a shilling a week, another war loan raised the equivalent of $1.9 billion in today's funds.[20] Yet even this was not enough. White placed a tax on business profits: 50 cents on a barrel of apples (almost $10 in today's money) and one-half cent on a gallon of oil. In 1917, Sir Robert Borden's Conservatives brought in a "temporary" income tax on salaries over $2,000 ($33,660) a year as well as a graduated tax on higher incomes.

Today welfare is largely a provincial responsibility. Prior to the First World War, by contrast, "relief," as it was known, was a local responsibility. Local governments were, however, unable to assume the burden of helping soldiers' families in straitened circumstances. To fill this void, the federal and provincial governments chartered organizations such as the Manitoba Patriotic Fund, which, though it received some provincial funding, also raised money as a charity. British Columbia's fund raised the equivalent of $25.5 million in February 1917.

Within months of their husbands going off to war, tens of thousands of Canadian wives were opening their lives to people other than their churches' leaders. Women like Lady Nanton, the driving force behind Manitoba's Patriotic Fund, "visited the homes of recipients to ensure that the money was needed." For the class satirized in plays like Oscar Wilde's *The Importance of Being Earnest*, a piece that was well known across Canada because of performances by amateur thespians, "need" was linked to the concept of the deserving poor. Hence, Nanton and other authorities inquired into the morals of the women in "the lower orders." A Mrs. Curran of Toronto, for example, was inscribed in the Canadian Patriotic Fund's "black book" of disgraced wives—"not only on account of her German origin, but on account of her character." In 1916, pushed by the number of common law relationships recognized by the Militia Ministry (which allowed the assignation of pay to a common law wife), the Canadian Patriotic Fund began making payments to common law wives. A year later, Herbert Ames, member of Parliament for a poor Montreal riding and muckraking journalist, thundered, "When the soldier goes to the front, he leaves his wife and family, usually, in trust to the government and the Patriotic Fund. Now if the woman becomes immoral and forgets the care of her children and becomes a drunkard, and those children are likely to starve or run wild, the country owes an obligation to the children as well as the wife."[21] Somewhat surprisingly, the funds' managers agreed.

While the patriotic funds helped the families of many POWs, all POWs were helped by prisoner of war committees and the Red Cross. Indeed, were it not for the food parcels these organizations sent, thousands of POWs would have suffered from diseases associated with malnutrition and many could have died. Since the earliest days of the war, Canadians had contributed to the Khaki Prisoner's Relief fund to help British POWs. In remembrance of her son, Guy Melfort Drummond, who died at Ypres, Lady Grace Julia Drummond devoted herself to providing succour for the Dominion's prisoners of war. She led the Red Cross in establishing the machinery to send letters and parcels to the prisoners and then to raising money for food parcels. Tobacco could be sent, as could remittances made by money order to the POW's account in Germany. Parcels could not contain newspapers or magazines.

Like the patriotic funds, POW committees were charities that raised their own money. In October 1915, the committee in Chilliwack, B.C., received twelve donations, the smallest being for $2.50, the cost of maintaining a POW for one month. In early August 1916, the Duchess of Connaught's Prisoner of War Fund transferred $1,000 to London, bringing its total to $15,225 (almost $300,000 in today's money). Just over three weeks later, the *Vancouver World* praised the city's Prisoner of War Committee for raising more than $5,000 (much of it small collections from places like Spencer's meat department, which raised $3.88).[22] Schoolchildren donated pennies, nickels and dimes. On 19 August 1916, at the bottom of the advertisement in the *Winnipeg Free Press* for a two-night fundraiser put on by the 141st Bull Moose Battalion Band for the Prisoner's Fund, was the plea: "Maybe you cannot fight but surely you can help ease the suffering of some poor prisoner." By publishing the name of each local donor, the papers in different parts of Canada created a direct link between them and the prisoners.

For the prisoners' part, the importance of this link is made clear in an article published in the *Free Press* on 11 April 1917. The article's curious title, "Eyes Down! Look In!," meant a consignment of parcels from the POWs' loved ones was ready to be distributed. Standardized parcels contained much-needed bully beef, Oxo cubes, sugar, razor blades and soap. But sentimental ties to family, friends and unnamed civilians who contributed money to prisoner of war committees mattered to POWs. "There is no nice parcel packed with the thoughtful care of a loving mother: no pleasant surprises" such as her homemade jam, wrote one POW. The POWs, who, of course, had no way of knowing how the creaking system had to function, had more personal concerns. They worried that now that they were not preparing parcels, "those at home [who] cared for us through the years 1914–15–16 . . . will [still] think of us as often as we do of them."[23]

* * *

MEN SUCH AS LIEUTENANT WILLIAM D. HARDING, who signed his Attestation Papers in July 1916 and arrived in France in February 1917, and who was captured at Vimy, would have known much more about the conditions they were going to face in the POW camps than the men captured at Ypres. While training in Canada and Britain, and when time allowed in the trenches and in rear areas, soldiers were inveterate readers of the newspapers. In Canada, news stories on fundraising activities routinely reported on the poor conditions in the camps. Some stories originated with the Red Cross, some came from American ambassador James Gerard (who, until Washington broke off relations with Germany in February 1917, acted as the "Protecting Power" for British POWs), and some from grievously wounded POWs who had been repatriated. Until mid-1917, Canadian soldiers in the field gleaned news of the camps from British papers; even when the men were in the trenches, some papers arrived only a day after being published in England.

Accordingly, Harding and men such as Private William N. O'Toole, who survived Ypres only to be captured at Amiens in August 1918, had the opportunity to hear how the Germans were violating the 1907 Hague Treaty on the treatment of prisoners of war. As does its more famous successor, the Geneva Convention, the Hague Treaty required that the "Detaining Power" provide rations similar to those in nearby garrison troops, banned torture and recognized the POWs' duty to try to escape. Two stories that appeared in the *Globe* in mid-1916 indicate the kind of information known by men captured later in the war. On 12 May, the paper reported that typhus had broken out in some camps. Two weeks later, even the humour of one of the two unnamed soldiers who was captured at St. Eloi but were so badly wounded that they were repatriated immediately could not hide the misery of the prisoners. The fish the Germans gave them to eat appeared to have been "cooked before the Flood," these last words, incidentally, showing how natural it was for these men to use Biblical imagery.[24]

From the point of view of the men who had been languishing in the camps, newly captured men brought much-desired news about both the war and Canada. In his secret diary, Lieutenant Frank Lawson, who was captured in May 1917, records speaking about the war to a British tank driver who had been captured at Amiens in August 1918. For obvious reasons, Lawson does not record the words that told him of the tank, its abilities or how it was used in conjunction with infantry—sadly, in the case of this British soldier, none too successfully.

The men of the First Canadian Division, who before the attack at midnight on 22 April 1915 on Kitchener's Wood that stymied the German advance against Ypres, were told to "follow the North Star." For them stories brought into the camps by the men captured at Vimy of maps being pushed down to the platoon level must have been scarcely believable. So, too, the development of the gas mask. Not long after Second Ypres, some thirty thousand mouth pads that were to act as gas masks reached the Canadians at Bailleul, France. By the end of May, the reinforced 2nd Battalion was training with the Black Veil respirator. Soldierly movements such as ducking, running or lunging dislodged the pad soaked in sodium hyposulphate, sodium carbonate, glycerine and water, so it provided little comfort to the men.

In mid-June the Allies had been joined by a brigade of what those who remembered translating *The Odyssey* might have thought of as Cyclopses. For that is what the men wearing the Hypo helmet looked like. The hood was impregnated with chemicals that neutralized phosgene and hydrogen cyanide, with a mica window in it. When properly sealed under a soldier's greatcoat while he breathed through a spout, the helmet decontaminated the air. But it had the psychological effect of isolating the soldier and making the battlefield seem ever more other-worldly.[25] By the end of 1916, Canadians were using the small-box respirator, a corrugated tube connecting the head piece (which had goggles) to a box filled with chemicals that filtered the air.

The hundreds of men who saw their Ross rifles jam under rapid fire at Ypres understood why the army would in 1916 undertake to re-equip the men with Lee-Enfields. (Senior Canadian officers winked at the many Canadians who did so on their own by picking up these redoubtable rifles from British soldiers who fell at Ypres.) While coughing through the chlorine gas attacks, men at Ypres used their heels to try to bully open the seized bolts of their rifles. One can only imagine what they thought when they heard about the sustained fire produced by the Lewis gun that was integrated into the Canadian army in 1916. The American-designed light machine gun could not match the fire of the heavier Vickers, some ten thousand rounds an hour, and, since the Lewis gun was air-cooled, could only be fired in short bursts. But the Lewis gun had the great advantage of being light enough to take across No Man's Land, and thus was at the sharp end, where men could see directly from where fire was coming.

Soldiers hated what were called "fatigue duties" (hauling supplies, digging trenches, stringing barbed wire and other hard, physical labour). To the men captured at Ypres, the regular patrols (called "stunts") carried out by bombers beginning in mid-1915 in the most desolate of places in the dark of night would have seemed a good trade-off. Shortages of manufactured bombs (grenades) meant that, like the British soldiers who freelanced making bombs in 1914, bombers found themselves acting like latter-day alchemists, mixing just the right amount of black powder and nails—albeit, of the metal variety—into old tin cans or jam jars. At the Battle of Givenchy in mid-June 1915, in areas neatly denominated on the map as H.1 and H.3, not all bombers had to light their "grenade's" fuse. Some bombers were equipped with the Mills No. 1 with the fuse set to five seconds, or the Mills 4, which was armed by pulling its pin. In the narrow trenches filled with a tangle of bloody dead bodies and body parts blown away, bombers fought a furious battle governed by both the zigzags they had to contend with and the ditty "Throw them high and drop them low and into the trenches they will be sure to go."

No matter which bomb they used, the goal was to blast jagged pieces of metal into German bodies. By 10 p.m., the battle—which began with the explosion of three thousand pounds of high-explosive ammonal that Allied planners hoped would destroy German trenches, but that wrecked a number of Canadian trenches and killed or wounded some fifty Canadian troops—was over. The fight for another useless splotch of France ended with Lieutenant Glen Gordon and a couple of dozen other men in the bag.

Perhaps even more important than news of the war, new arrivals in the camps brought news from home. Though POWs could send only two letters and two postcards each month, there was no limit on the number of letters they could receive. Neither letters to nor from POWs required postage. Regulations published in Canada and enforced by German censors meant that letters from home could not contain war or political news. Yet seemingly innocuous sentences about an aunt, a sister or a female cousin getting a job in a sector that before the war was dominated by men gave the POWs more than an inkling about both Canada's booming economy and the changing role of women.[26] Canadian POWs were not prevented, as the almost 2,200 German POWs in Canada were, from quoting poetry or referring to books, music or art works; presumably it was feared that these references could constitute a code.[27]

Only through new arrivals could the men hear that by mid-1917 New Brunswick, Saskatchewan and British Columbia had joined every province but Quebec in becoming "dry." Prisoners who belonged to the First Division would have had no trouble recalling the men's attitude toward Sir Sam's ardent temperance beliefs. On route marches on the muddy Salisbury Plain, a favourite song went:

D'ye ken Sam Hughes,
he's the foe of the booze;
He's the real champion [cham-peen] of the wet canteen
For the camp is dead, and we're sent to bed
So we won't have a head in the morning.[28]

The men who left Canada in 1917 and 1918 could tell of a very different country. Manitobans, especially, had an interest in the story of not only Premier Rodmond Roblin's fall in 1915 but also his indictment in mid-1916 over a scandal involving contracts to build the province's new parliament (which was not, in fact, completed until the early 2000s). Manitoba was also at the forefront of the fight for women's suffrage. In 1916, barely two years after Sir Rodmond had all but called McClung a "loose woman" for demanding the vote, Manitoba's new premier, Tobias C. Norris, went one better than the suffragettes by introducing a bill allowing women to sit in the provincial parliament. On the eve of the 6 August 1915 election, which Norris won in a landslide, the *Manitoba Free Press* praised McClung's "wit and eloquence," and thousands of Liberals applauded her for saying "women's desire for the suffrage is simply a desire to help" at an election-night rally. The extension of the vote to women had become so unremarkable that on 6 April 1917, the *Winnipeg Tribune* reported the signing of the bill enfranchising women in British Columbia on page three; page one reported that the Americans had declared war on Germany.

The complexity of the period's view of women can be seen by the juxtaposition of newspaper stories about women enlisting as streetcar drivers in Toronto and working in munitions plants, advertisements that stressed the traditional homemaker role, and advice columnists who told girls seeking a man "to be demure and deferential rather than forthright and positive."[29]

By December 1915, women were driving Toronto streetcars. Within a few months almost 700 factories in 150 different Canadian towns and cities were turning out munitions of all types. Much of the labour came from the more than 35,000 women who would work in the munitions industry, making not just fuses and other small components of shells (which experts believed were suited to their smaller fingers) but every size of shell—and being paid the same piecework rate as men.[30] The skin of many women turned yellow from absorbing TNT; in Britain they would be called "canary girls." Yet, even as the *Free Press* praised McClung's political savvy, it covered her in the society pages, noting, for example, that she wore a pretty dress decorated with pink carnations to a party where she was the guest of honour.[31]

The need for women in non-traditional jobs became so vital that in late October 1916 the *Ottawa Journal* asked, "If women are 'slackers,' what is going to be done about it?" The wives of Ottawa Valley farmers and those of workers in Mechanicsville, and the French Canadian wives, maids and washer women who lived in Lower Town or Eastview (later, Vanier) must have shaken their heads in disbelief at the paper's insouciance when it asked, "Are the women of Ottawa—the greater majority of whom have been accustomed to leisure hours—willing to rise at 6 o'clock in the morning and take their places in the factories at seven o'clock, there to labor all day as the men have done in the past?"

While the nursing sisters' desire to serve was obvious, judging from the papers, Canadians were unsure of what these women in uniform actually meant. On one day, pictures of twenty rather severe-looking women in uniform appeared only inches from "Fashion Tips" in the *Winnipeg Free Press*. The contested view of women in uniform can be seen in letters sent home by nursing sisters and letters soldiers sent home about them. Back in January 1915, the *Winnipeg Tribune* published a letter from Miss Alfreda Attrill, a nursing sister with No. 2 Stationary Hospital in Boulogne, France, in which she notes with pride that her hospital was the first Canadian unit "to touch French soil." She writes of the beauty of the hills around Boulogne and skilfully counterposes two things most Winnipeggers could only imagine: the "roar of the ocean" with the "boom of the guns" not far away.[32]

Attrill, who like every other nursing sister held the rank of 2nd lieutenant and thus merited saluting by men of lesser rank, assures her reader that such domestic chores as "taking stock of linen" were part of her day. Though speaking of a "Tommy," there is no doubt that Attrill expected her reader to assume that she, too, was emotionally affected: "You never saw such a delighted boy and pleased father, who was overjoyed to see his son doing so nicely." In the context of a hospital, the administrative simplicity of naming the wards for the provinces recedes behind their names as reminders of home. Phrases like "wounded soldiers" and "a great number of the surgical patients have frost bitten feet" partake of the bland rhetoric of the military communiqué and cloak the reality that Lieutenant-Colonel A. T. Shillington, the letter's recipient, knew to be Attrill's.

After Ypres, hospital beds had filled with men with "cyanosed" faces. Among the wounds Attrill saw in Europe were "heads shattered to pieces or limbs hanging by a thread of tendons," words recorded not in a letter meant for publication but in Nursing Sister Clare Gass's private diary. Those surgeries that were not for frostbite were like those on the "young boy with part of his face shot away and both arms gone."[33] The denizens of "Winterpeg" would have assumed that the surgeries for frostbite amounted to nothing more than the routine removal of a toe or two and not the stinking, swollen, black monstrosities cut off of young men whose wet feet froze in the trenches.

Men captured after Vimy would have brought even more alarming news about Canada, including the Conscription Crisis.[34] Claims, such as those made in the House by the MP for Maskinonge, Quebec—that "the first 150,000 men raised would have to be sent to the boundary [American border] to keep others from leaving the country"—were not included in either the news digests or the newspaper produced for the men in the trenches.[35] Many who had been in Britain or were newly arrived from Canada knew of Bourassa's and others' attacks on Borden and conscription. Some who arrived in the camps in mid-1918 would have known about the anti-conscription riots that rocked Quebec City during Easter of that year.[36]

By mid-1917, more than 500,000 men out of a total of eight million, some 18 percent of the male working-aged population, were on active service, had been invalided out of the army or were prisoners. Accordingly, in a way that is difficult to imagine today, Canada was a militarized society. For years headlines had blared out war news. Soldiers stood guard at canal locks, bridges, gasworks and other important sites such as the Victoria and Albert Pavilion in Ottawa, where Parliament met after the fire of February 1916 destroyed the Parliament buildings. Before it was determined that a cigar had caused the fire, speculation ran to German terrorism. Years of casualty lists translated into tens of thousands of women wearing black. Those who found the strength to put away the mourning clothes fought daily battles to keep the gnawing emptiness at bay. Young sons and daughters knew their fathers from letters, photos and family stories, which is all that tens of thousands of these children would ever have, despite the promise at the end of George M. Cohan's hit song "Over There": "We won't come back till it's over over there."

The language people spoke also changed. Words such as "platoon," which in 1912 appeared in nine newspaper stories—and then only to refer to two-man police platoons—became as commonplace as "gas attack," "killed in action," "missing," "tank" and "prisoner of war." "Front" slipped its military meaning and became a commonplace in weather reports. As suggested by its H. G. Wells–like title, the *Winnipeg Tribune*'s 1915 (dystopian) Christmas story had nothing to do with the nativity scenes set up in innumerable churches and homes: "Are European Ants, Driven to a Frenzy of Blood Lust, Following *Man's Mad Course* and Waging a War of Annihilation?"

Given the quasi-militaristic nature of Canada's schools before the war (Ontario's inspector of schools before the war was Sir Sam Hughes's brother, James), it is not surprising that military themes were common in school-leaving essays, as they were in German schools.[37] Another example of how deeply the war had insinuated itself into the fabric of daily life can be seen in the children's short-story contest run by the *Winnipeg Tribune* in early 1918. On 6 July, the paper published eleven war stories written by children in the *Tribune Junior*. The third prize was won by an eleven-year-old who wrote about a French boy who saved his father from the Germans, though afterward remained afraid of going to bed in the dark. Second prize went to an eight-year-old who wrote about his brother, who had been wounded at Vimy and was still "taking medical treatment." Willie Fillery of Toronto Street won first prize with a story of Mr. Gavin A. Gold, a former boarder in Willie's house who joined the 79th Cameron Highlanders in early 1915. After an attack, "everyone was accounted for as dead, wounded or unharmed, except Private Gold, who was reported 'missing.'" Sometime later Gold's name was moved to the prisoner of war list.

Willie hastened to add that Gold "would not have been captured if it had not been for an accident which happened to him in the midst of the battle." Three years of war and hundreds of stories about how prisoners of war suffered under the Germans had not entirely erased the stigma of surrender. Plutarch gave words to a Spartan mother two thousand years ago—"Come home with your shield or on it"—that thousands of Canadian soldiers would have seen in the original Greek in their high school classes. Private Gold's misfortune was not to be surrounded by an overwhelming German force. Rather, it was a hazard of bad fortune: he "fell to his knees under the weight of some heavy sandbags that had become dislodged and fallen on upon his neck." The fall blinded Gold in one eye. Though he was still a prisoner, young Fillery tells his readers, a recent photo of Gold shows him proudly wearing his uniform in the POW camp.

* * *

Canadian soldiers knew they were not supposed to see their artillery pieces captured. Neither were they to allow themselves to be captured. The knowledge that during the American Civil War more than 15,000 Confederate POWs had been imprisoned at Johnson's Island, a few miles south of Pelee Island, Ontario, did not lessen the opprobrium of being captured.

Canada's first POW was Joseph Burns, a private with the Princess Patricia's Canadian Light Infantry (PPCLI), who was captured on 16 January 1915. By the time the largest group of Canadians (1,383) was captured at Ypres, a few other Canadians and hundreds of thousands of British, French, Russian and German soldiers were already prisoners of war. For eight months papers had been carrying appeals for donations for the POWs and articles detailing their mistreatment and describing how the Red Cross provided aid.

Many of the articles about the Prisoner of War Relief Fund focused on the activities of women raising money for the men behind the wire.

Still, in the blink of an eye, men such as Lieutenant John Thorn, Lance Corporal Edward Edwards and Private Jack Evans went from being actors in the great drama of their time—and in some cases, officers and gentlemen—to being subjects under the control of a hostile authority that often did not speak their language. In the fevered moments after the Germans captured these men, within sight of their own dead or dying comrades, the captors often communicated with the point of a bayonet. Later, the guards turned to the butts of their rifles to compel men to work or silence their singing. In an age that privileged "manliness," such subjugation was profoundly emasculating.[38] Being captured, being a prisoner, partook of both notions of cowardice (for not fighting to the last) and effeminacy in that the prisoners were now under the control of stronger men.

The cultural bias against being captured was so great that the prayers said in memorial services in London, Winnipeg and other Canadian cities did not mention the prisoners. Nor did the editorial pages of the major papers say much about them. Captain Thomas Scudamore's father, himself a veteran of the Afghan War (1879), was so discomforted by his son's capture that he wrote to tell Thomas that Thomas's brother had been killed in battle and that he, Scudamore *père*, could only assume that the Canadian captain had been unconscious when he was captured and would not be writing again until he had such assurance. As it happens, such assurance soon arrived, for the ignominy of being captured was so great that the Red Cross reported that every Canadian captured at

Ypres had been captured unconscious. The elder Scudamore lived by a hard code: he did not put Thomas's picture back on his desk until his son was interned in Switzerland.

The men had, of course, never seen a B-movie Western in which a sweaty U.S. cavalry sergeant raises the white flag in surrender. Rather, they were animated by Admiral Nelson's admonition before the Battle of Trafalgar: "England expects every man will do his duty." They knew that even though Britain (acting for the Empire) had signed the Hague Treaty, which mandated that POWs be treated humanely, the British War Book under which the men served dictated that a Court of Inquiry awaited any man who was captured. At all events, there were so many prisoners returned to Canada that no Court of Inquiry was struck.

* * *

NONE OF THOSE CAPTURED expected to languish in dusty POW camps, in schools pressed into service by the war, or at labour camps doing backbreaking work of cutting peat or, worse, mining salt or coal without even the protection of gloves or helmets. Nor, of course, were the men whose stories I tell here able to fall back on tales such as Alfred J. Evans's *Escaping Club*, which is about his and other men's experiences during the Great War. They were not, however, without examples of escape.

Winston Churchill's bestselling *London to Ladysmith via Pretoria* (1900) provided an important model. In December 1899, during the Boer War, the subaltern climbed the wall that surrounded the school in which he was being held. After realizing that the train he had clambered aboard was heading for a collier region, he jumped from the train and hid in a wood. A few days later, as his supply of chocolate was running low, Churchill revealed himself to a farmer, who turned out to be an Englishman. The farmer hid Churchill for a few days before putting him on a train. On the way to Delago (Maputo) Bay, Churchill hid in a bale of woodchips, remembering beforehand to fill up a water bottle. By the time the steamer Churchill boarded in Delago Bay reached Pretoria, papers across Canada had published the first account of his escape, which he had given to a newswire.

Baroness Emma Orczy's *The Scarlet Pimpernel* (1905) also played its part. The Scarlet Pimpernel was not a POW, but his use of stealth and disguise was a model for prisoners. In the opening of the popular novel, the Pimpernel disguises himself as a cart driver, who secrets French aristocrats sentenced to death by the Revolutionary government in his cart. The key to their escape is the boy apparently suffering from smallpox who was riding with the Pimpernel. After seeing the pox, the guards waved the cart through the gate and out of Paris.

Even English history imbued these men with the mythos of hiding and escaping. Though now long gone from Canadian classrooms, the men discussed here would have learned about Queen Elizabeth I's spymaster Sir Thomas Hutchinson's efforts to find Catholic recusants and Jesuits hiding in "priest holes"; at the time, Catholics were considered a threat to the Queen and the Church of England. Teachers would have explained how during the English Civil War of the 1640s, Royalist gentry hid the future Charles II in the walls of their manor houses, in an oak tree and even disguised him as a servant. For this last ruse to work, the six-foot-tall Prince of Wales affected a most unroyal stoop.

Unlike many of the POWs who escaped in the Second World War, First World War escapers did not have access to M.I. 9–designed gadgets such as compasses hidden in buttons, blankets that were marked so that they could be cut and then sewn into passable civilian clothes, or maps printed on silk handkerchiefs. Instead of using a Gillette razor blade designed so it could be placed on a pin to make a compass, men cut razor blades into triangles and magnetized them to create their own compass needles. In at least one case, an escaper received a compass hidden in a cheese sent from home; as in the war still to come, authorities judged the food in Red Cross parcels much too important to the men's survival (because of the poor German rations) to risk using the parcels to send escape equipment.

Many escapers procured clothes, money, and in one case a gun by bribing guards. Most of the guards belonged to the *Landsturm*, made up of men as old as fifty-five. Among these men, as will be seen, were sadists. In almost every camp, however, some could be suborned with a little chocolate, sugar, tea or especially cigarettes. As the war wore on and the British blockade caused Germany's economy to weaken, bribing guards became easier.

Men such as Major Peter Anderson, the first and, as it turns out, highest-ranking Canadian to escape from Germany, and Private Frank MacDonald can be thought of as latter-day Robinson Crusoes. Everything that came within their reach was hidden for later use. The string around a parcel could be plaited into a rope; the can in which bully beef came could serve as part of a tunnel's ventilation system. In the later part of the war, the Germans tried to ensure that cans of bully beef and cheese or jam were not squirrelled away by requiring the men to open the cans and dumping the contents into the POW's bowl to form an edible slop; the Germans then sent the tin to factories.

Whether or not it was true, as one British officer told MacDonald, that Canadians were keen to escape because most were "more or less used to the open," he and the other escapers displayed excellent field craft skills.[39] One British soldier who escaped with a Canadian credited their survival—which included choosing ditches in which to hide and covering themselves with vegetation, and burrowing into a haystack to stay warm—to the Canadian's field craft skills honed in Algonquin Park. The hole in the deep snow that another Canadian dug so that he and his British escape partner could hide and huddle for warmth during the day is a further example of Canadian field craft.

Every escaper discussed here was forced to forage. In a few cases they had the luxury of being able to bake their potatoes or make what they called "beef tea" from Oxo cubes. Most of the time, the escapers ate raw potatoes, carrots, turnips and apples, many far from ripe, stolen from farms and orchards. Such food barely filled stomachs and never warmed men who swam canals and trudged through wind, rain, snow, bogs and swamps. Even in the summer, wet, exhausted and emotionally stressed men primed to listen for the breaking of a twig or the pulling back of a rifle bolt found the nights distressingly cold. The chill not only sapped their strength, it made sleeping difficult (as, of course, did damp uniforms, blistering feet and hard ground), which further weakened the escapers.

Still, despite these hazards and the very real possibility that a trigger-happy guard might shoot first and ask questions later, hundreds of the Canadians captured in the war risked escaping. Many, as we will see, escaped more than once, which means they had first-hand experience with both the terror and pains of life on the run and the cost of failure: days in dark, damp and cold cells and/or savage beatings. Between August 1917 and the end of the war in November 1918, the period for which we have the best numbers, 735 ordinary ranks were captured and 70, or 9.5 percent, escaped. Sadly, 76, or 10.3 percent, of the prisoners also died during this period. (Over the course of the war, 10.6 percent of Canadian POWs died.) For the same demographic as the soldiers, in the years before the war the death rate was 5 percent; even at the front, the death rate of 8.3 percent was lower than among POWs. While some men died of accidents in mines and others as the result of beatings and mistreatment, the largest proportion of men who died while prisoners of war were survivors of Second Ypres, which suggests that they were badly wounded and/or gassed in the battle.

One hundred and one, or 2.6 percent, of the Canadian POWs successfully escaped from Germany. The best estimate for the total number of escapes, however, is that 10 percent of Canadians, or about double the percentage of other British Empire troops, escaped. As will become clear, since almost every escaper was helped by a number of other men—to make clothes, pleat string into stout rope, steal food, keep lookout—the percentage of Canadians engaged in escape activities likely approached 30 percent.

A French POW described the effect of surrender as *le cafard*, the cockroach of disgrace that "crawled round in the brain, round and round and round." As their memoirs make clear, the men feared that their families and other Canadians would think they had "sold liberty for life" and thereby dishonoured their uniform, their families and themselves.[40] Indeed, their biographies sometimes have an air of expiation. Escaping—or simply planning an escape—which the Germans surmised the men were doing and thus had to devote scarce resources to foiling, helped "level the score against the hated enemy."[41]

As we will see, these men judged themselves too harshly. Their derring-do alone is worth remembering. But what is most interesting about these men is their mettle. Though off the chessboard, they remained men of war.

Prelude

Even before the German bombardment that heralded the attack at Ypres on 22 April 1915, the Canadians found themselves on a battlefield utterly different from one on which victory could be achieved by a dashing cavalry or a bayonet charge like those depicted in the bestselling works of G. A. Henty or the *Boy's Own Annual*. Nor did the 4,000 yards of trench the Dominion troops took over in mid-April bear much relation to what was shown on the maps French commanders handed over to Canadian commanders. The first 1,500 yards were all but vacant, with only portions of isolated trenches, firing pits and a few bits of rusted barbed wire. Some parapets were only waist high, which meant that anyone who stood up became an easy target for a sniper. To avoid losing men to "wastage," death caused by odd shots and shells, the Canadian field commander, Lieutenant-General Edwin Alderson, ordered his green troops to move into the trenches that arced to the north and west of Ypres only at night.

Even for men who (because of the prevalence of now curable diseases) were familiar with death and corpses—which were often laid out in family living rooms—the trenches and No Man's Land were almost unbearably gruesome. In many places, the ground oozed with the remains of French, German and British soldiers killed the previous October who had been disposed of at the bottom of those trenches. To at least partially alleviate the overwhelming stink of decay, Canadian engineers liberally spread around tons of lime. To cope with death, the men domesticated it. The men of the 10th Battalion treated a desiccated arm that stuck out of the trench war as a talisman, shaking it as they went by. Unexpected encounters with the grisly remains of battle, however, caused many uniformed men to vomit.

When they disembarked from the RMS *Franconia* in Plymouth, the Canadians refused to unload their equipment, calling it "coolie work."[1] At Ypres, fatigue duties became more serious, as the men strung miles of telephone wire, manhandled heavy crates loaded with thousands of rounds of ammunition and dug gun emplacements. They shovelled heavy, muddy Flanders earth into sandbags to build up the parapet in front of shallow trenches and the parados (the rear part of a trench) behind them. Because of the high water level around Ypres, the trenches that elsewhere were etched into the ground were in large measure built up from the ground, making them less effective in protecting the men against snipers and shelling. One officer's sardonic pen captured the men's feelings about fatigue duties, albeit in the somewhat drier trenches of France: "Most of our time is spent digging holes in France to fill other holes in other bits of France. Much of the country is now contained in sandbags. The rest is in our boots, our pockets, our rifles and clareted thick all over our uniforms."[2]

On the other side of No Man's Land, the Germans, too, were busy. Those belonging to *Pionier-Regiment* 35, a specially trained engineering unit, wearing modified Dräger underwater breathing apparatus, buried 5,700 steel cylinders in the parapet facing Ypres. The men in the trenches did not know that these cylinders contained deadly chlorine gas or that Duke Albrecht of Württemberg, who commanded the German 4th Army, awaited only the right wind conditions to unleash *Operation Desinfektion* and add gas warfare to the miseries of war.

The wind the duke needed came on the afternoon of April 22. Within seconds of the "Stink Pioneers," as the Germans would later call them, opening the valves on the tanks, a wall of greenish chlorine gas blew toward the French colonial troops on the Canadian left. And within minutes, hundreds of French troops lay dead or dying from asphyxiation as the chlorine they inhaled combined with fluid in their noses, mouths and lungs to create hydrochloric acid that burnt their throats and lungs. As the few remaining *Zouaves* ran for their lives yelling "*Gaz, gaz!*" hundreds of Canadians in positions abutting the French found themselves under the gas cloud. A number recalled enough high school chemistry to know that if they breathed through urine, which would neutralize the chlorine, they might just survive, so they urinated on their handkerchiefs and breathed through them. And Major D. Rykert McCuaig quickly ordered his men to bend their line on a right angle so that they would be perpendicular to the onrushing Germans and thus able to fire into the German flank as they advanced into the four-mile hole the gas tore in the Allied line.

Over the next two days, the untried Canadians would hold the Germans back as the British rushed up reserves. At midnight on the 22nd, two battalions attacked a small wood in the centre of the German advance, which helped sketch a patchy and thin defensive line. Even more importantly, as Lance Corporal Fred Frost, who was captured on the northern edge of Kitchener's Wood, would have seen, the night attack convinced the Germans that the Canadians had more reserves than they in fact did; this gave the Germans pause. After finding his troops unable to punch through to Ypres on the 23rd, on the 24th Albrecht ordered the opening of the canisters of chlorine facing the Canadian position on Gravenstafel Ridge. The cloud of gas and the subsequent attack shattered this part of the Canadian line. And though in the end Ypres did not fall, this attack killed hundreds of Canadians and ended with more than a thousand of them holding up their hands in surrender here and in positions closer to Ypres.

Approximate Locations of Major Prisoner of War Camps

Chapter One

April 1915

24 April 1915: Ypres, Belgium

As Private Harry Howland learned when a number of Germans broke into his 7th Battalion trench, which was protecting a "Locality C" between Gravenstafel Ridge and Ypres, surrender bore little resemblance to what top-hatted statesmen had imagined when they signed the Hague Treaty in 1907. For them, surrender was a clear, legal act and prisoners of war were "in the power of the hostile Government but not of the individuals or corps who capture them."[1] On the battlefield, however, things were different. In his memoir of the war, *Storm of Steel,* Ernst Jünger could have been describing the *Feldgrauen* (German soldiers, named for their field-grey uniforms) who bayoneted a number of gunners near Howland who had raised their hands in surrender: "A man cannot change his feelings [about the enemy] during the last rush with a veil of blood before his eyes. He does not want to take prisoners but to kill."[2]

When he realized that his position was surrounded, Captain Thomas Scudamore ordered his men to stand up, putting them at risk of machine gun fire and shrapnel. To Scudamore's surprise, the Germans who jumped into his trench readied to use their bayonets. One of Scudamore's men, Private George Scott, credited his and his comrades' survival to the fact that though faint from a blow to his head, Scudamore was aware enough to yell out in half-remembered German, "*Halt!* You can't shoot me. I'm in command here."[3] Killing men who have surrendered may have violated the Hague Treaty, but accorded with the German military code, *Kriegsbrauch im Landkriege*, which said, "Prisoners can be killed" when the "exigencies of war" demand it.[4]

Surrender touched off emotional storms that rankled former POWs decades later. Private Mervyn Simmons felt that raising his arms in submission was "bitterer [by] far than to be shot," a judgment that Scott, who had been shot, agreed with when he spoke of being "hopeless and helpless before our enemies."[5] For Major Peter Anderson the awful feeling of humiliation culminated in the worry, "What will people at home think about me"?[6] Private Fred McKelvey felt the emasculating impact of surrender: "This is the thing my father told me never to let happen."[7]

The Canadians may not have been battlefield lawyers, but they knew that the Hague Treaty required their captors to provide medical attention and refrain from pilfering personal effects. Woozy from loss of blood, Private James Mackie was treated well, as was Private John Finnimore, who was lifted into a wheelbarrow and brought to a medic.[8] By contrast, when the officer questioning Arthur Gibbons called him a *Goldsoldat* (mercenary), he dragged the wounded man forty yards behind the German trench to a field on which shells from British guns burst. At a dressing station where Simmons hoped his bullet wound would be treated, he saw a Canadian Highlander lying unattended on a stretcher in the corner as "blood dripped horribly and gathered in a red pool on the dusty floor." The soldier found the strength to say, as if in apology, "It's no use, mother—it's no use."[9] Simmons was tagged for later treatment, though not before the forty-five francs in his paybook were stolen and he was forced into the building's airless basement, where he collapsed into sleep on a pile of rat-infested straw.

The Saxon troops took Private Nathan Rice's surrender correctly, with one even asking, "Englanders, English men, why do you fight Germany? We are your cousins," referring to Anglo-Saxons' ancient "racial" link to Saxon tribes. Another man, however, was concerned with more personal family ties. Though Rice did not speak German, the words the man sputtered out sounded to him like "My brother's been killed" as the soldier swung the butt of his rifle at the man in front of Rice. He ducked, and Rice "got it on the back and went down."[10]

Toward dusk, Howland and a group of other prisoners were handed over to a detachment of Uhlan Guards, who used their lances to hurry along the prisoners, including the walking wounded, and enforce demands to hand over watches and rings. Surprisingly, the soldier who had found Anderson's camera returned it to him after exposing its film, though he kept both Anderson's paybook and the address book filled with names of people that, Anderson knew, would be wishing him a happy birthday on this 24th day of April 1915, the 263rd day of the war.

24 April 1915, Night, Roulers, Belgium

THE CANADIANS' FIFTEEN-MILE MARCH to Roulers ended in front of a caricature come to life. The Prussian officer's face was "swollen and blood red" as he walked up and down the ranks of the POWs.[11] Scott did not understand what he was yelling but knew the meaning of the sword whipped toward their faces.

As if to underline their willingness to use violence against unarmed, exhausted, hungry and thirsty men—many suffering from the effects of the chlorine gas or having been wounded—the officer ordered his men to bring a young Belgian man forward. A short time earlier, the Belgian had run up to a Canadian, shouting "*Bravo les Anglais*," and handed him an apple. The whip-wielding German guards grabbed the Belgian and held him while their *Kameraden* beat him almost into unconsciousness. The officer, for his part, whipsawed the boy's head with his riding crop and then handed this "friend of the British" to his men, who continued to beat him.[12]

Their captors herded them into a large building, where they were given water and their first ration of *Kriegsbrot*, hard, sour "war bread" that over the next few years would be augmented with potato and turnip peelings and even sawdust. Having heard stories of German atrocities in Belgium in the first days of the war and how German civilians had thrown nails at the British captured at Mons the previous August, the Canadians must have thought they had caught a bit of a break when they became only something of an overnight attraction, as Germans in Roulers came to see the POWs. Scudamore was, however, taken aback when one German gawker commented on the "comparative whiteness of our skins" and when another said, "So you are Canadians, and yet you speak English!"[13]

24 April 1915: Midnight, Roulers

The bright-eyed girl with the radiant smile wore a pink dress and white shoes. As the stabbing pain in his wounded shoulder woke him, Simmons was hardly surprised that he had seemingly met her in church. For, since sometime after midnight, he and scores of other Canadians had been held in the basement of St. Michael's Catholic Church. Had there been light in the basement, the pre-war carpenter could hardly have missed the differences between this church, with its deep stone footings put in place hundreds of years ago—which accounted for the damp cold that tormented him—and the small clapboard Presbyterian church in his hometown of Verschoyle, Ontario. In the tomb-like darkness, he could not help but think of the irony of using a church as a prison.

In the moments before a German cavalry officer wrenched him from his post-dream daze, Simmons imagined bashful boys outside the church waiting to walk pretty girls home. The officer found Simmons's groggy request for water funny. And, using English honed while working at the Dunsmuir Colliers in Ladysmith on Vancouver Island (where his brother still worked), the German told Simmons, "You Canadians are terrible fools to fight with us when you don't have to. You'll be sick of it before you are through."[14]

But at least this cavalry officer was not threatening like the one who ordered that Rice and the men captured with him be shot. This officer took umbrage when one Canadian prisoner said he came from the town of Hindenburg, British Columbia, because he thought the Canadian was mocking General Paul von Hindenburg, who had triumphed over the Russians at the Battle of the Tannenberg eight months earlier. Fortunately, as the Canadians were being marched away, another officer ran to the column and countermanded the order.

26 April 1915: On Trains to Germany

Because they were officers, men such as Scudamore and Anderson were taken to Bischofswerda POW camp near Dresden in fourth-class carriages, while the ordinary ranks travelled in cattle cars to Giessen, the POW camp near Frankfurt. The air in the cars headed for Giessen smelled of horseshit, dried blood, sweat and the stink of the mud of Flanders that stuck to their heavy woollen greatcoats, tunics and trousers. Each cattle car held dozens of thirsty men, yet the Germans provided only two bottles of water per car. When the train stopped in a small town and Belgians tried to bring water to the prisoners, the guards opened fire on the Belgians. Once in Germany, however, a few of the guards arranged for beer for several of the imprisoned officers.

The Canadian officers took some solace from the fact that Lieutenant Edward D. Bellew was among them. Bellew had provided machine gun cover, allowing Scudamore and six other men to withdraw before they themselves were captured. On the afternoon of 24 April, a hastily convened battlefield court heard that Bellew had continued to fire his machine gun after a white flag had been raised. If true, this could have merited a death sentence. Bellew's life was saved because the prosecuting officer could not produce enough evidence.

As rumours of the thousands of casualties at Ypres spread and countless Canadians passed the first of hundreds of sleepless nights, four postcards, two written by Scudamore and two by Anderson, sat in German Military Post canvas bags. After being checked by censors, the cards would go to Switzerland or Sweden, and then to London. Anderson's arrived in Canada in June and told his family "the disgusting news" that he had been captured.[15] Scudamore reached his father on the Isle of Guernsey some time earlier, and his words discomfitted his father severely. Since the Germans did not have any Red Cross information about the Canadians, such as their real names, Scudamore was able to slip a message past a German censor by signing "Your affectionate son, Tom Hungry."[16]

27 April 1915: Giessen POW Camp, Germany

Howland first heard "*Raus*! *Raus*! *Komm . . . Schweinehunde raus*!" (Get up! Come . . . Pig-dogs up!) near midnight when the train arrived at Giessen. He quickly learned to hate these words that every morning preceded the slamming open of his barrack's door. As the Germans counted them on their first *Appell* (roll call) on the parade ground, the Canadians heard the German numbers that went well into the hundreds before they received their ration of *Brot* and coffee. The famished men ignored the order to save some of the sour bread for later. The *Kaffee* had neither milk nor sugar. Indeed, it did not contain any coffee, being made from burnt chicory and acorns.

The fact that the British POWs wore clean uniforms was a hopeful sign for the Canadians. However, a Tommy with a bandaged leg supporting himself on a crutch called out, "You'd be better off in a home, mates," hinting at a dim future, as did the sight of prisoners with arms in slings and bandaged heads. The British soldiers' thirst for news seemed more of a concern than their injuries, which showed how within the wire prisoners "lost touch with events."[17]

As they walked through the camp to their 150-foot-long barracks, Howland and his comrades displayed a studied nonchalance toward one another, in an effort to defeat the Germans' attempt to separate comrades who appeared close enough to want to try to escape together. The barracks held one hundred men, who slept side by side on straw mattresses on the wooden floor. For years to come, Howland would recall the soup that was ladled out for lunch after they arrived as the only decent meal he had in Germany.

28 April 1915: Ypres

THE GERMAN MEDICAL CORPS amazed Gibbons. "No sooner was a man wounded than a stretcher bearer rushed up to him, even under fire, bandaged his wounds and placed a tag on one of the buttons of his uniform."[18] So, too, did the trench digging system of the *Feldgrauen*, which produced strong positions in less than an hour. (Five days earlier, the Germans had produced one such system on top of Mauser Ridge—which overlooked Ypres from the northeast—that allowed them to repulse two attacks. The high-water mark of the second attack was Lieutenant Colonel Arthur Birchall falling dead on the German parapet after a dash, complete with cane, during which his men could see the blood spurting from several bullet wounds.)

Gibbons marvelled, too, at the cook-wagons, which at night came right up to the trenches to provide the men with hot soup and coffee. Gibbons saw all of this and, in the first hours after he had been dragged back onto the battlefield, he also saw two other "wounded boys done to death" while lying on a field raked by machine gun bullets and shaken by exploding shells.[19]

On the night of the 25 April, he dared to hope that the soldiers he could hear in hand-to-hand fighting with the Germans nearby might drive the enemy back and rescue him. Gibbons endured kicks and mock bayonet thrusts, the rough pulling off of his boots and the theft of personal items, and the degradation of having his insignia and even his buttons cut off. At one point, one German had to stop another from cutting off one of Gibbons's fingers to get at a gold ring. No one—including the medical corpsmen who walked past him—gave the badly wounded soldier who had been lying in his own waste for days food, water or that soldier's longed-for joy, a cigarette.

Finally, on 28 April, a stretcher-bearer took the dazed Canadian to a dressing station in the ruined village of Langemarck. A heavy artillery bombardment began soon after. Lying out in the open, Gibbons watched the bursts of hundreds of shrapnel shells and felt the blast waves of the high-explosive shells that destroyed a house nearby wash over him. He saw the terror in the eyes of the Germans, defenceless before tremendous forces that pulled whole trees from the ground and eviscerated bodies.

An able-bodied prisoner bringing Gibbons food and drink said, "Look at the effect of those shells . . . our boys are sure giving these Huns hell now, eh?" Gibbons could not see the soldier's brassard, but the telltale "eh" signalled he was a fellow Canadian. "Hell is right," Gibbons responded. "I hope they keep it up."[20] Not long after, Gibbons was loaded into an ambulance and driven away from the battlefield.

29 April 1915: Winnipeg

Under a leaden sky, twenty thousand Winnipeggers assembled in the cold at Happyland Race Track for a memorial service. Hundreds of the families gathered, including that of Sergeant Major Frederick William Hall, were in mourning. Hall, who had told his mother he would die on the battlefield, earned a posthumous Victoria Cross for braving a hail of gunfire while trying to save a wounded man stranded several yards from the trench. Though he praised the Canadian feat of arms, Reverend G. B. Wilson told the faithful that their sons, husbands and fathers were "not filled with the lust of conquest." The men of the CEF had "no chant of hate to sing." How the "victories of peace" over adverse weather, the stubborn prairie sod, the very land of Canada, had prepared this "commercial people" for the eventualities of war was presumably clear to the gathered thousands.[21]

Ten days later, the Right Reverend Arthur Foley Winnington-Ingram, the bishop of London, conducted a memorial service at Westminster Cathedral before senior Canadian commanders and hundreds of men wounded at what was already being called Second Ypres. Winnington-Ingram was known for his blood-curdling sermons. On one occasion, he said it was the "British soldier's duty to kill Germans, the good as well as the bad, to kill the young as well as the old, to kill those who have shown kindness to our wounded as well as those fiends . . . I look upon it as a war for purity, I look upon everyone who died in it as a martyr."[22] He did not disappoint.

Drawing from General John French's report of the battle, the bishop explained how the "Canadians saved the situation." He repeated the story of the early hours of the battle, when Major Edward C. Norsworthy, who was "already almost disabled by a bullet wound, was bayoneted and killed while he was rallying his men with easy cheerfulness."[23] He told the story of Chaplain (Canon) Frederick Scott, who just before the attack on Kitchener's Wood near midnight on the 23 April, went up and down the line saying, "It's a great day for Canada, boys."[24]

The bishop said nothing of the confused welter of orders before the attack on Kitchener's Wood that saw men taking off, then putting back on, their sixty-pound backpacks and twelve-pound overcoats, fixing and unfixing their seventeen-inch bayonets and then fixing them again to their Ross rifles. Nor did Winnington-Ingram tell that the 16th Battalion's officers considered the attack over unreconnoitred fields, without artillery support, to be a sacrificial charge, which it almost became when the men encountered a fence about halfway between their starting point and the wood. Nevertheless, the Canadians' first attack of the war was so audacious that it recaptured four heavy British guns (which had been incorrectly reported to be Canadian) and re-established something of a defensive line. Furthermore, it made the Germans think that there were more reserves in Ypres than there were, which caused them to become more cautious.

Literary scholars use the term "high diction" to refer to words and phrases like "perish" to mean die, "peril" for danger or "the fallen" to mean the dead on the battlefield. As the lists of dead mounted into the thousands, this type of language undergirded the rhetoric of churchmen in Canada who sought to provide transcendent meaning to the grieving. This language was also used by editorial writers and the (amateur) poets published in the newspapers.

Among themselves and in letters home, the men who had seen their friends shot to death or blown apart spoke their own euphemisms, such as "gone west" and "made the supreme sacrifice." Conn Smythe's praise of the "Man up there" for saving him when he was shot down and captured was a very familiar way of referring to the deity; this language would have shocked the great and the good in Smythe's Anglican and Protestant Toronto.[26]

Neither Winnington-Ingram nor other churchmen in Canada spoke of the bodily feeling of fear experienced by men under bombardment. Nor did they speak of the morale-destroying delay between the time a shell was fired and its arrival, "during which their screams intensified, forcing soldiers to brace themselves, and [of] the nerve-jarring effects of the subsequent explosions" that caused men's eyes to seemingly pop out of their sockets, their hearts to race so quickly that breathing became difficult and their tongues to stick to the roofs of their mouths.[27]

Absent, too, from the sermons and all but absent from the editorialists' columns and the ephemeral poetry that followed Ypres were words like those written by an American YMCA delegate about the German POW in England: "Though living, he is dead, and dead with little glory."[28]

* * *

A few days later, a cable from a London-based friend of George Alexander arrived at a stately brick home on Toronto's Elm Street, green with newly budding trees. It said that the 15th Battalion captain had been taken prisoner on 24 April. The captain's almost jocular words, "Taken prisoner yesterday," are of a piece with the words Alexander called out after being buried by a shell explosion. Another man had shouted that Alexander had vanished. "No, Alexander is not gone, but he is pretty badly hurt," came the words from beneath the earth he was soon dug out of.[29] The telegram continued "Fortunes of war. I am quite well," hiding the fact that one of his legs was badly injured, while "being well treated" was meant to calm fears. Since the start of the war, Canadians had read dozens of stories of German mistreatment of prisoners. The cable ended "Germans say we did well in fight," which shows Alexander's awareness that though his family would be elated he had survived, they would soon demonstrate concern, perhaps even shame, that he had violated the injunction pasted on the back page of his and every other soldier's paybook: avoid being captured.[30]

Chapter Two

May–September 1915

8 May 1915: Frezenberg, Belgium

The light of day revealed a scene of unimaginable horror. The battlefield was nothing like that sketched by lithographers or imagined by those who visited the trenches in London's Hyde Park, where the sandbags stood in orderly rows as if on parade and did not sag into the Flanders mud. Nor was the burlap stained brown with blood, singed by the touch of a red-hot splinter from a high-explosive shell or holed from speeding shrapnel balls. In the lithographs, zigzags designed to contain explosions and delay attackers who might break into the trench were clean lines. They were not bulges that threatened to collapse into what soldiers likened to an open sewer at the bottom of the trench that often included the remains of decayed bodies. Beyond these trenches lay mounds of unburied dead and the "small-pox appearance of the shell pitted ground."[1]

For Lance Corporal Edward Edwards, "the ball commenced" at 6:30 a.m. when a shell exploded behind the trenches held by Princess Patricia's Canadian Light Infantry.[2] A moment later a barrage of high-explosive shells fired from concealed batteries to Edwards's right collapsed parts of the trench in bursts of flame that incinerated wooden supports and some wildflowers. Such flowers' humility, Canon Frederick Scott had found some days earlier, "mocked . . . the world of men which was so filled with noise and death."[3]

Groups of men were obliterated while others were stupefied by the "terrible pulsation[s] of the atmosphere," unable to avoid the enfilading stream of lead from Maxim machine guns.[4]

Amid the maelstrom of flying metal, remnants of logs that had shored the trench, and the acrid smell of cordite that seemingly ate into their brains and lungs, somehow Edwards and a few other men produced enough fire to force the vanguard of the German attack to go to ground. The same, however, was not true on Edwards's left and right, and soon the order came to retire. It was impossible to retreat over this swath of Belgium swept by machine gun fire. Held together by a few fragments of chicken wire, the communication trench that led back from the front line was not much better. Edwards long remembered the screams of those men who were only partially buried by the detritus of their blown-in trenches. But because he was running for his life, he could not pause to help.

The rifle fire may not have had the emotional impact of shellfire, but it signalled that the Kaiser's infantry, many of whom wore belt buckles saying "*Gott strafe England*" (God punish England) had again thrust forward. A short distance ahead of where the Germans, now standing on the parados, speared men with bayonets, Edwards turned and tossed his rifle to another man before picking one up from the mucky trench floor. Unlike hundreds of other Ross rifles at Ypres and to Edward's left and right this one did not seize up. Edwards managed to squeeze off one shot—before a German bullet smashed through his rifle's bayonet, just as a troop of Germans swarmed into the trench.

Edwards saw a German soldier blow off Private Harold J. Cosh's head and, when Private George Brown collapsed after seeing this, another German blew his head off. A blast from a Mauser rifle at almost point-blank range left "only a broken and bloody mass" hanging from the end of an arm raised in surrender.[5]

The Germans who shot at Edwards as he climbed out of the bloody trench were poor shots. Moments after he flung himself into a shell hole an angry voice and rifle trained on him ended his attempt to play possum. As he marched into captivity, Edwards saw that as Germans reversed the Canadian parapets, they enacted a ghastly Teutonic version of the words Shakespeare gave to Henry V: the *Pickelhaube*-wearing soldiers "close[d] up the wall with our English dead."[6]

8 May 1915: Morning, Bischofswerda POW Camp, Germany

THE HAGUE TREATY DICTATED that prisoners' lodgings be comparable to those of men of the same rank in the detaining power's army. Accordingly, the Canadian officers were imprisoned in a former cavalry barracks surrounded by two fences: one wooden, one barbed wire. Unlike the ordinary ranks at Giessen, officers at Bischofswerda could pay a woman to do their washing. Instead of being crammed into a barracks with a hundred men, Lieutenant John Thorn shared his room with nine officers, their straw mattresses lying on bunks and not on the cold, damp and often dirty wooden floor. Shortly after the Canadians arrived at the Bischofswerda, the American ambassador, James Gerard, acting in his capacity as the representative of the Protecting Power, visited the camp and found flowers on the tables. The complaint that the men were fed horsemeat upset the *Kommandant*, who denied the claim and said he ate the same rations. The flowers were a one-time pleasure.

The prisoners had no grounds to complain about their haircuts, but that did not lessen the effect of the "prison crop," which made them look like common criminals. The Hague Treaty made clear that POWs were not criminal prisoners by, among other stipulations, banning the holding of POWs in civilian jails. However, by eliding the physical distinction between types of prisoners, the Germans sought to undermine the POWs' esprit de corps and view of themselves as soldiers who happened to be behind the line. This, in turn, added to their feeling of hopelessness. Unlike criminal prisoners, who would know when their sentences ended, POWs found themselves running on what seemed an endless treadmill. At Giessen, with the absence of the military chain of command, the glue that holds units together, and the absence of regular mail, POWs were cut off from vital psychological supports.

Even in the somewhat more salubrious conditions of Bischofswerda, Thorn found that within days, "time [began] hanging very heavy on our hands."[7] This effect was more pronounced because it followed the telescoping of time inwards during battle or the psychic reaction of being anaesthetized. One soldier described his state of "non-thinking, not-feeling, not-seeing . . . Past and future were equidistant and unattainable, throwing no bridge of desire across the gap that separated me from my remembered self and from all that I hope to grasp."[8]

Not long after the *Appell*, the morning of the 8th became sullener in proportion to the verve of a band celebrating another German "victory," the sinking of the RMS *Lusitania*. A few days later, responding to international outcry over the fact that 1,191 men, women and children had died eleven miles off the coast of Ireland, the *Continental Times*—an English-language propaganda newspaper distributed in the camps, nicknamed the *Continental Liar*—reported that *Lusitania* was a legitimate target because thousands of Canadian soldiers were secreted in her holds. As Arthur Gibbons lay in a Belgian hospital awaiting an operation on his untreated, shattered thighbone, a triumphant German medical orderly showed him a medal commemorating the sinking.

9 May 1915: Roulers

After what Edwards had seen when the 21st Prussian Regiment stormed into his trench and the hours he and other prisoners spent crouching low as the Germans practised sniping, he had little doubt the officer nonchalantly smoking his pipe told the truth when he said, "Our orders were to take no Canadian prisoners."[9] By contrast, the soldier who later guarded Edwards and his comrades seemed bemused by the fact he was guarding Canadians and not *Engländer*.

One of the marks of how green the Canadians were was that they did not know to give interrogators only their name, rank and service number. Thus, when asked how many divisions of Kitchener's New Army were in the reserve behind Ypres, Edwards said that they had not come over yet and that the armies totalled between five and seven million men. In fact, as the Germans probably well knew, they totalled some two million men. Saying that he had not fought at Ypres because he had been wounded, Edwards pled ignorance when the German told him that the Canadians had cut the throats of German wounded.

More importantly for the German intelligence, which saw every piece of information as part of a jigsaw puzzle, Edwards volunteered that he had been in the 2nd Gordons in the Boer War and had served several years in the reserve. Edwards did, however, keep silent when an officer said that since the death of Colonel Francis Farquhar (which had been reported in the press), the PPCLI had been under the command of Lieutenant-Colonel Herbert Buller. Buller, Edwards knew, had been blinded, and command now rested with Major Hamilton Gault, the millionaire who had helped raise the regiment in the first days of the war.

After spending a night in the same befouled church Mervyn Simmons had, Edwards stood before a high-ranking officer who had asked to speak to a member of the "Princess Patricia's Canadians." To Edwards's surprise, the immaculately dressed officer said in perfect English, "Well, the Princess Patricia is my niece—awfully nice girl. I hope it won't be long before I see her again." Edwards told the German that in a happier time he had been in the Princess Patricia's honour guard at Aldershot in Hampshire, England. The Hohenzollern prince ended the interview by promising that the Canadians would be sent to a good camp and would "be all right if you behave yourselves."[10]

Early May 1915: Vancouver and Giessen

The sequence was cruel. First, the communiqué published on 3 May listed Captain Robert V. Harvey as being "Killed in

Action." Two weeks later, the *Vancouver Daily World*, Harvey's hometown paper, said he was a "Prisoner of War and wounded (formerly reported killed)." Then, on 11 May, Robert's brother Edward in Liverpool received a telegram saying Harvey had died of his wounds in the Giessen hospital on 8 May. Two days before that, Private William Keith Dickson, also of the 7th Battalion, had died of his wounds.

The Germans allowed funeral parties befitting each man's rank. Dickson merited six pallbearers and a guard of three men on 8 May, five days before his family back in Alberni, B.C., invested their hopes in the 13 May report that he was among the missing. Harvey's casket was also carried by six pallbearers and was accompanied by a nine-piece band. After twenty Germans fired a volley in salute, Harvey's casket was lowered into the ground so far from home.

Early May 1915: Giessen

Giessen may have been something of a show camp, but as Edwards soon learned, his captors did not provide prisoners with the same rations as nearby garrisoned troops. The daily ration of half a pound of sour potato/rye bread for five men and the bag of small, rotten potatoes boiled in two hundred gallons of water for eight hundred men did little to fill stomachs. The Limburger cheese they were given some days was so rancid that the Canadians preferred hunger pangs and gave it to Russian prisoners. Meals cooked with decayed vegetables and ham soup made from ten pounds of ham rinds—some with hair on them—made a mockery of Berlin's pledge in April to provide a "plentiful diet."

It mattered little to Edwards and others whose stomachs ached whether, as the Germans claimed, they provided short rations because the Red Cross parcels topped them up or because Berlin was unprepared for the number of POWs they had to feed (by mid-1915 close to 700,000). Some men suspected that the Germans kept them underfed in order to weaken them and thus make escape less likely. The Reich's policy on dealing with food shortages caused by the British naval blockade had, in fact, been announced the previous February when Germany publicly declared, "Prisoners of war must starve first."[11]

14 May 1915: Handzame Military Hospital, Belgium

ARTHUR GIBBONS FOUND *HERR DOKTOR'S* bedside manner lacking. Instead of comforting the patient who had a smashed right thighbone, the doctor approached him carrying an amputated leg still dripping blood, and placed it on the ground before asking in perfect English where Gibbons had been wounded. After hearing "Ypres," the doctor smiled and said, "Well, well, you Canadians fought in your own graves," before asking why they had come to fight Germany. Gibbons's answer, that they were patriots who loved England, prompted the doctor, who had done his residency in London, to exclaim in a latter-day version of Napoleon's dismissal of Britain, "Love England? Why do you love that nation of grocery clerks? Bah!"[12]

In his addled state on the gurney, Gibbons was in no position to argue, as over the next few minutes the doctor provided a short lesson on how the Germans viewed the war. "England was jealous of Germany's commercial power," he declared, which was not untrue. The *casus belli* was, however, Germany's violation of

Belgium's neutrality.[13] The German Foreign Office dismissed this, saying that the British had committed "race treason." The German foreign office on Wilhelmstrasse had, for its part, declared that the Germans would never "forgive the perfidy of the British government in betraying common blood in favour of uncivilized pan-Slavism. It is the most criminal faithlessness in the world's history, this taking advantage of our difficulties to vent long pent-up spite against the German commercial rival."[14]

Mid-May 1915: Canada

The Canadian and British reaction at the Germans' use of poison gas three weeks earlier at Ypres was encapsulated in an Australian cartoon. It showed the devil arriving late to a classroom at the "Academy of War Kultur–Torment Section–Poison Gas." A stern-looking, monocled professor tells him, "I am sorry, we have no further openings for instructors." The devil replies, "Ah, you misjudge me—I come as a pupil!"[15]

At Giessen, Edwards heard the horrifying story that the Germans had mimicked Calvary by pinioning two men on each side of a Canadian who was crucified on a barn door. Though he could not vouch for the story, he gave it a soldierly respect. For his part, Canon Scott doubted the story but suggested the man who told him he had seen it file an official report.[16]

Aware that this story could be seen as rumour mongering, on 5 May, the *Vancouver World* assured readers, "This is not mere camp gossip, a general vouches for the fact."[17] Two days later, the paper ran a short story on its front page quoting a British member of Parliament saying that the ancient-style executions were payback for stymying the Germans before Ypres. On the 15th, the *Globe* reported that the crucified body had been found. Remarkably, there were no statements from Sir Sam Hughes and few letters to the editors. Nor did Canadian papers report on the debate on the story that began in the British Parliament on 17 May.[18]

Canadians did not lack, however, for grisly stories of Second Ypres. On 19 May, the *Toronto Star* published a letter from a private to his sister that must have left many breakfasts uneaten.

> We had about 1,500 yards to go over absolutely open ground . . . Believe me, if hell is anything like Friday, I'm for reforming . . . How I lasted as long as I did I hardly know, as at every rush the fellow next to me copped it, and once when we were lying down the man next to me got it square through the head . . . the fellow next to me was hit in the arm. I sat beside him to get out his bandage . . . when I got it myself through the back.[19]

Late May 1915: Giessen and Handzame Military Hospital

PRIVATE SIMMONS HAD RECOVERED enough from his wounded arm that he was able to go out in the May sunshine and walk in the hospital's enclosure at Giessen. As his strength come back, he turned his mind away from the English soldier whose leg had been amputated without chloroform and the agonizing moans of another who had died of lockjaw. (This death is somewhat surprising, since wounded POWs were routinely inoculated for tetanus.) Instead, since Simmons had a compass, he began considering how to escape.

Gibbons, too, was getting stronger, thanks in large measure to Belgian nurses who risked severe punishment for secretly giving him apples, oranges or pieces of chocolate. *Herr Doktor*'s idea of German *Kultur* ensured the prisoner would not even think of escaping. For, as Gibbons discovered to his horror once the chloroform wore off, his foot was turned completely around and the leg was now significantly shorter than the other; what would later be considered a war crime was the result of the surgeon overlapping Gibbons's broken thigh bones.

Early June 1915: Giessen

The previous two weeks had been pretty good. After insect powder and cold-water washes failed to eradicate the lice infesting men's uniforms, the *Kommandant,* fearing an outbreak of typhus, called in a fumigator. He also allowed the POWs to have the first of what became monthly baths. Then Red Cross parcels arrived carrying food, cigarettes and, equally important for Simmons, new uniforms. Before he left the hospital he had been given the uniform of another prisoner, which fit him poorly.

While the prisoners dismissed most of what they read in the *Continental Times*, some stories hit close to home. Since Zeppelins had bombed the London dockyards the previous January, perhaps the story of a mid-May bombing of London was true. The one about Zeppelins bombarding the "shores of America," which, because the United States was still neutral, the Canadians took to be Halifax, made it difficult to keep their spirits up.

For men who remembered the world before the Wright Brothers had flown at Kitty Hawk (just over a decade earlier) and knew how flimsy the biplanes that passed over their trenches were, the 400-foot-long, 38-foot-high, lighter-than-air Zeppelins represented the "very embodiment of might and power." Yet one day in early June, recalled George Scott, the men felt that "even the stars in their courses fought for us." Scott then used language learned in a Church of England church in Ottawa to describe the wind that "rolled and crashed down, and with wild exuberance smote the proud work of man and destroyed it utterly."[20]

Mid-June 1915: Bischofswerda

THE BRITISH MILITARY CODE OF 1907, under which the Canadians served, required POWs to try to escape. The Hague Treaty recognized this when it declared, "Escaped prisoners who are retaken before being able to rejoin their own army or before leaving the territory occupied by the army which captured them are liable to disciplinary punishment." German lawyers, however, put more emphasis on the treaty's stipulation that prisoners of war were "subject to the laws, regulations, and orders in force in the army of the State in whose power they are. [And that any] act of insubordination justifies the adoption towards them of such measures of severity as may be considered necessary." [21] Since the Germans declared escape to be illegal, doing so amounted to mutiny. Thus the poster in all camps that read on top, "Prisoners have no RIGHTS only DUTIES" and then listed a number of offences, followed by the words "THE PUNISHMENT FOR THIS IS DEATH."

Peter Anderson's escape took months to prepare. Many days were spent with a needle and thread making passable civilian clothes. Others were spent studying conversational German, some pleating rope into a ladder he would use to climb out the riding school's window. The grappling hook that would hold the ladder in place came courtesy of a major in an Irish regiment who, unmoved by Sir Roger Casement's appeal to join the Irish Legion, secreted a fireplace poker in his peg leg. Intending to "relieve Fritz or Hans of a little chicken or pig," Anderson hoarded the salt the Germans provided for him to soak his feet after he reported that walking so much on the hard-packed earth of the parade ground had injured them.[22]

As would other escapers, Anderson planned to stay out of sight, travelling at night and using Germany's forests as cover. However, since he did not have a map, Anderson needed to learn which forests were nearby. His information came from a surprising source: the camp *Kommandant*, who was keen to compare big-game hunting in Germany and Canada.

Late June 1915: Giessen

Private Frederick Dent avoided going to a punishment camp because a German doctor believed him when he said he was sick. Private James F. Whittaker, also captured at Ypres, was not as lucky.

A few weeks earlier, Whittaker and some other men had exercised their right under the Hague Treaty to volunteer for work for which they were to be paid at the same rate as German soldiers. For the first while, their work in a nearby ironworks provided what the POWs desperately wanted, a respite from the mind-numbing boredom of the POW camp. Then, by chance, Whittaker saw shells being shipped away from the foundry; though he could not have known this, both Canada and Britain were, coincidentally, gripped by shell crises at this time. The treaty forbade any work that "had connection with the operations of the war."[23] After Whittaker told the others what he had seen, they immediately refused to work. The Germans, in turn, cut their rations. When the POWs still refused to work, each was made to hoist a heavy sack of bricks on his back and, at bayonet point, march up and down a steep hill. After a few days, they were sent back to Giessen, where they were tried for mutiny and sentenced to eighteen months in a punishment camp.

At the iron foundry or the railway that Private John Keith worked on near Giessen, the Germans enforced their will with gratuitous pain. A German drove his rifle butt into Keith's face. The guards responsible for Harry Howland's barracks at Giessen, nicknamed "Mutiny" and "Shrapnel," were bullies, with the former, and uglier, delighting in pitching cold water over the face of a man he caught in bed after reveille. Mutiny also slapped the prisoners for minor infractions or drove his hobnailed boot into their buttocks.

1 July 1915: Giessen

Compared with Dominion Day celebrations the POWs could remember that featured picnics and ice cream, it wasn't much. But by giving the Canadians sweets they had managed to save, the Canadians' British comrades at Giessen did what they could to soften the pain of being a prisoner of war on the anniversary of Confederation.

Scott and a few other Canadians could not even enjoy this simulacrum of a holiday because they were serving punishment sentences for feigning physical and mental illnesses in order to avoid work. Despite the day's importance for Canadians, each prisoner was given only a small amount of water. But, as Scott noticed on 2 July, Private Fred R. Ivey had it the worst. In addition to bruises caused by a baton, on the day Canadians celebrated the 48th anniversary of Confederation, the Germans had tattooed an Iron Cross on Ivey's nose and forehead.

19 July 1915: Giessen

The code for "Do you want to try to plan an escape?" was "Have you a compass?" and Mervyn Simmons did. Even before Lance Corporal Thomas Bromley asked the question, Simmons had realized previous failures had nothing to do with escapers lacking vigour. Rather, their "plans had been frustrated by their unwise confidences." In the large man "with a strong attractive face" who had proved his mettle at Ypres, Simmons saw another soldier who would agree to take security seriously. Accordingly, when together, each was keenly alert to eavesdroppers.[24]

Of his own imprisonment during the First World War, the French scholar Robert d'Harcourt wrote, "Upon arriving in a camp, a prisoner's first care is to get to know his enclosure."[25] Giessen was an open book. It was surrounded by a high wooden fence topped with barbed wire. Set back from that fence was a barbed wire fence; between the two was a forbidden stretch of No Man's Land, where a prisoner could be shot without warning. Each compound was divided from the others by two barbed wire fences. Sentries marched beats around the barbed wire. Guards manned towers that offered a clear field of fire into the camp.

The fractured English on the notice posted on the 19th after the recapture of a French officer did not detract from its message. "Owing to the evasions recently done, we bet to inform the prisoners of the following facts. Until present time, all the prisoners who were evased, have been catched." The threat that "any evasion give place to serious punition (minima) fortnight of rigorous imprisonment after they go in the '*Strafebaracke*' for an indeterminate time."[26] The notice did not, however, have the intended effect. A few hours after it was posted, Simmons and Bromley volunteered to work on a farm in Rossbach, from which they planned to escape and make their way to Switzerland.

29 July 1915: Giessen

The letter from Lord Kitchener confirmed that Mr. Moncur's namesake son, David, a British private, had died as a prisoner of war. But for ten other families named in the *Globe*'s page-six article, enduring the war had changed. Bugler Frederick Allan and Sergeant W. Ellis were alive—wounded, but alive. Their families' hopes and prayers rested now on such stories as the one on the 24th, which quoted the American ambassador as saying that the conditions at Bischofswerda, albeit the officers' camp, were good—rather than with the fears generated by a story on the 29th that said that POWs were being "badly fed."[27]

Story after story said that Red Cross parcels prevented starvation, something they were never meant to do. Contrary to Red Cross rules, the Germans included the calories, fats, vitamins and minerals in the parcels as part of the prisoners' diet. Even with the food contained in Red Cross parcels (money for which was raised by organizations across Canada) and in those sent by friends and families, most POWs lost a significant amount of weight.

The gnawing emptiness in their stomachs, something known only to the destitute in Canada and unknown to Canadian soldiers, pushed proud men such as Edwards to desperation. Once, after seeing a piece of French loaf cooling on a windowsill and realizing no one was around, Edwards quickly pocketed it. He sold the stout boots that had shod his feet and provided much-needed purchase in the mud of Flanders to a Frenchman for an old pair of his boots and sixty pfennig, with which Edwards bought a single extra bread ration. Those in Britain and Canada who complained that German prisoners were too well fed would have been even more vociferous if they had known that at Giessen, hungry POWs "picked over the sour refuse in the [garbage] barrels," or that on some days, what flavour or small amount of protein the broth had came from the marrow of dog bones.[28]

Mid-Summer 1915: Torhout Hospital, Belgium

The behaviour of the German nurses at the military hospital in Torhout, Belgium, shocked Gibbons. They shook their fists in his face and called him a "*Schwein Engländer*!" One enjoyed tearing off his bandages. The doctor charged with caring for the men in Gibbons's ward violated his Hippocratic oath by taking hold of one man's wounded limb and wrenching it, "causing the unfortunate man to writhe and scream." Before leaving the ward, the doctor tried to further undermine morale: "Yes, yes, my friends; that will make you realize that you are at war!"[29]

The doctor's effort had failed, he discovered, as he twisted Gibbons' damaged leg. "You devil," the Canadian yelled, "why don't you torture your own men as you torture us? You are a typical German; you torture and maltreat those who are helpless and unable to hit back."[30] His *dignitas* impinged, the doctor dropped Gibbons's leg, turned and left the room. An orderly told Gibbons that he had barely escaped being shot, and Gibbons believed him, though German military law would have sanctioned a hard *Strafe* sentence.

At first, the chaplain who came to visit Gibbons was little different from other Germans who failed to understand why Canada had come to Britain's aid.[31] He was better informed than most, for he knew that Canada's soldiers were volunteers. When Gibbons didn't agree that he was seeking adventure, the chaplain asked how much the British paid him. Gibbons answered, "Nothing. We receive our pay as soldiers from Canada." The chaplain asked, "How much?" "One dollar and ten cents ($23) a day," said Gibbons, stunning the chaplain. The Lutheran man of the cloth did some mental arithmetic and started yelling. "Four marks a day! . . . Murderers."[32] As other Germans gathered around Gibbons, the chaplain worked himself up into a towering rage, pointing toward Gibbons, yelling "Four marks a day!" in German.

4 August 1915: Ottawa

THE CABLE AMBASSADOR GERARD sent to Canada saying that most of the food parcels were getting through to the POWs was meant for people such as the friends of Lance Corporal Michel J. Jenkins in Ottawa, who had received a letter from Jenkins saying, "Send anything in the way of eatables."[33] As soon as parcels arrived, the POWs sent letters thanking those who had sent them. Indeed, to keep senders from thinking "What's the use?" even when expected parcels did not arrive, POWs sent thank-you letters.[34] Many POWs who did not have family or friends who could send them food and clothes were "adopted" by such organizations as the Women's Canadian Club. It cost $2 ($42) to adopt a POW for a year, and one man in 1915 adopted four prisoners.

Boxes could not weigh more than ten pounds and had to be tied with string. They could not contain newspapers, but tobacco, food, clothing and personal items such as razors were allowed. Those who found the regulations difficult to follow could turn to the Timothy E. Eaton Company, which would send something tasting of home "to the unfortunate lad who is a prisoner." Eaton's Overseas Chocolate came pre-packaged in one- and four-pound boxes, the latter costing $2. Eaton's guaranteed that this specially formulated chocolate would not cause thirst or melt and "will keep indefinitely."[35]

Mid-Summer 1915: Bischofswerda

DESPITE WHAT THE HAGUE TREATY said about recaptured prisoners not being "liable to any punishment on account of the previous flight," Anderson had nightmares of being executed after being recaptured.[36] These did not, however, slow his plan for escape. For a number of reasons, men normally escaped in twos or in groups. One man could sleep while another kept watch, one man could keep up another's flagging spirits, and different men usually had complementary field craft skills. Anderson, for his part, pinned his hopes not on an escape partner but on his experience as a big-game hunter in Canada to carry him across Germany.

Since he would not be able to escape with a sufficient stash of food, Anderson set about accumulating money. When he arrived at Bischofswerda, he turned over £7 in gold ($292) and 25 francs, which the Germans placed into an account. He had another £4 hidden in his clothes. To increase his bankroll, Anderson borrowed RM 40 from Lance Corporal Frederick E. George. Anderson could pay the 3rd Battalion officer back because POWs could have money wired to their POW accounts. An agreement reached in the second week of August between Canada and Germany resulted in a portion of a soldier's pay being sent to the American ambassador in Berlin, who then deposited it into the prisoner's German account. Money from home could also be transferred to the prisoners' accounts.

After the £10 Anderson had requested from home arrived, he asked the quartermaster's officer to transfer 40 marks to George's account. The clerk who recorded the transfer in a big leather-bound double-entry accounting book ignored the regulations against gambling and likely smiled at the reason Anderson gave for transferring the money: a poker debt. Somewhat more difficult to hide, but equally important, were the woollen balaclava, biscuits, chocolate, Oxo cubes and small enamelled cooking pot other men donated to Anderson's cause.

Late Summer 1915: Giessen

GIBBONS EXPECTED THE TAUNTS from the train and from those who saw him being marched to Giessen. But he was shocked at the condition of the men he saw in the hospital.[37] Men with dirty, festering wounds lay unattended, many in their own filth. Men with terrible wounds to their backs lay on straw, which worked its way beneath their paper bandages and caused at best irritation and at worst excruciating pain. Though the hospital was filled with scores of men, the doctors changed only a dozen bandages, and these, Gibbons saw to his horror, had been taken from other patients and washed and rewound.

At times, such as after being beaten for singing, the POWs in the general compound experienced physical pain. Most of the time, however, their pain was psychological. Likely because he was so hobbled, Gibbons was spared the "mortification" of having an orange stripe sewn onto his pants. These stripes acted like a latter-day scarlet letter, bespeaking the moment of iniquity when they surrendered. He was not, however, spared the effect of being enclosed behind barbed wire. At the front, where barbed wire protected your trench, wire was blessing, and when you tried to get through the enemy's wire, a curse. Every POW had seen bodies hanging grotesquely limp, decomposing on the wire, bones lying on the ground, picked clean by vultures and rats.

Strung around unarmed men, barbed wire dehumanized, shaking the prisoners' "certitude that they are human. It confirms their fate: like beasts, they are to be worked or slaughtered."[38] As one German POW in England put it, "Yesterday I was a gentleman, to-day I am a monkey behind iron bars."[39]

At the front, fatalism carried men through the misery of the trenches and the horror of bombardments.[40] In many cases, however, fatalism could not survive the corrosive effects of the monotony of camp life. The tension of "living in the hands of enemies . . . and hearing nothing of what is going on in the outside world" turned some men's hair white.[41] Others succumbed to "barbed wire disease"; like their comrades who experienced shell-shock on the battlefield (what today we recognize as post-traumatic stress disorder, PTSD), these men stared vacantly into the distance, their expression signalling that they had abandoned all hope.

Some long-term POWs horrified Lieutenant J. Harvey Douglas, for they had become "despondent, nervous wrecks and often go stark staring mad, or commit suicide."[42] Historian Jonathan Vance reports that another POW captured in mid-1916 suffered from hallucinations and "fits of mania"; even the much-desired Red Cross food was not enough to coax him from his bunk.[43]

It can easily be imagined what the men suffering from PTSD in the camps would have made of the fact that years later, Sir Andrew McPhail would write in the official history of the Canadian Medical Services: "'Shellshock' is a manifestation of childishness and femininity. Against such there is no remedy."[44]

Late September 1915: Giessen and Rossbach, Germany

WHAT EDWARDS CALLED the "cunning of the oppressed" was as central to Gibbons's escape from Germany as it was to Simmons and Bromley's plans.[45] Gibbons was in no condition to escape from a farm. However, after hearing that the Germans planned to repatriate men unable to contribute to the war effort even as clerks, Gibbons played the Hamlet card and feigned madness. He was helped along by his youthful face, hair that had not been cut since he was captured, and the fact that in addition to being wounded in the leg, he had been wounded in the head. When asked about Canada, the U.S., England, France and his own regiment, Gibbons shook his head hard enough to make his hair fly. He "star[ed] in a bewildered fashion at the doctors and officers."[46] After a few weeks and several performances before German and Red Cross doctors at a POW camp near the Dutch border, Gibbons left Germany.

End September 1915: Rossbach

Simmons and Bromley's first move toward freedom came courtesy of the Germans, who trucked them to Rossbach. After the drabness of Giessen, both enjoyed seeing the pretty country in which some low stone houses dated back centuries to when the crusaders made their way across the German lands. In Rossbach, the POWs slept in a house in the village. After the meagre prison diet, they appreciated soup with meat and vegetables. Also on the farmer's table were cheese and potatoes that were boiled in their skins and fried. His *Kaffee* may not have contained any coffee, but it did have milk and sugar.

After the casual brutality of Mutiny and Shrapnel, the attentions of Lena, the comely farmer's daughter who spoke English, were especially welcome. Simmons enjoyed telling her that in Canada women did not do heavy labour. Rather, they had the leisure to read books, play the piano, and make pretty clothes to wear while visiting and going to parties. This sketch of women's lives, which belonged more to an Evelyn Waugh novel than to the reality of Simmons's labouring class in rural Saskatchewan, seemed designed to provoke envy and lessen the morale on Germany's home front.

Lena taught Simmons some German and told him about her beau in Sweden. A week after Simmons arrived in Rossbach, he and Lena were joined in the fields by Lena's friend Fanny Hummel, an attractive sixteen-year-old who spoke excellent English. After hearing that her brother was an army officer, Simmons pushed to find out her thoughts about the war. He was not surprised by her reticence, thinking rather that "Fanny was a properly trained German girl, and didn't think in matters of this kind."[47]

Chapter Three

October–December 1915

Early October 1915: Outside Spremberg, Germany

His "*Guten Abend*" (Good evening), German-style backpack, pipe and cloth-covered buttons made Peter Anderson look enough like a civilian that not even the two policemen he walked by on his way through Spremberg took much notice of him. Not wanting to try his luck in the full light of day, he spent the first day after escaping from Bischofswerda dry and warm in a hayloft. The Canadian big-game hunter's second sanctuary was surprisingly familiar, a plantation of jack pines protected by a sign saying "*Verboten*" (Forbidden).

Three days earlier, with the help of two officers, Anderson had carried his escape kit to the corner of the riding school building and buried it in the sand. Just after evening roll call, shielded by Edward Bellew and another officer, Anderson slipped into a well. After darkness fell and Anderson heard the sentry's steps die away on this particular beat, he began sliding open the well's lid, but found it was too heavy to move at one go. He had to hold it partially open as the sentry marched by—hoping his efforts would not be seen. A few moments later, Anderson climbed out of the well and dug up his escape kit. He then sneaked over to the disused stable, which he entered through a window he jimmied open. Since the window ledge was high, he used the fire-poker-cum-grappling-hook to secure the rope ladder so he could climb through the window.

The seven hours it took him to leave the stable and clear two barbed wire fences ticked by agonizingly slowly. To get to the fence, he ran into the gap created when the two sentries had turned their backs to each other and began goose-stepping in opposite directions. Once beyond the wire, he pulled off the socks that muffled his steps and made false tracks, starting off toward Switzerland. To nudge the Germans into searching for him in that direction, he had asked another officer to rip off that section of the map of Europe posted in their common room. When he came to a hard road on which he would not leave footprints, he changed direction. Meanwhile, to ensure that the German shepherd tracking dogs that would be soon be brought to Anderson's bed to get his scent would be useless, Bellew sprinkled cayenne pepper around it.

The jack pines may have smelled and looked familiar, but they provided much less protection than the hayloft Anderson had slept in the previous day. At one point, the deserted stand seemed to come alive with a terrifying noise quite unlike anything Anderson had ever heard hunting or in the trenches. When he realized he'd been startled by hundreds of pheasants walking and flying through the pines, Anderson relaxed and ate some biscuits and chocolate.

3 October 1915: Frankfurt, Germany

Under other circumstances, a man filling his water bottle, as Anderson was doing just outside Ketbus (Cottbus), might have gone unnoticed. But when he noticed that two men were following him, he realized that he, an unkempt man lying down at ten o'clock at night in apparent exhaustion, had drawn unwanted attention. Thinking he might be able to scare them off, the infantry officer ran toward the men, prompting them to turn and run, giving him the opportunity to jump into a ditch. A short while later, as he sneaked around a nearby house, Anderson heard what he took to be the two men talking. To distract them, he took a handful of large pebbles and threw them into a bush some distance away. As these armed civilians turned and fired into that bush, Anderson made for a nearby wood.

The rain that began that night assured him that the hounds loosed on him could not find him. It also explained why the following day, people who passed on the road about 150 yards away from Anderson were too preoccupied to notice a drenched man hiding in the thinning autumn underbrush. Later, as Anderson walked down a road, a man came up to speak to him. When the man said simply, "*Ja, ja*," Anderson knew that the scarf wound round his neck had helped make his hoarse voice (which he hoped would cover his accent) believable as he said gruffly, "The doctor has forbidden me to speak, *Halsschmerzen*."[1]

At 4:30 a.m. on 3 October, after waking up shivering and then walking through still another windy and rainy day, Anderson reconsidered his plans. Heartened by the fact that, save for the men who had followed him out of the village, his presence on the roads of Germany had elicited little reaction, he decided to buy a train ticket. Near 9 a.m., having gotten rid of anything that indicated he was a Canadian soldier, he walked into the town of Guben, armed with a believable story. He was now Peter Jansen, a Swede who had lived in Minnesota and whose business partner, Hans Schmidt, had recently been killed in battle. Jansen was on his way back to Copenhagen, where his wife and children awaited him. To support this part of his story, after destroying papers with his handwriting, he wrote a couple of tender letters from his "Mrs. Jansen" to himself.

Augmented by Jansen's un-neutral support for the Kaiser, Anderson's cover story worked so well that the normally reticent Germans provided a surprising amount of military information. The woman in a shop where he bought a rain cape and an umbrella asked about business conditions in America. After he assured her they were good, she told him not to worry about having lost his passport because they were checked only when nearing the frontier. Anderson spent the afternoon in another stand of jack pines before walking to the train station, where he bought a third-class ticket for Frankfurt. With his new raincoat, worn trousers and cloth hat, he fit right in with the soldiers in mufti waiting on the platform. No one noticed that when he joined in their patriotic shouts of "*Hoch der Kaiser*" (Up with or praise the Kaiser), Anderson's lone voice changed the *H* into an *F*.[2]

3 October 1915: Near Rossbach

MERVYN SIMMONS NEVER FOUND out how Fanny Hummel took the news that despite having walked her home, he did not consider her his girl, because the next day he and Thomas Bromley escaped. Since the POWs were not guarded in the fields, the guards assumed that any escape from Rossbach would occur from the farms. Accordingly, the guards were less than vigilant when the POWs were in the boarding house. Still, as the minutes ticked down to the moment when Simmons and Bromley planned to escape, they had to consider one particular guard. At 10:30 p.m. they heard the expected commotion caused by the change of shift of POWs working in a nearby mine. But the creaks caused by the unaccountably restless guard "tramp[ing] up and down the . . . floor" surprised them and almost caused them to abort their escape.[3] By 11:30, however, the guard seemed to have settled down. Even though other POWs urged Simmons and Bromley to reconsider their plans, the two Canadians pushed the wire away from the window and dropped to the ground below.

For a few moments after the window slammed shut, the escapers ran into the inky darkness, "as if the whole German Army were in pursuit." The rain that added to the weight of their greatcoats was more than offset, however, by the "weight [that] had rolled off [their] souls."[4] Unable to see more than a short distance ahead, Simmons led Bromley by following his compass, remembering each time he checked it that in Germany the needle was 16° off true north.

Their training to drop noiselessly to the ground came back quickly when, not long after a train whizzed by, they saw people they assumed had gotten off at the nearby station walking toward them on what they had hoped would be a deserted road. As the party passed and one man sang "The Joy of Life," a popular song Simmons recognized, the "desperate game against terrible odds" the Canadians were playing behind enemy lines seemed less dangerous for a moment. “I can't work up any ill-will to that good old soul going home singing—and I don't believe he has any ill will toward us,” remarked Bromley.[5]

The road ran through a village that seemed easier to walk through than go around, especially since the road was dirt and not cobblestone, so their steps did not echo in the darkness. They made so little noise that not even a dog barked at them. The three clangs of the village bell told them that nautical twilight would soon rise and with it, German peasant farmers. The marshy ground around them offered little cover, so they kept moving until they saw a thick wood, where they hid throughout a miserably cold and sodden day. Unable to sleep, they ate the carrots and turnips they stole from all-but-empty gardens. Simmons's and Bromley's lieutenants would have been pleased, for to protect their feet, the two soldiers remembered to take off their boots, rub their feet until they were dry and then put on dry socks before putting their sodden boots back on; to dry their sodden socks they placed them between their stomachs and their shirts.

4 October 1915: Berlin, Germany

ANDERSON ATE HIS FIRST real meal in months surrounded by German soldiers and travellers in the ornate Frankfurt station, famed for the steel and glass roofs that covered the platforms. On the train to Berlin, he had his first dry sleep in days. Under a sign reading “Soldiers beware of spies, especially women spies. Do not discuss military matters with strangers. Be loyal to the Fatherland,” soldiers talked loudly and spoke openly about where they and their heavy guns were going.[6]

Since the train to Wittenberg, from where he planned to catch a train north toward Hamburg, would not be leaving Berlin for two hours, Anderson decided to hide in a cab—and do a little sightseeing. The Berliners, he saw from the window of the cab, seemed nothing like the loquacious soldiers or the shopkeeper in Ketbus; hardly anyone was smiling. Though alone in the enemy's capital city, Anderson felt quite safe since "no German would expect me to visit [Kaiser] Bill's home town under the circumstances."[7]

4 October 1915: Near Frankfurt

Simmons and Bromley cut a different path through Germany. Instead of making for Frankfurt, they stayed away from the metropolis and most roads. Accordingly, they found themselves splashing through streams. Bromley had lost the sixth sense that, as Sergeant Fred Bagnall recalled, allowed a man in the trenches to "guess where there is a wire overhead hanging to catch your rifle, for here the field telephone lines must be strung."[8] He tripped over a railway signal wire, setting off dozens of alarm bells. Mercifully, the darkness that hid the wire cloaked the escapers as they ran down the track that anyone who came rushing out of his house would have looked down.

On their third night out, when the North Star was obscured by clouds, Bromley's worried tone signalled that he did not believe Simmons when he said that they were heading west. Even after Simmons showed Bromley that he had been guiding them by a light patch in the sky that had not moved, Bromley insisted that they light a match and take a compass reading. This showed that they were, indeed, heading west.

Keeping that direction became ever more difficult when they reached a bog. Moving forward here was so unbelievably difficult that even a soldier who had endured the winter of 1914/15 on Salisbury Plain and then the mud of Flanders described it as a place "where travellers could be lost forever." They found their way out of this "dismal swamp" thanks to a narrow-gauge railway that led toward the small city of Hanau.[9] After taking shelter in thick bushes, they again changed into dry socks. Then they choked down some of the raw potatoes, sugar beets and apples they had stolen that night.

5 October 1915: On a Train and Near the River Main, Germany

FOR A FEW MOMENTS after seeing railway officials asking passengers for their papers, Anderson readied himself to run between the cars so he could jump from the train. Then he noticed that they questioned only men in uniform, and rested easier. After arriving in Hamburg, he walked into the same small hotel that he had stayed in two years earlier on business, cheekily signing the guestbook "Peter Jansen, bricklayer, Lübeck," before having a good meal, bathing and climbing into a warm bed.

Several hundred miles away, again unable to sleep because of the rain, Simmons decided to explore the area around the wood in which he and Bromley hid. The soldier laid down a trail of broken twigs, which he later followed back to Bromley and told him of wondrous things: deer, a vine-covered lodge that could have served as an illustration in a Grimms' fairy tale and, especially, the blue smoke rising above its chimney, which had made the hungry and chilled Simmons think of a warm room and a breakfast of bacon and eggs.

Though Simmons feared he had been spotted by at least some of the people in the lodge, he was so exhausted that immediately after telling Bromley what he had seen, he fell asleep. A short time later, a bugle call woke him and he heard shouted commands ringing out from the direction of a nearby hay meadow. At first, the escapers took these harsh sounds to be nothing more than an infantry training exercise. Then they heard the men charging into the wood. As the Germans surrounded them, the escapers showed the same sense of self-control they had needed to survive the stress of battle as they "lay close to the earth and hardly dar[ing] to breathe."[10] At one point, a number of soldiers passed a mere ten feet from Simmons. After a second combing of the wood in the afternoon, Simmons and Bromley made their way to a meadow.

Climbing out of water-filled ditches in the meadow was so difficult that when the escapers reached a road, they decided to risk using it. Several hours later, they found themselves heading south on a road that ended at a stream so swollen by the heavy rains that they could not swim across it. They walked along its bank until they reached what their map told them was the Kinzig River. Unable to find a path along this tributary of the Rhine, they chose a place to hide, ate some chocolate and biscuits, filled their water bottles and lay down to sleep.

7 October 1915: Near Hesse, Germany

The 6th of October had been another teeth-chatteringly cold, wet day, but Simmons and Bromley were heartened when they passed into Bavaria. The next afternoon, the heavy rains gave way to bright sunshine, and the escapers slept in its warmth. After resting they set out again. Not long after, they came to a railway track and could see a station not far up the line. The stationmaster's dog noticed them, but in the gathering dark, the man who came rushing out did not. As dawn on the 8th approached, the escapers became worried. They were "in an open and treeless stretch of land," words that evoke the desolation depicted in the opening to Edgar Allan Poe's famous short story "The Fall of the House of Usher."[11] They were hidden by the heavy mist that soaked them through, but it could lift at any moment. Hoping to find a wood, they turned east. The large, dark shape visible through the mist turned out to be a hill, at the top of which was the cellar of a collapsed building. With daylight near, they had little choice but to climb into it and cover themselves as best they could with some rubbish.

8 October 1915: Schleswig, Germany

Anderson was surprised at the cursory security on the train taking him across the Kiel Canal, the strategic waterway that allowed Großadmiral Alfred von Tirpitz to move his High Seas Fleet from the Baltic to the North Sea without going around Denmark. Instead of officious Prussians asking for each passenger's papers, there were a number of policemen who ensured only that the curtains in the car were drawn.

Now in Schleswig, the Danish-born Anderson became a Danish bricklayer trying to get home. The truculent population that still remembered how the Kaiser's grandfather had ripped the duchy from the Danish crown in 1866 gave the man who spoke their language food, shelter and directions.

On the afternoon of the 8th, on a less-travelled road leading toward the border, Anderson was surprised when a guard stepped out of the trees and asked him for his papers. As Anderson fumbled for the nonexistent documents, he bet his freedom on his ear and said, "You don't come from this part of the country. You are from the south." When the guard answered, "Yes, I'm from Silesia," Anderson said how nice the country was compared to the bleak north. When the guard asked again for his papers, the escaper went for broke. "You have some great forests in Silesia and great sawmills," he prompted, leading the guard to speak of them with pride.[12] Later, fearing that the guard was again about to ask for his papers, Anderson started speaking about the depth of snow in Silesia, at which point the guard forgot about the papers and waved Anderson on. In a village inn that evening, Anderson fended off another guard's demand for his papers by buying round after round of beer, one of which was flavoured by ashes from Anderson's cigar.

9 October 1915: Aschaffenburg, Germany

After hours of remaining motionless, Simmons noticed Bromley pointing toward the rim of the cellar, where he saw a boy of about five whom he took to be the child of one of the farmers they had heard working nearby. A few minutes later, a little girl and some women peered down at them. When the escapers heard the sound of soldiers running, they stood up and surrendered.

To Simmons's surprise, they faced nothing more hostile than the indignity of being paraded through the streets. The commander of the Aschaffenburg military base was by turns inquisitive and incredulous. When asked why Canada was even in the war, Simmons claimed that Germany's "violation of Belgium had set Canada on fire," which cut little ice with the red-cheeked officer. He was even less impressed with Simmons's answer to the question of why he wanted to get out of Germany: "No free man enjoyed being a prisoner."[13]

Cut in the Prussian style, the commander's grizzled whiskers suggested that his battles had been staff rides, not shooting wars. German propaganda that stressed that the Kaiser's soldiers were protecting their homes and women (from the Slavic hordes) partially explained his reaction when Bromley said that he had escaped so that he could rejoin his wife and children. "This is not time for a man to think of his wife and children!" barked the commander.[14] Though Canadian soldiers called the Germans "Huns" and, as every army does, dehumanized its enemy, the Canadians also knew that, individually, Germans were not caricatures. Neither Bromley nor Simmons knew a certain Eugene Küpper, but neither would have been surprised at the sentiments contained in a letter to his wife back in Germany: "You wouldn't believe how the consciousness of your love, of the harmony of our hearts and souls strengthens me and makes me feel cheerful and confident in this din. I am always delighted to get your letters, far more so [now] than ever before."[15]

9 October 1915: The Danish Border

Anderson was fed by a woman whose husband had been drafted and who was left to support her five children and mother by herself. A farmer that Anderson had stopped on the road recognized from the escaper's accent where in Denmark he came from, and offered to walk Anderson partway toward the next village. A farmer who lived a few miles from the border advised the escaper to hide near there for a day and study the beats of the sentries. But anxious to get out of Germany, Anderson disregarded the advice and put his faith in the soldiers' age-old ways in heavy rain and storms.

His steps muffled by the storm, Anderson passed a customs house in which he saw a number of guards keeping themselves warm and dry, unaware of the POW sneaking right by them. After stepping through a gap in the hedge on the other side of the customs house, Anderson silently slipped back into the gloom to avoid the beam of a sentry's flashlight. When the light from the flashlight told him that the sentry was far enough away, Anderson crept to the road that led beyond a hedge, where he saw a sentry whose marching beat was so precise that the Canadian officer had little trouble following a few yards behind him. When this sentry was about to turn around, Anderson vanished into a ditch.

The admonition by a British staff officer that "no British soldier crawls into battle on his belly" mattered not a whit to escapers like Anderson, as he crawled through the four-foot-deep trench that separated Germany from Denmark.[16] Anderson could not help thinking that despite the storm, the three sentries he had stalked "should have been more careful looking after the interests of the Fatherland."[17] No one came running after the bell started ringing when he touched an unseen wire entanglement. Anderson assumed the sentry he had just passed credited the disturbance to the wind and not to an escaper who would soon cut through the wires and sneak into Denmark.

Late October 1915: Giessen

Simmons's stint in the *Strafe* cell was not the hard time his jailers had intended. True, the cell was only six by eight feet and there was only a shelf to sleep on with no pillows or blankets. Simmons had only water to drink, and his jailers brought him vile, cold food and never enough of it. However, a few minutes after the door to his cell clanged shut, the Canadian learned that no matter what the Germans thought, the cell was not completely dark, nor was he alone.

As soon as his eyes adjusted to the dark, Simmons noticed a ray of light coming through a crack in the wall. On the other side of that wall was a French prisoner, who told Simmons that on the opposite wall of his cell there was a batten that, when opened, furnished more than enough light to read, albeit while standing. The French prisoner, who had the ironic name of Malvoisin ("Evil Neighbour"), initiated Simmons into the ways of the punishment cell, which included leaving notes in lavatory number 8, ensuring that books, chocolate, biscuits, cheese and cigarettes would be smuggled to Simmons. Standing on the cell's platform, Simmons was able to read three or four books in the week or so before the cell that had furnished the light was itself darkened. After that, Malvoisin, who wore the circles (effectively bull's eyes) the Germans had painted on the front and back of his tunic with pride, did what he could to lighten Simmons's mood by regaling him with stories of his escapes.

25 October 1915: London, England

The War Office's Special Intelligence Department was so impressed by the information Anderson brought out of Germany that the major debriefing him thought that Anderson was gung ho to go back to Germany as a special agent. To protect other would-be escapers, the War Office would have wanted to keep the story of Anderson's means of escape under wraps for a time. That, however, is not the reason why Anderson's exploits were never the subject of Max Aitken's (purple) pen, which he wielded as "Canada's Eye Witness," telling of Canadian exploits in battle.

In August 1914, when the government received a report saying Germans were massing to invade from Minnesota, and in February 1915, when a bridge in New Brunswick was bombed by a German agent, Ottawa's heads stayed cool.[18] In late 1915, the upper echelons of Canadian Overseas Mission, which was responsible for Canadian soldiers in Britain, France and Belgium, lacked such good sense.[19] Even after Anderson was placed back on active duty, some senior Canadian officers who believed he could not have made his way out of Germany on his own whispered that the Danish-born Canadian was little more than a German plant. Thankfully, the official in the paymaster's office whom Anderson saw on the 25th was more trusting. After looking over the paper Anderson had filled out, the pay clerk stepped away and came back with a cheque for £39 ($7,250) made out to Major P. Anderson for "travelling expenses in Germany and elsewhere on Government business."[20]

Late October 1915: Giessen

Edward Edwards was humiliated because the Germans did not even know he had escaped. Taking their cue from Simmons and Bromley, Edwards and his escape partner had volunteered for a railway work party. The appropriate moment to flee arrived when the men were having lunch on an embankment near a wood. The escapers' comrades wished them Godspeed and they stepped into the darkness of the wood. But a few moments later, Edwards "noticed a curious change come over" his companion.[21] The barking of a dog broke what was left of his nerve. "There's too many dogs about," he pleaded, "and look at all those houses." Edwards tried to reason with him, saying, "Germany's full of houses and people. That's no news. Come on." Stronger language and pleas failed. "He had conjured up all the dangers that an active imagination could envisage. Every bush was a German and every sound the occasion of fresh alarm."[22] Had the Germans known of this, they would have been pleased, for in this case at least, the threats that escapers would be shot undid a soldier's pride.

Early November 1915: Giessen

THE WEEKS IN THE *Strafe* barracks were worse than the two weeks in the *Strafe* cell. The mattress and two blankets and the same food as the rest of the camp mattered little when set against what today we would call Psychological Operations, which Simmons recognized as a deliberate plan to weaken bodies and minds with weeks of "deadly monotony and inaction." Simmons's indeterminate (to him, at least) sentence meant that the Germans had stripped away the knowledge of when he would be "nearing the end" of his time in isolation. By depriving prisoners of books and even the risible *Continental Times*, the Germans aimed to produce mental stagnation, "to break us down to the place where we could not think for ourselves."[23]

During the long hours when Simmons was forced to remain sitting on a stool without speaking or moving, he fell back on his own inner resources. Recollections of his childhood intermixed with political thoughts, which compared the "heritage of liberty, of free speech, of decency" with the "strutting, cruel-faced cut-throat who was our guard." The German Lutherans around him, not to mention his Presbyterian minister back in Buchanan, Saskatchewan, would have been shocked at his layman's gloss on the phrase found so often in the Old Testament, "the Lord had commanded." Simmons thought it meant, "'Get the people together; let's have a mass-meeting; I have a message from God for the people!' When the people assembled, the king broke the news: 'God wants us to wipe out the Amelkites!' . . . and the show started."[24]

When a guard pricked him with his bayonet, Simmons did not respond with a stripped-down version of one of Bishop Winnington-Ingram's blood-curdling sermons that he had heard on church parades. Instead, Simmons thought that love and "not force and killing and bloodshed and prison-bars" would bring the days of peace. With the veins of the guard's neck swollen with rage and his eyes "red like a bull's," yelling in "his horrible guttural tongue" and thrusting his bayonet toward him, Simmons—who had used cold steel himself—thought of how "the image of God had been defaced in this man, by his training and education."[25]

Mid-November 1915: Giessen

"After the monotony of the cells in the *Strafe* barracks, the camp seemed something like getting home for Christmas," recalled Simmons, even though he could find none of the family parcels his sister's letter told him had been sent and had to content himself with one from a friend.[26] So that he would receive more mail,

Simmons made a deal with some Russian POWs who had no one to write to. Using their postcards, he wrote to friends under the names of Private Paul Rogowski and Private Ivan Romanoff. This last soldier, who shared a surname with Nicholas II, czar of all the Russias, was delighted to receive an unexpected letter from an Ontario woman, even though he could not read it.

The resourceful Simmons risked another *Strafe* sentence by sending a letter to a friend with whom he used to do puzzles, asking for a compass. The key to the code was the words slipped into the address, "Seaforth Wds," which meant "See fourth word" and not, as the censor probably thought, "Seaforth Highlanders of Canada." Simmons also sent a second message to his brother in the flap of an envelope that the POW had steamed open; he signalled the presence of the message by saying in the letter, "look into this for me." The secreted message read, "I tried to escape, but was caught and my compass taken away from me. Send me another; put it in a cream cheese."[27]

What Simmons calls the "pleasure" of reading was more than simple entertainment. In an overcrowded, noisy barracks in a drab POW camp, reading provided men with a means to carve out a personal (albeit internal/imaginary) space. This psychic space went beyond what can be thought of as a bubble apart from chronological time, as suggested by Bing Crosby's standard from the next war, "I'll be home for Christmas . . . if only in my dreams." Since this theatre of the mind was formed by the conscious choice to read Shakespeare, Sir Walter Scott, Robert Louis Stevenson and even middlebrow writers, its creation demonstrated that the POW had "some element of control over [his] life behind the wire." Reading allowed the prisoners to withdraw "from foreign geographical spaces [i.e., Germany] surrounding them."[28] If not precisely an act of rebellion, at least it was proof that the camps had failed to break the men's minds and spirits.[29]

Simmons is clear on how he viewed the act of reading what was once called the Great Tradition of English literature. For "imperial nationalists" like Simmons, words penned by Shakespeare, Milton, Dickens and others formed the "heritage of liberty, of free speech, of decency . . . which Fortune has thrown into our laps." [30]

Early December 1915: Rennbahn POW Camp, Germany, and Giessen

At Rennbahn, a camp located on a race course near Münster, Lance Corporal George W. Hinks, who had been captured at Ypres, had "no goddarn use for bawling hymns and pestering the Almighty with prayers." Yet, when asked to wield a hammer for the Anglicans, he replied, "If the poor guys that go in for that kind of thing want a few bits of furniture knocked together, I guess I'm the boy to do it."[31] At Giessen, the Church of England–confessing Scott was not the only one impressed by the French Catholic POW's life-sized painting of St. Patrick. It was so lifelike that when a guard caught a man hiding in the chapel to avoid a work parade, through the dim light the guard pointed to the painting, saying, "Bring him too." When the POW objected, "But that's St. Patrick," the (obviously Lutheran) guard responded, "It makes no matter who he is. He must work also."[32]

Simmons, however, was more concerned with the soldier who ingratiated himself with the guards by painting their portraits. To calm them as they posed, the POW engaged them in light conversation, asking seemingly innocuous questions about the area and

Germany. Once his patrons had left his studio, the painter turned to his real work, sketching maps. He gave one of his best works to Simmons as he and Bromley readied themselves for another escape.

Early December 1915: Canada

So that their letters would get past censors and keep up their respondents' morale, prisoners wrote in bromides. In his 2 October 1915 letter to his wife, Emma, Edwards told her he'd received her parcels, asked how their boys were, expressed sorrow for what had happened to his friend Hector, mentioned the cooling weather and ended by saying, "I have really nothing to tell you, only write soon and often."[33] Such letters conflicted with news stories like "Dogs and Typhus Fever British Prisoners' Lot," which claimed incorrectly that the POWs were made to wear uniforms that had been put on dogs, and correctly that typhus had broken out in camps.[34]

Letters home also conflicted with the reports from men who had been so badly wounded at Ypres that they were repatriated in early December. Hinks told of being left on the battlefield for two days before he was picked up and then transported all the way to Siegburg, Germany, before receiving treatment for the bullet and bayonet wounds to one of his legs. The food in the hospital where he was operated on was "such as a healthy soldier could not eat unless ravenous with hunger." The *Winnipeg Tribune* said that another emaciated soldier "declared that but for the parcels of food received, some of the prisoners would not have survived."[35]

21 December 1915: Rennbahn

Christmas came early for Private Gerry Burk, who had been captured at Ypres, and the other POWs at Rennbahn. Agog with the heady realization that a squadron of Allied aircraft were bombing near the POW camp, the prisoners ran out of their barracks into the cold afternoon air. The rolling thunder was followed that night by a "great glare in the sky" above Münster. The prisoners realized the bombing raid had hit an ammunition dump when, to their great joy, the "glare became brighter and the concussions more violent."[36] The crackle of exploding small-arms ammunition and the shriek of debris squealed through the air, thrilling the POWs.

The unaimed fusillade broke the nerve of the guards.[37] After the POWs sang a chorus of "La Marseillaise," which the guards knew was the French national anthem, the guards, shouting with rage, drove the prisoners back into their barracks at bayonet point. Had the Germans known that the French national anthem included the words, "Let the impure blood / Water our furrows," referring to their fathers, who had fought the French in 1871, much worse could have happened.

Christmas 1915: Giessen

Simmons enjoyed the plum pudding he had been allowed to boil in the cookhouse as part of his Christmas dinner. To ensure that Canadians would receive Christmas parcels on time, organizations like the Winnipeg War Service Association arranged to send them the first week of October. Simmons hoped his family had experienced the same joy in reading the Christmas card he had sent them a month earlier as he had felt in writing it.

However, what absorbed Simmons's interest was the new greatcoats he and Bromley had been given a few days earlier. Their coats differed from the hundreds of others distributed under the watchful eyes of the German quartermaster. A few days earlier, a friend of Simmons working in the parcels office had secretly moved two coats from the pile of "uncensored" coats (coats that had not been tampered with) to the pile of "censored" ones (that is, ones that had already had a brown stripe sewn on them). After being handed their (apparently censored) coats, Simmons quickly sewed on a stripe and prepared a cocoa-based paint that, when dried, was a fair approximation of the stripe on the POWs' trousers. Both the sewn on and painted stripes could easily be removed after they escaped, so they would not look like runaway prisoners.

Chapter Four

January–May 1916

1 January 1916: Rennbahn

The cold, easterly wind that drove rain and hail against the windows of their barracks heightened the emotions of Gerry Burk and British private Herbert Tustin. For them, smashing Prussian autocracy, something neither they nor their millions of comrades would have given much thought to eighteen months earlier, no longer involved the hypnotizing horror of explosions and seeing comrades "lying about in all attitudes, their faces yellow and ghastly, mucus flowing from their mouths and nostrils."[1] Rather, their war had been reduced to defying petty discipline, meted out by fists and kicks, and furtively sitting next to their room's stove, which threw off little heat as 1915 slipped into 1916.

The captured privates thought not of their families but of their comrades in both the CEF and BEF who at that very moment were shivering in the trenches a couple of hundred miles to the west. The experiences of those soldiers on the line were made all the more miserable by the water pumped toward them by the Germans, who held the high ground. Even had they known of these conditions, the two POWs would have willingly exchanged their cold, dry barracks for the trenches.

Mid-January 1916: Bischofswerda

The sound of the truck leaving the camp signalled that the second part of Thomas Scudamore's plan to reach Dresden was underway. In the first part, Scudamore had secreted himself in a laundry basket that was then carried onto the truck. After only a few moments, however, the truck stopped and Scudamore could hear guards unloading it.

Soon he could hear and feel the guards struggling to open the lock on the basket. A moment later, they threw the lid back and tipped the basket on its side, and Scudamore ignominiously spilled out. The guard in command did not believe Scudamore's story that the whole thing had been a lark. Nor was he fooled by Scudamore's attempt to escape judgment: after taking a few steps to get the kinks out of his legs, Scudamore started down a corridor that led to the main courtyard, where he could have vanished into the crowd of POWs.

An hour later, Scudamore found himself in an unheated guard room standing before the *Kommandant* and several other officers and guards. After being ordered to strip, he watched each piece of his "civilian" clothing being torn to shreds as the guards searched for money and maps. The cold, which produced a most unmilitary shiver, was bad enough. Worse by far was the fact he was standing before the "gorgeously dressed individuals *in puris naturalibus*," though holding his hands bashfully in front of his penis. Still, Scudamore kept his sense of humour, saying as he stood naked, "Herr Kommandant, you have forgotten this," as he took off his signet ring and held it up.[2]

The *Kommandant* was not amused and ordered Scudamore, now re-clothed, to a prison cell, where he spent his first night shivering on a plank that served the office of a bed without a blanket. Oddly, the *Kommandant* also refused to allow Scudamore to shave, so three days later he sported an unofficer-like shadow when he was tried by a colonel and a major from Dresden. Though the trial found him guilty, Scudamore thought it to be fair, and he was especially thankful that the two officers allowed him to shave and ordered that his bedding be sent down to him. At first, the *Kommandant* refused Scudamore's request for a pack of playing cards or a book. After Scudamore's vigorous protest, the *Kommandant* relented and allowed him both cards and a copy of *Handley Cross*, a comic novel published in 1843.

Thanks to a bit of cheek, John Thorn's ten-day *Strafe* meted out for aiding Scudamore ended a few days early. On the sixth or seventh day, the *Kommandant* summoned Thorn to his office for what the Canadian expected to be another dressing down. However, to his surprise, the office was empty. After waiting a few minutes, Thorn assumed that the *Kommandant*, who was known for partaking freely of his favourite beer, "must have been in a generous mood" and ordered him to be released. He left the office and walked to his regular room.[3] At that evening's *Appell*, the camp's second in command was confused to find one officer too many, until Thorn stepped forward to tell the German that he, Thorn, had been released. The next morning, in order not to lose face, the now-sober *Kommandant* accepted that Thorn had played the better hand.

Mid-January 1916: Vehnemoor POW Camp near Oldenburg, Germany

Mervyn Simmons was nervous as he and Edward Edwards were searched before leaving Giessen. Simmons wasn't worried about the guards finding contraband cans of food in his pack because they had none. Rather, he and Private Edwards wore the incriminating materials: the poorly sewn stripes on their greatcoats and faux stripes on their pants.

For hours on the train that took them to another camp, Simmons marvelled that the guards failed to notice that after each lurch of the train, their pants gave off a brownish puff. As pieces of red paint flaked off their pants, Simmons reproached himself for not having used sugar to create a stronger binder.

At Vehnemoor POW camp, Simmons and a number of men who stood around a soldier named Bert when he read a letter from home learned how POWs were being treated in Canada. The ones that Bert's female friend had seen the previous July at the Kingston Road Internment Camp (near Toronto) had enjoyed strawberries and ice cream.* Such tastes were but unimaginable to men

* In reality, these prisoners were some of the thousands of the Ruthenian civilians interned at the beginning of the war, but in the parlance of the day they were called prisoners of war. Having ice cream and strawberries was, nevertheless, an unusual luxury.

who choked down *Kriegsbrot* and held their noses while putting spoonfuls of vile fish soup into their mouths. The idea of leisurely sitting in the sun was now foreign to men who wore uncomfortable wooden clogs (to prevent them from escaping) yet cut peat in bogs at gunpoint.

Neither Bert nor the other men could quite believe that his friend had written, "I am so glad, dear Bert, that you are safe in Germany and out of the smoke and the roar of the trenches." She had worried about Bert before seeing the POWs in Canada. Recalling what she had been told by his parents after their pre-war trip to Germany, she told Bert, "The German ways are so quaint and the children have such pretty manners, and I am afraid that you will be awful hard to please when you come back." These words caused Bert to burst out dejectedly, "Lord! What do they understand?"[4]

The four hundred men who shared the barracks lit by a single bare lightbulb sustained their morale by small acts of disobedience. Some came early; after giving their name, rank and service number, a number of Canadians told the Germans they were piano tuners, keepers in asylums, secretaries, supreme court justices and, in one case, a lion tamer. Small acts of sabotage—smashing shovels or losing tools—may not have broken the Germans, but these minor victories were vital to the prisoners' mental health. So was singing, which carved out a small space of their own. Even though the guards could not understand the anti-German lyrics, they ferociously stamped out singing at every opportunity. Singing bound the men together. Songs like "It's a Long Way to Tipperary" linked them to distant armies, recalling the camaraderie and esprit de corps.

22 January 1916: Vehnemoor

The arrival of some two dozen more guards in camp gave one man cold feet. But Simmons and lance corporals Edwards and Bromley went ahead with their planned escape without him.

On Saturdays, Vehnemoor's eastern barbed wire fence was festooned with laundry, which, the three men hoped, would hide their attempt to get under it. Getting to, let alone through, the wire required careful choreography. As night gathered and other men screened them from the guards, the escapers ran to the fence to a spot beyond the harsh glow of an arc light just moments before a sentry turned to march past that point. At Frezenberg, the air had pulsed with explosions and the shrieks of wounded men and incoming shells. Now the swishing sound came only from Edwards's own blood rushing through his ears. The blood's speed was caused by the same adrenalin spike that made the fine motor control needed to snip the wires all the more difficult. In his heightened state, Simmons equated the twang heard when Edwards cut the last wire to a rifle shot.

At least one guard noticed something, for as soon as they were through the wire, shots rang out. The bullets might well have felled them had the escapers given in to the urge to rise and run, and not remembered the infantryman's mantra (still taught today): Dirt is your friend. For the first twenty yards, they hugged the ground. The crack of rifle shots told them the bullets were landing well past them. A few moments later, they heard dogs, but they were far enough ahead that they could plunge into the bog beside the camp to mask their scent. Through the long, cold January night illuminated by a silvery moon, they struggled through the bog. As dawn approached, they crawled into a thicket of spruce and, as they breathed the stink of their wet clothes impregnated with bog scum that constricted on their skin as it dried, they fell asleep.

Late January 1916: Near Oldenburg and Near the River Ems, Germany

---

SIMMONS AND EDWARDS WOULD have acted the same way to ensure the other men's escape. Hobbled by the constriction of his legs caused by the shrinking of his half-dried underwear, Bromley surrendered when they heard a voice call "*Halt!*" Noting that the guards had momentarily focused on Bromley's raised arms, Simmons and Edwards gambled that the three civilians who were some distance away in another direction were not armed and that the guards would hold their fire if the escapers ran toward the civilians. As Simmons and Edwards threaded their way among the civilians, the soldiers realized why none of them moved to try to stop their dash to freedom: the figures were, in fact, three bare trees swaying in the wind. Throughout the rest of day, the escapers hid in a grove surrounded by spruce trees that crackled in the cold wind.

They did not have any food. Simmons had been hungry before, but in his excited state, he found that this bout of hunger gave him "a view of things that will never happen when the stomach is full." The Simmons even found himself thinking that Catholics were on to something by having the faithful "come fasting to mass, for that is the time to get spiritual truths over to them!"[5] The extreme cold foiled their plans for one man to sleep while the other kept watch.

* * *

Some days were spent hiding in a copse; all were cold and miserable. During the nights, the little warmth the haggard, hungry men felt was generated by walking and watching for the glow in the sky or a dog's bark, which indicated they were nearing one more village that they had to avoid. The few people Simmons and Edwards saw on the roads were despatched with indifferent grunts or avoided altogether by stepping into whatever darkness providence provided.

In 1916, the Dutch border lay some six miles beyond the Ems River, which the escapers reached on 29 January. Too deep and wide to swim, the river's waters were partially iced by the coldest winter in decades. Accordingly, Simmons and Edwards built a raft, but unlike the one in *The Swiss Family Robinson*, which both men recalled, theirs barely floated. Hours later, they had to risk rushing across a bridge. The fact that the high waters of the Ems partially submerged the bridge's roadway gave them hope that the bridge would not be well guarded. Twice over the past few days they had been able to run from capture, but now, lit up by arc light and hearing the sharp clatter of rifle bolts rammed into place, they had no choice but to surrender.

Early February 1916: Meppen, Germany

The gendarme who questioned them proved a puzzle, not least because of the two beautiful women who incongruously fawned over the fat man. To Simmons's dismay, the gendarme knew enough of his business to find the compass hidden in Simmons's shaving brush, though he missed the map hidden in Simmons's paybook.

The gendarme also had a sense of humour, a trait the sergeant major who soon joined them lacked. When Edwards, in white-hot fury, spouted, "I've seen what you have done. I have boys of my own—little fellows—just like the ones [in Belgium] you've cut the hands off—and I tell you why I want to get back—I want to serve my country and my God—by killing Germans—they are not fit to live,"[6] the gendarme only smiled. For his part, the sergeant major turned red with anger.

Their civilian jailers in Meppen provided hot food and a bed with mattresses and blankets. By contrast, the guard charged with taking them back to Vehnemoor tied the POWs together and then brandished his gun to make them dance, while "occasionally putting it against [their] heads and pretending he was about to draw the trigger."[7] These mock executions violated the Hague Treaty. The eleven days in the *Strafe* cell were made bearable by the "invisible brotherhood" that again swapped an overcoat hung outside the latrine with one filled with sardines, cheese, biscuits and books. After Simmons told one guard that he was a carpenter, the guard said he was both a bridge builder and a socialist. He brought Simmons hot soup ladled from the bottom of the pot, which ensured it had more meat and vegetables.

The weeks Simmons and Edwards spent in the cold and damp of the *Strafe* barracks at the punishment camp at Oldenburg drove both men close to the edge. Simmons dreamed of a turkey dinner, only to awaken to the cold reality of the inedible German bread accompanied by globs of fat. To keep his mind sharp, Simmons cast himself as an NCO preparing for a route march by pacing off the 120 steps back and forth across his cell to make 5,280 feet, or one mile.

Simmons worried that he was the only man on earth. In his

darkest moments, shrouded in silence, he thought, "Edwards was dead—everyone was dead—I was the only one left." Simmons began to think that this punishment sentence would do what German bullets had not, and that all his family would ever see would be a report in the Toronto papers: "Died—Prisoner of War No. 23445, Pte. M. C. Simmons."[8] When Edwards was not worrying about whether his wife was receiving her separation allowance or how his boys were doing at school, he emptied his mind so that time would pass all but unnoticed.

Mid-February 1916: Fort Zorndorf, Germany

STRUCTURALLY, FORT ZORNDORF, a former Prussian fort sixty miles northeast of Berlin, was everything that Bischofswerda was not. Long, poorly lit underground tunnels extended in every direction. Not far from the punishment prison was a deep forest in which an escaper could easily hide, but a thirty-foot-wide ditch and a high brick wall lay between the prison and the fort's forbidding stone walls.

John Thorn had been held prisoner for ten months behind barbed wire and surrounded by sentries, but he had lived in barracks and, save for the time in the *Strafe*, could see both the world beyond the wire and the sky above. As soon as the gates closed behind him, Thorn felt he was no longer "a prisoner of war but a criminal."[9] After being searched on his arrival, Thorn was taken to a part of a tunnel that had been turned into a room that already held forty-two Russians. The floor was covered with dirt and the area was stuffy. A few hours later, when the dinner of hard, dried herring arrived, the smell of the fish combined with the stench of the room made Thorn's stomach turn. It would turn again on the many nights when the prisoners were given this vile food.

After eating, the Russians staged a two-hour impromptu dance and the room became stifling. Each time Thorn tried to open the window, the Russians, who were scared to death of a draft, rushed to close it, so Thorn smashed the glass. Surprisingly, the *Kommandant* was sympathetic and ordered Thorn moved, but it was to a room with French POWs, who also had a reputation of being afraid of drafts.

Escape from Fort Zorndorf seemed impossible. Just weeks before Thorn arrived, the noise of tunnellers had betrayed them. One man, "whose head had been a little turned with his long captivity," had planned on using a balloon to float over the walls, while two others had schemed to fly out while holding on to the tail of a kite.[10]

Mid-February 1916: Vehnemoor

"We are not Russians. You won't push us around. And you won't scare us," called out one of the self-styled Fannigans, a group of recalcitrant POWs that included Harry Howland, as they were marched from the train to Vehnemoor POW camp.[11] In the test of wills that followed, the brute of a *Kommandant* believed he held all the cards. He commanded men with guns and bayonets, and thought nothing of pulling his sword and yelling "*Halt*" when the Fannigans started moving too quickly and the guards appeared to be losing control of the column. The Fannigans began stopping every fifty yards and lying down on their packs. The ploy worked, for now the *Kommandant*, worried that the men would not reach the camp before sundown, agreed that if they marched there before nightfall, he would send a wagon for their kit on the morrow.

A few days later, the *Kommandant* forced the Fannigans to run a gauntlet while carrying stretchers heavily laden with earth. He got his personal revenge by swinging the flat end of his sword at their heads, including Howland's, while a lesser officer using either his fist or the butt end of a revolver pummelled the other side of the POW's head. To the Russian POWs' amazement and great joy, when the *Kommandant* called out, "I will break your spirit, you swine," and held up his revolver, saying in poor English, "Is for Englander swine," the Fannigans made extremely rude remarks about the Germans on the Western Front.[12]

22 February 1916: Dienstedt POW Camp, Germany

SIMMONS UNDERSTOOD WHY the little girl who had seen him and Edwards in the train station became so frightened that she ran back to her mother. A father of two young girls himself, he knew that she had seen only two filthy, emaciated men with long, matted hair. Fortunately, the guard escorting them from Oldenburg to Dienstedt took pity on his charges and bought them some bread, coffee and an orange. Simmons was also heartened that the guards who searched them did not leaf through his paybook and, thus, his map remained undetected.

For a few moments after they walked into the large hut that was to be their new home, Simmons and Edwards worried that they were being housed with Russians. Then they saw some British POWs. One reached up to his bunk and pulled down a parcel, offering them bit of cheese and biscuits, the same type of twice-baked biscuits that innumerable tars in the British navy had eaten over the past few centuries. The camp was flea-ridden, at least until the day after the censor came into the barracks to warn them not to write about the fleas and left, scratching himself. The fumigator's chemicals did nothing, however, about the disgusting brackish water the POWs were given to drink. That a man who had defecated in small, foul-smelling muddy saps (short stretches of trenches dug into No Man's Land) and urinated either directly into the ooze of a Flanders trench or into a bottle that was thrown over the parapet found the latrines at the camp terrible speaks for itself.

The Russian POWs soon became objects of pity. After Simmons and Edwards began receiving parcels, they gave their thin cabbage soup to the Russians in exchange for their boiled water, which the Canadians used to bathe in. They gave the Russians their portion of black bread in exchange for doing their washing. Since their parcels alone could not sustain them, Simmons and Edwards learned to down the soup made from fish roe. One night each week they knew they would be especially hungry. The raw herring soaked in brine was too disgusting to eat, and they gave it to the Russians.

Early March 1916: Canada

THE CUTLINE "FRENCH GUNS [at Verdun] pound second and third line positions" made something of a mockery of the *Ottawa Tribune*'s lead story on 1 March: "Lull in fighting over whole Front, Experts puzzled as to reason." In fact, the experts knew very well why over the course of 750 miles of trenches from Switzerland to the North Sea major fighting was confined to the area around the fortress system at Verdun. The battle that would rage until the end of the year and would involve a combined 2.3 million soldiers and result in almost a million casualties unfolded across the nation's kitchen tables with metronomic regularity.

The "lull in fighting" meant little to the families of men like John F. Clarke of Muskoka, Ontario, or Frederick S. Paddington of Wood, Saskatchewan, who were reported as "Killed in Action" on 3 March, or to Joseph M. Maybin's family in Scotland, who learned on 5 March that the 7th Battalion private captured at Ypres had suffered the fate that Simmons had feared would be his when he was locked in the *Strafe* cell.

Early Spring 1916: Halle POW Camp, Germany

SCUDAMORE REMAINED UNFAZED WHEN the guard escorting him to Halle-am-Saale, the officers' punishment camp, pulled back the bolt of his rifle and showed his prisoner the bullet in the breech. When he'd been marched to Bischofswerda, gawking civilians had made him feel "dreadfully conspicuous and ashamed."[13] After a year in a POW camp, he had gotten used to surveillance. Indeed, to borrow structuralist historian Michel Foucault's words, he had "inscribed himself [in] the power relation in which he . . . [became] the principle of his own subjection."[14] Accordingly, the shabbily dressed prisoner (comically carrying a cage with two canaries) barely noticed the looks he received.

The conditions at Halle were dreadful. What food there was was provided in rusty tin basins, though for a fee of $5 ($100) one guard arranged for a prisoner to have a good chicken dinner. The building, which had been an iron foundry before it was condemned, had no ventilation. Because there was no proper latrine, the camp was as rat-infested as the trenches. Using an overflowing latrine struck at the POWs' sense of military order and their sense of self; it was also a health hazard. Only when a British medical officer pointed out to his German counterparts that the swarms of flies would not respect the barbed wire and would spread typhus and diphtheria to the surrounding blocks of workers' apartments was a proper latrine established.

Though Easter did not occasion a formal church service, in the run-up to Holy Week, Scudamore enjoyed some of what many children and their parents did across Canada. Courtesy of Russian POWs, the camp was awash with coloured eggs. The holiday itself occasioned celebrations quite unlike those in Canada: drunk on bathtub gin, Russian POWs kissed one another and other POWs on the cheek.

Not long after, Scudamore hit on a plan to relieve his boredom. A feigned eye problem bought him a trip to an eye specialist in Halle. The doctor was more amusing—and, as it turns out, helpful—than Scudamore could have imagined. On the major's first appointment, the ecstatic doctor "marched up and down the room, throwing his hands in the air and exclaiming in a paean of praise: 'God be thanked. Verdun is ours for the first time in a thousand years.'"[15] (In fact, though the Germans expended more than 400,000 men, Verdun had not fallen.)

The nonplussed Canadian seized the moment, congratulating the German patriot, who took an immediate liking to Scudamore and asked what the POW camp was like. Scudamore stressed how boring life in the camp was. Before he was through, the doctor offered to "tell the authorities that it was necessary to see him at intervals," which allowed Scudamore to get out of camp regularly.[16]

Early April 1916: St. Eloi, Belgium

THE STORIES BROUGHT into the camp by many of the eighty-four men captured in the Battle of the St. Eloi Craters started differently than those of the Kaiser's other guests. The battle began with the detonation of six huge mines, the largest being 95,600 tons of TNT at 4:15 a.m. on 27 March. The explosions (which were heard as far away as England) did more than blow up the German trenches. They utterly changed the landscape.

When the hundreds of tons of earth and the body parts of some two hundred Germans had settled, British troops rushed forward into a moonscape of seventeen craters. One was more than half a football field across and sixty feet deep. Worse for the heavily laden Tommies, the ground had been turned into a porridge-like sea of mud that, together with German small-arms fire, slowed them enough that the Germans occupied the key position of Crater 5. Days of hard slogging and hand-to-hand combat won the craters at the cost of one man for every ten feet. It almost broke the British, as Private Donald Fraser heard in the early hours of 4 April when the Canadians were rushed in to relieve them. Fraser's efforts to pep up a dejected British soldier brought this response: "You'll be downhearted when you see what's up there: I have lost my best chums."[17]

As at Ypres, the "line" existed only on the divisional map. There was no barbed wire; eight of the twelve machine gun positions were unmanned. Unable to dig trenches because of the shelling, the men of the 27th Battalion took what shelter they could in shell craters. By the next morning, every other man in the battalion's forward companies had been wounded. The watery trenches were filled with British dead. The line that Canadians such as Private John Campbell and a Sergeant O'Brien were tasked with holding consisted of shell holes that provided "no continuity, no communication." This meant that "platoons and smaller bodies were cut off from their Company Commanders, and were obliged to act on their own responsibility," Canadians read in an "Eye Witness" report published on 17 April.

Stories such as this one made clear the Canadians' mettle: Sergeant Recce steadied his men in a shell hole until forty Germans were close enough that rapid fire could kill them; these isolated units performed well. The seventeen-hour bombardment, sometimes totalling hundreds of shells a minute, killed some of Major Daly's men and wounded others, many of whom were buried alive, and "shattered [some men's] nerves." The men stood for two days in putrid water, and many were forced to seek medical attention. Yet on the 16th, Daly's men mustered enough rifle fire to kill twenty-five Germans and drive back more than a hundred. At other times, the Canadians were entirely overmatched by the weight of numbers.

What words were used by men such as Campbell and O'Brien, two of the eighty-four men captured at St. Eloi, are unknown. Some were able to tell of the confusion of men found fighting without maps or aerial photos while slogging through the mud, limited to a narrow field of vision that was less than that of most Roman legionnaires. On the night of 13 April, a group of bombers tried to reprise the German success of a few days earlier and squeeze through the gap between Craters 4 and 5, but they were chewed up by a machine gun. The next night, Canadian bombers stopped a

German party intent on retaking Craters 6 and 7. Unable to tell one set of craters from another, one group of bombers sneaked their way to a set of craters only to find Canadians already held them. More doleful were the stories like this one from a man who was not captured: "Heads, arms and legs were protruding from the mud at every yard and dear [God] knows how many bodies the earth swallowed. Thirty corpses were at least showing [in] the crater beneath its clayey waters."[18]

26 May 1916: Bokelah POW Camp

WHAT STARTED AS A work slowdown just before noon, when the POWs were working on a rail embankment a thousand yards from the camp, escalated quickly into a full-blown strike. Responding to the POWs' calls of "bread, bread," the *Landstürmer* in charge promised bread if they returned to work. Led by Private Francis Armstrong, who had been captured at Ypres, the work party ignored repeated orders to work and marched back to the camp.

At a time when 60 percent of labour in Germany came from POWs, the *Kommandant* could not let the prisoners refuse direct commands from his officers.[19] He ordered Feldwebel Busch to bring up twenty-one guards. When the POWs failed to cower at the sight of them, Busch ordered his men to load their rifles and fix bayonets, which prompted the men to run around whistling and bawling while making rude gestures. According to the German charge sheet, Armstrong stepped forward far enough that Busch felt threatened by the prisoner's raised arm and pushed him back. After the POWs refused another command to return to work, Busch ordered them driven back to camp at bayonet point.

At the POWs' trial, which an American observer judged to be fair, the military judges believed a guard named Szymezak, who said he had felt threatened enough to justify bayoneting Armstrong when he appeared to bend down to grab a log. Armstrong testified that he had extended his arms while speaking, that he had been thrown forward by three guards and that "to break his fall, he had stretched out his hands."[20] The judges also disregarded Private Herbert Corby's claim that he had not been close enough to a car loaded with logs to have reached for one.

Each of the accused was sentenced to ten years' imprisonment for mutiny. Pegged as the ringleader, Armstrong could have received a longer sentence. But the prosecution soft-pedalled his role—while providing a fascinating glimpse into Prussian notions of class and race. The Germans believed that Armstrong was the ringleader because of his education and "finer physique," meaning, for the Germans, that Armstrong closely resembled what racial theorists were already defining as the Teutonic type. As well, the Prussian officers found something of themselves in Armstrong's behaviour, which was "particularly remarkable to every German witness."[21]

Chapter Five

June–July 1916

2 June 1916: Morning, Sanctuary Wood, Belgium

The shells that began exploding just after 8 a.m. dismembered some men and produced blast waves that broke other men's spines and burst their lungs. The blasts also prevented J. Harvey Douglas of the 4th Canadian Mounted Rifles from eating the plate of eggs, fried bacon, and prunes just laid before him. As the torrent of shells turned their protective berm into "a cloud of dust and dirt, into which timber, tree trunks, weapons and equipment were continually hurled up," Douglas led twenty men over the parapet in a dash for what remained of a communication trench.[1] A moment later, a shell landed directly among Douglas's party, killing thirteen men; a fusillade of trench mortars wounded Douglas and four others.

Field dressings absorbed their blood and morphine tablets eased their pain. But nothing could be done about their mounting fear when they saw that "Canada Street," the way to the battalion headquarters, no longer existed. Nor were there any able-bodied men left in their sector to hold back the Germans when, in a desperate bid to save themselves, Douglas and his men ran, if that be the word for how a man wounded by a shell blast hobbled his way across a stretch of pockmarked ground amid machine gun fire, toward a small bit of trench. When Douglas reached it, he saw that only Private Barclay had made it with him. A moment of silence, save for the leftover aural effects of the explosions, followed.

Then a deafening blast caused the ground to sway as if they were at sea, as "bits of trench and parts of what had once been soldiers" billowed into the sky, blotting out the sun. A large piece of timber drove Douglas's wide-brimmed Brodie helmet down on his head. When he came to a few minutes later, he urged Barclay to save himself, but Barclay refused to leave his lieutenant's side. From the shelter of a shell hole, they watched the Germans advance. The enemy, rifles slung over their shoulders, were much more concerned with "the swampy uneven ground that had been torn up by shell fire" than with any resistance the Canadians might offer. To avoid capture, the two men feigned death. Through half-closed eyes they saw a German flare rise a hundred feet as one solid ball of smoke before "burst[ing] into two small balls which flew off at a tangent . . . the signal that their objective had been reached."[2]

"Look here," cried Corporal Fred McMullen to his friend Flynn as they lay on a trembling patch of ground not far from Douglas. "A shell doesn't often hit in the same place," he said, leading them into a crater. A few minutes later, a German gunner pulled a lanyard, setting off the charge that propelled a "Jack Johnson" artillery shell through the air at more than twice the speed of sound. Its blast knocked McMullen unconscious, sparing him the first moments of pain from the two-inch piece of shell casing that tore into his side just above his hip and the shard that drove into his right eye. When he came to, McMullen saw that "poor Flynn had disappeared."[3]

Even though he saw the enemy moving off to his right, McMullen began inching his way back toward the battalion's headquarters. He felt as if "the whole earth was turning upside down," and the explosion from a detonated mine knocked him out. When he regained consciousness, he saw a number of Fritzies "'*digging in*' *not more than ten feet away*."[4]

2 June 1916: Sanctuary Wood

To deaden the pain of the wound caused by a shell splinter that had ripped flesh, tendon and bone from his body, Douglas downed a large shot of whisky and soon passed into unconsciousness. When he came to sometime in the afternoon and looked over the edge of the trench where he and Barclay crouched, his heart sank at the sight of a new German trench between them and Canadian lines. Not long after, a German mopping up saw them and, despite being rather rough looking, treated the POWs he captured properly. Douglas gazed in awe at the German trenches; unlike the mud-packed trenches on the Allied side, they were built of logs laid on top of one another. "The fire bays, fire steps and traverses . . . were carefully and strongly built as if they had been completed before the war."[5] At a dressing station, a medic put a wire splint on his arm and gave him some coffee. At a second station, the splint was replaced, and he was given a tetanus shot.

The *Feldgrauen* who captured Private David S. O'Brien nearby were, by contrast, cruel. Despite the obvious serious wound in his side, O'Brien was dragged and kicked back to the German trenches, where he saw other Canadians being kicked and pistol-whipped with rifle butts. In the moments after another German, who had seen them in a shell hole, stood over them with his shovel yelling "*Engländer Schweinerei*," Private Frank MacDonald had thought those with him would die from rifle fire or on the end of a bayonet. He credited their survival to the fact that the Germans were somewhat cowed when, in the best NCO voice he could muster, MacDonald made a show of impressive authority in much the same way Scudamore had at Ypres a year earlier.

Mercifully, the orderly at the dressing station cared more about pulling splinters of shrapnel from his eye than about the red and black badge on MacDonald's shoulder that identified him as a bomber; bombers were almost as hated as snipers. The stupefied soldiers found the fifteen-mile march to Courtrai a horror that was made worse when the Uhlan Guards' steel lances pushed back the civilians who offered the Canadians bread, water, chocolate and cigarettes. Finally, near 10 p.m., "broken, ragged, bloody and hopeless," the men who had staggered through ancient streets so far from home arrived at a barn, where they were given a small square of almost sour black bread and a bowl of black, bitter *Kaffee*.[6]

Since the battle still raged around them, McMullen understood why the first German to see him had taken the time only to give him a cigarette and a swig of water, and did not bandage the Canadian's wound. He even understood why the Germans digging a trench refused to come to get him, for even in the dark of night, such movement in No Man's Land would likely attract sniper fire.

Knowing, however, that he could not last until morning, McMullen crawled toward the enemy's trench in agony. The *Feldgrauen* who pulled him over their parapet risked their lives doing so, and then let him fall to the bottom of the trench like a sandbag. He might as well have been one to the men who over the next half-hour stepped on him as they walked through the trench.

Finally, two big men came to get McMullen. But rather than use a stretcher, they grabbed him by the arms and legs, ignoring his screams of pain as they carried him to a dressing station in the Germans' second line, where he slipped into delirium. When he woke, he heard the voice of Corporal Peter S. Thornton, who had also been wounded. As they waited for treatment, McMullen looked up and saw hanging from the ceiling "a lot of R.I.P. crosses . . . all ready for use on the graves of the poor beggars who are planted around in the vicinity." In mock admiration, he said, "Oh yes, the Germans are good organizers, all right."[7]

3 June 1916: Mount Sorrel, Near Ypres

THE DAY BEFORE, Private Jack Evans had seen good friends die and his parapet blown in. Now, shells were landing every six feet in his trench. After one intense barrage, he noticed his unit's No. 3 machine gun position was silent. A moment later, the position itself vanished into a flash and a tremendous wind. Then, a barrage of trench mortars destroyed the parapet, half burying Evans. When he had dug himself out, he saw the reasons for the piercing pain in one leg: shrapnel had pierced his foot, knee and back. The pain in his head was explained when he took off his steel helmet and found that it had been dented.

Under the garish light of star shells fired at 1:30 a.m., it was all about to begin again for the men who had neither slept in a day nor had any food or water. As the Germans advanced, Evans squeezed the trigger of his Colt machine gun and fired off bullet after bullet for just over half a minute. Some of the two hundred rounds hit home, but there were hundreds more Germans to take the places of the first in the mud of Flanders. With all of Evans's officers dead or captured, it was every man for himself. Evans and a few other men climbed over the back of the parados only to see "four Fritzies with fixed bayonets," who pulled their triggers a moment after he jumped back into the trench. Any thoughts of escaping down the trench ended when four other bayonet-wielding Germans came rushing toward them. Instead of yelling "Shove up your hands," the Germans made their commands clear by jabbing the Canadians "in their most convenient portions with their big bayonets."[8]

4 June 1916: Menin, Belgium

Douglas and the other men captured at Mount Sorrel knew that more than a thousand of their fellow Canadians and hundreds of thousands of other soldiers had become POWs. Yet, none of them had "ever dreamed of being captured."[9] MacDonald's claim that a few hours' respite from battle against a cold, damp wall renewed their spirit such that the prisoners were determined to carry on the fight behind German lines was likely written with an eye to helping the home front's morale, but it nonetheless accurately depicts his career as a POW.

In Menin, an officer told them, "You are now under German martial law, and if you do not give up any papers or any other information in your possession, you will be shot." Evans tore up the pages of a pocketbook on machine gunnery into little pieces that he dropped down a drain. As they waited for the train to take them to Dülmen POW camp near Münster, German officers interrogated the men about the number of soldiers held in reserve at Ypres. Evans hid behind a predictable Prussian belief: "I'm only a common soldier. It isn't for me know such things." Private William Raeside earned a stiff kick in the rear for saying "about four million, I think."[10]

Near 4 p.m. at a train station, Douglas finally saw men with Red Cross brassards. They quickly arranged for stretchers for the worst off, including men with protruding bones around which blood had congealed into rough crusts. A railway guard who looked at Douglas strangely meant no harm, the Canadian realized when the guard handed him a pocket mirror. The sight of his face, begrimed with mud and clotted with blood, made Douglas "glad that no one who loved me could see me at that particular minute."[11]

Early June 1916: The Hospital in Cologne and Dülmen POW Camp, Germany

At first, the police corporal charged with delivering Douglas and scores of other wounded men to the hospital in Cologne was more concerned that the officers did not have their commission papers than with the mute testimony of browned, bloodied bandages and anguished moans. After a lengthy wait, he admitted them and assigned each an iron bed in what had once been the classroom of a girls' school. On a postcard to his sister in England, Douglas asked for new kit. He sent his other postcard to his father in Canada. To ensure that Douglas received plenty of mail, his father typed the complicated address on a number of envelopes and gave them to anyone interested in writing to his son.

Douglas's medical care was better than what O'Brien received at Dülmen. Douglas's doctors X-rayed his wound and explained to him that pieces of bone and tendon had been destroyed, before wrapping his arm in flannel and putting a cast on him from his shoulder to his fingers. When, the next day, gas gangrene inflated Douglas's arm, doctors considered amputation but agreed to wait another day to see if the infection would subside. Fortunately, it did. By contrast, O'Brien heard the screams of men being operated on without chloroform and suffered the discomfort of paper bandages that became as hard as plaster after they were soaked with blood.

In neither camp did rations come anywhere near what the Hague Treaty required. Breakfast was normally one four-inch-by-two-inch square of tasteless *Brot*; lunch, watery potato cabbage soup, sometimes with a shred of horsemeat. Once a week they were given awful-smelling fish, complete with the heads, eyes and tails. At Dülmen, Evans recalled, they existed on granular porridge, nicknamed "sandstorm," and turnip soup.[12] MacDonald found that the bitter bread burnt his stomach and that some days what flavour the soup had came from ground bones. Both Evans and MacDonald felt the degradation of hunger that drove them to search through garbage pails filled with potato peelings and vegetables that even the Germans judged too rotten to be fed to the prisoners. Both were mortified to learn that foul-tasting meat in one day's ration of soup came from a dachshund whose bones were still in the soup.

The POWs' hunger would have been partially alleviated by the cabbages they were forced to plant—had MacDonald and others not "pinched the tender plants with the thumb nail just at the junction of the root and the stalk." Within days, the plants had withered and died, and the POWs had scored a minor victory against the Kaiser.

Early June 1916: Parnewinkel POW Camp, Germany

BOTH MERVYN SIMMONS AND Edward Edwards were relieved, even a little giddy, as they left the *Kommandant*'s office.

To their surprise, he had not gotten wind of their escape plans. Rather, what he wanted to do was comply with the Hague Treaty. While Edwards knew he deserved the pay for work he had done at another camp, Simmons was less sure that he had worked the one-and-a-half days that merited 27 pfennig, or 6¾ Canadian cents. As they left the *Kommandant*'s office, Edwards said with some disbelief, "They starve us, but if we work they will pay us, even taking considerable pains to thrust our wages upon us."[13]

6 June 1916: Kemmel, Belgium

JACK O'BRIEN HAD HIS leave pass in his pocket, but superstition told him not to think too much about Blighty lest fate take away his chance of reaching England. Not that he had much time for thinking, for instead of his usual duty in a "listening post," he was ordered to accompany a corporal into a tunnel that stretched under No Man's Land. At the end of the tunnel, the corporal put a listening tube to a rock and whispered, "I heard them [German sappers] yesterday, and I think they are close enough for us to get it now, we will lay a torpedo for them here."[14]

Shortly after O'Brien and his corporal began digging the hole for a torpedo, the war above intruded into a world that had not changed much since 1667 when the besieging Turks and the defenders of Vienna dug tunnels for mines and countermines. The sands around Kemmel, Belgium, transmitted the blast waves of a heavy fusillade so completely that they generated a wind strong enough to blow out their candles. Unable to dig, the two men started groping their way through the darkness toward the tunnel's entrance, only to hear a few moments later the anxious calls for help from other men trying to make their way through the dark toward them.

After learning that these infantrymen had taken shelter in the tunnel, and that the bombardment had blown in the entrance, the corporal, who knew the tunnels' layout, began leading the party toward an exit. They had not gone far before "there was a terrific explosion, [and] the props of the tunnel gave way," sending a huge pile of earth onto O'Brien. After pulling him from what seemed like "half of Belgium," the corporal found that a shell had blown in the top of the saphead, through which he had hoped to escape the tunnels.[15] With the sap and entrance blown in, the only air they had to breathe was the air trapped with them in the tunnels. Unable to find shovels, they began digging through the blockage with their hands.

A half-hour later, a sapper named "Nobby" whispered to O'Brien, "Do you see those lights?" The trapped men's sixth sense told them the flashlights were carried by German sappers and not Canadians. So while the corporal and another man continued to dig, O'Brien and Nobby, armed only with pistols, quietly made their way toward the lights.[16] In a gallery—the walls of which were ribbed by two-by-fours, with a low, rough-hewn rock ceiling area—suddenly lit by bright beams from flashlights, O'Brien and Nobby fired at the men just a few feet away. As they lay, readying to shoot the next man who came through the narrow passageway, a high-explosive shell burst directly above them, collapsing the tunnel on the Germans.

When O'Brien and Nobby returned to the corporal, they found that the men had managed to dig their way to a shaft. Their appearance was so unexpected that O'Brien described the corporal's reaction when he saw them by punning on the proper way to refer to their king, George V, "He thought we must have some connection with his Satanic Majesty."[17] After almost four hours underground and with the air becoming less and less breathable, they dug their way out through the bottom of a huge shell hole.

Once on the surface, O'Brien saw an apocalyptic scene—trenches blotted out, churned up ground across which dismembered bloodied bodies were strewn—that offered little hope and almost no shelter from the continuing shellfire. They were now behind the German advance. Nevertheless, at 2:30 p.m., O'Brien and the others started to dash from one shell hole to another. The British gunners fired shells to stem the German advance, and two of the men dropped—dead or injured, O'Brien never knew.

O'Brien and another man jumped into a shell hole and saw a number of Germans facing the other way. O'Brien's momentary advantage vanished when his revolver jammed just as a German lunged at him with his bayonet-tipped rifle. O'Brien dropped his revolver and sidestepped the bayonet before grabbing the man's rifle. After a brief struggle, he kicked the German in the stomach. As he let go of the rifle and fell backwards, so did O'Brien. O'Brien never knew who recovered first, for "one of our boys settled the combat by blowing the big Boche's head off."[18] Meanwhile, the other men with him killed the rest of the Germans. Once their battle for a shell hole was finished, O'Brien realized Nobby was dead. The corporal's command had ended.

A short while later, the men jumped into another shell hole and found themselves surrounded by about a dozen German rifles.

8 June 1916: Dülmen

THE POWS WELCOMED Jack O'Brien to Dülmen camp with hard tack, bully beef and jam. The men were desperate for exactly the same thing the Germans interrogators wanted: information. In addition to longing for news from home, POWs wanted to know how and why escapes had failed; the Germans, of course, were interested only in the latter.

The officers who interrogated O'Brien treated him well when compared with the Uhlan Guards, who had used their lances to prod the POWs along. One stabbed a Belgian woman who tried to give O'Brien water. The Uhlans did not provide medical care or even water. Toward evening, they herded the POWs into a filthy horse stable. By contrast, after giving the prisoners a small breakfast the next morning, interpreters offered them cigarettes, cigars and wine. They turned down the wine even as they accepted the smokes.

Later, after asking some general questions about Canada, an interpreter helped an officer turn to the business at hand. "Show me, on the map, the position your machine gun was holding on the Ypres salient." One soldier answered, "I am sorry Sir, but I can't read a map." When asked how many guns were in the salient, one man answered, "A million and a half." From this Scottish soldier's insignia, the Germans knew he was a sapper. After parrying a number of questions about the location of the mines, he appeared for a moment to break. O'Brien had to struggle to keep a poker face when the sapper said that he had been given a stick with a nail on it, an empty sandbag and the orders to "go through the trenches picking up all the paper, cigarette boxes and tin cans."[19] For his "dumb insolence," Jack O'Brien suffered the same fate as some other men: he was thrown down a small staircase.

Private David O'Brien's pain came from his wounds and a dulled hypodermic needle a German doctor thrust into his chest after doing the same to a number of other wounded men; the injection was almost certainly for tetanus. Like many of the other wounded men who had not been attended to in the days since they were captured, O'Brien was feverish. Mercifully for him, the infection was minor. Other men were so badly infected that they "required skillful treatment to save limbs and lives"—skillful, but not considerate, for many were operated on "without chloroform or anything to deaden the pain." O'Brien's wound required several operations; after one, "the bandage was soaked in blood, and when it dried it was almost like a plaster cast."[20]

On his second day in the camp, David O'Brien, who would soon find that the thought of food almost drove him mad, met a Russian prisoner who had lost both legs and one arm. "He would lie on his stomach [on a small wagon] and pull himself along by poking his good arm in the ground." Countless times it would be the Canadians who helped feed the Russians. This time, however, this "very pitiful" man gave a Dominion soldier a few crusts of bread. "I was hungry," O'Brien recalled, "and it tasted good, and was more precious than diamonds to me."[21]

19 June 1916: A Hospital in Jülich, Germany

PRIVATE HARRY LAIRD, who had been captured on 2 June at Mount Sorrel, assumed that an exploding shell did not kill him because it had burst only after burying itself some distance in the Flanders mud. Still, the explosion had driven a number of steel splinters into his left leg, preventing his escape from the onrushing Germans.

The doctor at the dressing station had no trouble reaching Laird's wounds, for his uniform had been shredded by the blast. Laird's tattered state may help explain why a *Soldat*, who Laird took to be no more than seventeen, paused when walking by him and furtively dropped a few cigarettes and several pieces of sugar. The stretcher-bearers tasked with taking the wounded man further back were neither brave nor kind. "Every time they heard a shell overhead, these fellows dropped me and ran for some sheltered spot," remembered Laird.[22] The following day, at a hospital in Iseghem, Belgium, Laird could no longer spare much thought for the wounds of Brigadier-General Malcolm Williams—his brigade's commander and the highest-ranking Canadian to be captured—because the infection in his own wounds had brought on bouts of delirium. The doctors operated on Laird early enough to avoid the fate of another Canadian, whose leg was shot off and who died from an infection.

Over the ten days Laird was in hospital, he and some British patients managed to keep one another's spirits up. Nothing, however, could mask the dispiriting hours he spent on the train to Germany. He had been ordered to travel, though he was in no condition to do so. Within a few hours, the worn blanket that covered him was drenched with blood. Breathing the fetid air of the sealed train car was as much of a trial. As the train crossed into Germany, he was so weak from lack of food, loss of blood and pain that his "surroundings were tinged with unreality, the bumping of the train alone arousing [him] from time to time from . . . lethargy."[23]

Late June 1916: Duisburg POW Camp, Germany

The good meal of vegetables and beef stew that McMullen had eaten on the train to Germany was now a distant memory. Moved by an achingly empty stomach, he asked the hospital's *Kommandant* for a larger bread allowance. "More bread? You can thank [British prime minister] Lloyd George for what you have got. At that you are getting as much as we are. All we are allowed is a half-pound a day."[24]

McMullen did not share MacDonald's disdain for his fellow French prisoners, who used the food in their Red Cross parcels as currency to "purchase" greatcoats and boots from the Canadians. The *poilus* (French POWs) that McMullen met, by contrast, shared their tobacco and food as well as the money that a bakery back in France secretly baked into their biscuits. Local women came to view the POWs, and McMullen told them about life in Canada. The willingness of the local children to earn a few pfennigs by buying the prisoners cigarettes (with money they threw down from the veranda) showed the POWs that the German economy was under severe stress.

6 July 1916: Pasewalk, Germany

The first of the wounded from the "Big Push" on the Somme arrived on 6 July. They told Douglas very different stories from the ones splashed across the front pages of Canada's papers. These British POWs did not know the details of the 60,000 casualties, 20,000 of whom had been killed on the first day of the Somme on 1 July, or of the destruction of the Royal Newfoundland Regiment at Beaumont-Hamel (which was not even hinted at in Canadian papers for a month). But they knew that the British had not "hurl[ed] the Germans back along a 20-mile front." As one paper reported, by the time the Canadians had entered the line toward the end of August, the British had lost almost 275,000 men for gains measured in some places in the hundreds of yards and in others by a few miles. When the POWs arrived at Simmons's camp, stunned by what they had seen, some veterans of the Somme told him they expected the war to last another five or six years.

Two of these soldiers in casts asked Douglas to write letters for them. Both were pleased by Douglas's words, which told their wives how much they were loved. For the soldier named Clark, Douglas wrote how much he missed his daughter. The letter had probably not even left the camp when Clark died painfully from gas gangrene.

After only six weeks of being a prisoner, Douglas wrote home begging, "Please write me often and tell me all the news, and ask anybody I know who would care to write me to do so." "The horrible monotony of the existence," compounded by the existential "fact that no one around you cares whether you live or die" wore at his morale.[25]

* * *

Douglas's words are important. He did not say that his captors did not care whether he lived or died, but rather that "no one around you cares whether you live or die," which included the men he mucked (shared food) with. His point was not that his comrades were heartless. Indeed, he knew from his shared experience in battle and the stories of escapes what one man would do for another *in extremis*. His point pertained, rather, to the day-to-day strain of being thrown together without the clear lines of authority. Shorn of this matrix, prisoners like Douglas felt a loss of agency, or what historian Tim Cook refers to as "the unwritten contract that underpinned the relationship between leaders and the led."[26]

The emotion invested in the Australian word "mate"—and hence in "mateship"—was real. But as one German historian of men in battle notes, the "consciousness of comradeship represented more of an exception in the everyday experience of the soldier."[27] What another historian calls "professional solidarity" exists in moments of high tension—in battle or during the drama of escaping a camp—but cannot be maintained on a day-to-day basis; even the fellowship of escapers could fray.[28] No less than in the battlefield, the POWs were in a "cold . . . lonesome place which men may share together."[29]

The tension of being surrounded by the armed enemy only added to the pressure. A British POW observed, "Trifles, which in ordinary life one would absolutely ignore, assumed mammoth proportions when one was herded up in a small space for an indefinite period with three hundred men drawn from every walk of life." The British lieutenant, imprisoned at Holzminden POW camp at the same time as a number of Canadians, continued, "It was incredible the intensity of dislike one could work up in a very short time for a man's face, the way he did his hair and his habits and hobbies generally."[30]

Mid-July 1916: Jülich Hospital

DESPITE THE WRETCHED FOOD, Laird had begun to feel stronger. Still, he found a way of hinting to his family in a postcard just how hungry he really was.

As his strength returned, Laird fought other enemies. The first was boredom, and it quickly gave way to something much worse, the "fear that his mind would give way." For his captors, he quickly realized, wounded prisoners (who could not work) were "mere bits of useless human material that must not be allowed to take up time, consume food and otherwise enjoy the prerogatives of active and useful beings."[31] The struggle to keep this Teutonic view of men like himself at bay was made all the more difficult by the "scorn and neglect" they endured.

Laird credited singing with "combatting the mental bug-bear." Unlike other POWs, however, he noted that hymns were so important they "exhausted the entire repertoire of each member of our gang." Accordingly, the men found the words of the hymns dispelled their "darkest moods." Laird had no doubt that an English-speaking minister would forgive the soldier who took advantage of the German Lutheran pastor's weak English by ending a prayer with the words, "that the Germans would be shot to Hell."[32]

Late July 1916: Rennbahn and Giessen

Herbert Tustin acted quickly but as nonchalantly as possible. Even as he answered "Geography" when a guard who had entered the barracks unexpectedly asked what the POW was studying, Tustin pushed some books over the paper on the table before him. The German's words, "Ah! Geography! That is good!" said with a patronizing satisfaction that suggested stroked national pride, told Tustin he had just saved his escape map.[33]

Tunnelling out of Rennbahn had been tried and had failed. The fences were not electrified, Tustin told Gerry Burk, who like him had been captured at Ypres, so he suggested that on a wet and windy night they might snip a few wires and crawl out of the camp. Burk was less sure. "You can't tell what this fucking German weather will do until it does it. And the sentry that night might be a leather-skinned old guy who likes rain and wind and never uses his [sentry] box."[34] Still, they began saving chocolate and bartering for cans of bully beef for their escape. Another POW sewed them shirts with extra pockets to hold these supplies. Worried that they had grown soft in the camp, Tustin and Burk volunteered to work on a farm outside Rennbahn.

At Giessen, Simmons and Edwards had come to the same conclusion and also volunteered to work on a farm. Since they would be searched before leaving the camp, they could take almost none of the food they had been stockpiling. Simmons took the compass that his brother, as requested, secreted in a tin of cream cheese. They shared meals of vegetables, potatoes, real bread and coffee at the farmer's table, an unexpected benefit.

Late July 1916: Hospital, Cologne

Moved by the POWs' testimony on how well German prisoners of war were treated in England, Inspector Driessen, the director of the hospital in Cologne, agreed to allow parole walks. Anxious to make a good impression on the townsfolk, Douglas and the other men polished their buttons and carefully wound their puttees around their legs. Their kit cut little ice with the local children, who "made cutting remarks about England" and threatened the recuperating men. After the prisoners had won the right to sit on the hospital's veranda, "people in the street would often stop to stare at the caged animals pacing up and down" as they tried to regain strength after months of idleness.[35]

Unlike most POWs, who learned of the bloodletting on the Somme from newly arrived prisoners and from what they could glean from the *Continental Times*, Douglas first learned of the battle from the *Kölnische Zeitung*; later, British soldiers captured on the Somme filled in the gaps. Like most of the stories in German newspapers, the *Zeitung*'s stories were little more than reprints of communiqués issued in Berlin and edited versions of British communiqués. The paper announced "bloody defeats" of the British with much the same regularity Canadian papers announced important advances (that never turned into the hoped-for breakthrough). Near the end of July, Douglas procured a copy of the *Volkszeitung*. In one article, a careless censor had missed an important sentence in a communiqué issued in London saying that the British "had taken several thousand prisoners."[36] Later that day, Douglas marked his secret map, likely at Pozières Ridge, which the Australians had captured at the cost of 5,708 casualties, 400 of whom were POWs.

End of July 1916: Dülmen

WHILE PRISONERS WERE ALLOWED to request parcels from home, they could not even suggest in their letters that the food was needed to keep them alive. One prisoner got around this by asking a seemingly innocent question: "I say, dad, have you seen my old school chum, W. E. R. Starving? I haven't heard anything of him for a long time." For his part, MacDonald wrote about the kind and thoughtful German people who treated him quite the same way he remembered being treated during that summer he'd spent in "Stony Mountain." His parents could not miss the reference to one of Canada's most notorious prisons. In an unsuccessful attempt to tell them he was all but starving, MacDonald wrote about a friend who loved his mother's cooking: "But I do miss poor old Chuck. I am afraid he has been killed. I haven't seen him since the day I was taken prisoner."[37]

For a short time after hearing that prisoners were going to be sent to a farm, MacDonald's spirits rose. Then some of the men returning from the *Arbeitskommando* dashed his hopes. MacDonald was not being sent to a farm but rather to a *Kokerei* (a coke plant). It was intimately tied to the German war effort and labour there was extracted by beatings. Even worse was the "Attention punishment," during which men who refused to work were forced to stand at attention for hour after hour until they collapsed. As soon as the men came to, a bayonet-wielding guard would make them stand, and the torture started again. If after twenty-four hours of this the prisoners still refused to work, they were kicked out of line and beaten unconscious.

Chapter Six

August–September 1916

2 August 1916: Auguste Victoria POW Camp, Hüls, Germany

Frank MacDonald's march to the train station was a melancholy experience. The sight of the harvest being taken in, complete with a McCormick reaper (common on farms across Canada) rusting off to the side of a field, stirred his emotions, but "scenes of peace and beauty bring no joy to the heart of the slave."[1]

At Auguste Victoria, "the Black Hole" of Germany, MacDonald and Jack Evans saw hundreds of POWs of various nationalities with sallow complexions who slaved away in a coal mine or at scorchingly hot coke ovens. As the POWs marched toward the ovens, the doors opened and a great cloud of steam and gas shot out. MacDonald could just make out "gaunt figures working like mad" pulling the red-hot coke from the eight-ton oven. Because of their intense heat, the ovens stood on a huge steel platform that rested on twelve-foot-high concrete piers.[2]

The coal mine where MacDonald, Evans and a number of other inmates were taken a few nights later had been sunk during the Franco-Prussian War a half-century earlier. Before entering it, the prisoners were searched for food, maps and compasses that they might have been hiding for a future escape, and then ordered to don coveralls.

The half-mile drop in the rough metal cage caused MacDonald to turn green; he asked an English prisoner if he'd become sick his first time in the mine. The man said he didn't know because when he and other POWs had refused to enter the cage, the guards beat them senseless and threw them in. The older galleries in the mine were not ventilated and thus smelled strongly of gas. Unlike the civilian workers, the POWs were not given goggles or any other protective equipment save for heavy boots. Even worse, the pressure of hundreds of tons of rock had bent or shattered many of the timbers supporting the mine. Some of the unsupported overhangs were so low that MacDonald bruised his knuckles when his hands were caught between a car loaded with coal and the unyielding rock.

Summer 1916: Fort Zorndorf

AFTER THE WAR, a German officer recalled that to escape, the Poles "always storm the wire, the French disguise themselves, usually as nuns . . . but the British [and, hence, the Canadians] always dig."[3] As if to prove the German's point, not long after arriving at Fort Zorndorf, John Thorn teamed up with a Royal Navy officer, and they soon used Thorn's jackknife to cut through the two-inch wooden floor. Pieces of iron wrenched from a bed frame worked quite nicely to scrape through the hut's cement foundation.

After several days of digging, the men found that the tunnel's face was too far from the head of the shaft for fresh air to circulate. The waste-water pipe that the tunnel was following was larger than the volume of water running through it. The tunnellers punched holes in the top of the pipe so that it would carry fresh air into the tunnel. Later, when the tunnel reached beyond the pipe, the POWs produced more piping using tin cans. A propeller was set up to provide the pressure needed to push air down the pipe.

To light the tunnel, the men made a small hole and used a well-turned piece of napping to turn tins of Williams Shaving Soap into lamps that were strategically placed in niches, making the tunnels seem like a fair imitation of early Christian catacombs. To remove the spoil efficiently from the ever-lengthening tunnel, they devised a pulley system. Bags made from stolen mattress coverings attached to a rope rotated into and out of the tunnel for twelve hours a day, dragging up two hundred sacks of earth. The men pulled on another rope to send messages back and forth. They packed the spoil into spaces under the flooring.

The single-minded efforts of the officers were probably their undoing. Unnerved by the lengthy period since the last escape attempt, the Germans guessed something larger was up and inserted a "Russian" into the camp. His "perfect knowledge of German" soon alarmed the Vigilance Committee, but it was too late.[4] A few days after the "Russian" inexplicably vanished, the Germans found the tunnel. Thorn took some comfort, however, in the fact that it had taken the Germans a full month using picks and shovels to dig up the tunnel. The Germans poured sand and broken bottles into it to deter another escape attempt.

11 August 1916: Auguste Victoria

Private James E. Flanagan, Evans's closest friend, had survived the blasts of high explosives, the pepper of shrapnel and the vectors of machine guns at Mount Sorrel only to die in a cave-in on 10 August.

Angered by Flanagan's death, the Canadians on the next shift refused to go into the mine. The beatings that followed did not break their spirits any more than the *Continental Times* story that said "Everyone in Canada had starved to death."[5] The Germans upped the ante by ordering Attention punishment. MacDonald, Evans and the others were still standing with bayonets at their backs almost twelve hours later—hours marked not by a ticking watch or tasteless, skimpy meal but by the sounds of another man being beaten by a rifle butt when, to ease the strain of standing, he moved the slightest bit.

Toward morning, MacDonald blacked out and fell face-first into the barbed wire fence. The Germans let him hang for a while, a horrifying effigy of what the weakened men had seen in battle. Finally, "anxious lest they lose a slave," they ordered two Tommies to take MacDonald off the wire and revive him.[6]

As Evans shivered on that unusually cold August morning, the holes in the line caused by MacDonald's and other men's collapse were more than made up for by men from the day shift who also refused to enter the mine. Day passed into night. Evans fainted and was revived by a bucket of cold water before being returned to the line. He was one of the lucky ones. When revived, others were marched to the *Kokerei* and made to stand in front of the red-hot ovens until they collapsed from the heat and fumes. The guards threw cold water on them to revive them and then repeated the process. After thirty-six hours, the Germans finally broke the will of the POWs, who again shovelled coal used in the making of shells they knew would be aimed at their comrades.

Late August 1916: Schwelm POW Camp, Germany

FOR THE FIRST FEW DAYS that Private David O'Brien spent at Schwelm POW camp, he thought that the officer in charge was fair. Then, after he caught the Canadian stealing a pear, the officer administered rough justice, knocking out two of O'Brien's teeth and breaking his nose.

Each morning, the hungry and increasingly dirty O'Brien forced himself off the straw. On those mornings following days when he'd managed to save a bit of the vile *Brot*, his stomach was less empty as he marched to the brick factory to start work at 6 a.m. For the next twelve hours, his world contracted to the muscle-straining act of wheeling twenty-five bricks, weighing almost as much as he did, to drying racks.

Knowing that this regimen would soon so weaken him that escape would be impossible, O'Brien decided to escape by himself. He slipped the leash of the brick factory by climbing into a disused smokestack and waiting long hours listening to the guards searching for him and counting and recounting the prisoners. At about 9 p.m., he climbed down from the smokestack and headed north toward Holland.

The next day O'Brien took shelter in a concrete drain. The following dawn, he passed a woman on the road and put his faith in his weak German and the half-light of morning, which he hoped would hide the telltale stripes on his clothing. Neither of these things were enough to save him, he realized, when the woman approached the bush he hid in shortly after with five men carrying cudgels. During the two weeks he spent in a *Strafe* cell, subsisting on *Brot* and water and recovering from being beaten with a rifle butt, he would think often of the hot breakfast he had been given as he awaited the guards who would take him back to Schwelm. Once there, O'Brien could barely push the cart laden with bricks and was soon transferred to the camp in Münster.

At Münster the food was so bad—the meat in one meal being, apparently, cat—that the Germans allowed the prisoners to make slingshots to hunt the crows that alighted on the camp's barbed wire for extra food. Only the intermittent arrival of parcels kept the men from starving. Still, some men were strong enough to put on plays. When a character required civilian or women's clothing, it was rented from merchants in Münster. To prevent the clothing from being used by escapers, the guards carefully counted the items after each performance.

The camp included a shoe factory, where O'Brien came into his own. His, however, was not the cobbler's art. He had forged his mother's signature so he could enlist in 1914; had become well known to the military police in London, who regularly arrested him for unauthorized leaves and; after learning that soap had become all but unattainable in Germany, bribed a guard to bring him a compass in exchange for a small bar of Castile soap. At the factory, he turned his attentions to the pretty stenographer, though not for sex. He convinced the *Fräulein* to bring him food, a civilian suit, a shirt and a cap. The cap was essential in a time when men rarely went outside without some sort of hat. Before O'Brien's next escape attempt, she gave him RM 15, and he promised to "send for her after the war."[7]

27 August 1916: Near the River Hunte, Germany

Strengthened by the work on the farms and the wholesome food, Mervyn Simmons and Edward Edwards were ready to try their luck. Getting away on 21 August from the farmhouse in Seedorf where they were billeted was surprisingly easy. As the sound of the other POWs eating fried potatoes told them that all was normal, they stepped outside, ostensibly to light their pipes, and slipped away into the gathering dusk, made darker by an approaching large black rain cloud.

They turned around the front of the house and walked down the street, taking care to stay under the trees, where the darkness was even greater. Once out of the village, they made for a wood and passed through it until they reached a ditch overgrown with heather, where they hid. Soon the heavens opened up and the ditch began filling with water. Knowing that the storm actually provided cover, they stayed in the ditch with "only the smallest portion of their faces projecting" so they could breathe.[8] Near 10 p.m., the soaked men climbed out and began making their way south toward Bremen, which they planned to skirt before heading west toward Holland. In their memoirs, each man's sense of propriety led him to stay silent about the terrible discomfort that followed when his wet underwear constricted against the tender skin of his crotch. Nor did they describe the itching that they felt as their clothes went from cold and wet to damp.

Three days later in the afternoon, Simmons was awakened by a loud whistle. After wiping the sleep from his eyes, he saw a man's legs through the buckthorn-like bush in which he and Edwards had bedded down. Then, a dog darted past them before stopping a few feet away. The escapers held their breath. Fearing that even a wink might make too much noise, they shut their eyes. In this self-induced darkness, as they wished they could cease to be, two escaped prisoners in tattered clothes hugged the ground six thousand miles from home.

As the dog came nearer, Simmons could hear his soft steps and imagined "the brute was stepping high—as they do when they see something." Then came the silence of a dog pointing—broken by the man's whistle, which did nothing to move the dog. The words that Simmons imagined as German for "Come here, you fool!" had a different effect. With a yelp, the dog began walking away.[9]

After a week, they had walked almost a hundred miles. A few small, raw potatoes and a handful of oats (both stolen from a farm), leavened with dirt from their unwashed fingers, barely kept the hunger pangs away as they walked through another cold and rainy night. But even more worrisome to Edwards were the painful blisters caused by his wet boots. In an effort to save Edwards's feet, Simmons cut one of Edwards's shirts into strips, which he then wound, puttee-like, around his feet. This helped, though without this shirt Edwards was even more chilled.

A long stretch of boggy country ended at the River Hunte. After his experience near Meppen, Simmons was understandably shy of bridges. So, again, the escapers made a raft. After stripping in the chilly air, they placed their clothes and boots on the raft and began swimming across the river.

Late August 1916: Hospital, Cologne

As 1916 wore on, Dr. Henri Béland, the member of Parliament for Beauce, Quebec, who had been interned at the Stadtvogtei prison in Berlin shortly after the war broke out, noted the decline in the quality of the rations, which included "soup" undeserving of the name. Horsemeat was a luxury. More often, Béland found something called a "sausage" made up of bones, gristle and offal floating in his bowl.

During the long weeks that seemed to consist of "eight meatless days," the British and Canadian patients in the Cologne hospital Harvey Douglas was in relied on their parcels and on the twice-weekly arrivals of bread from Switzerland that made up the more than 25-million bread parcels the Red Cross supplied during the war. Since the beginning of the year, the POWs had been helping to pay for these parcels because, as one historian noted, according to the ideology of the period "it helped a prisoner's morale to contribute to his own upkeep and not be entirely reliant on charity."[10] Because of the delay caused by checking the bread for contraband in Wahn, it often arrived with large parts green with mould. On those rare occasions when Douglas did not need to cut off any mould, the bread was still dry and hard. But when mixed with water or Oxo soup, it was edible. Many shipments, however, arrived with their centre "all eaten out and sometimes containing a rat's nest."[11]

Late August and Early September 1916:
On a Road Near the River Ems, Germany

THE HEAVY RAINS AND peals of thunder kept people indoors, even as the bolts of lightning illuminated the way for Simmons and Edwards. A day earlier, the sun, though weak, had lifted their spirits as they pushed on through swampy country and across a number of small canals. Raw turnip, peas and apples barely sustained them. Worried that their scraggly, haggard faces would frighten anyone they came across before they could get out a calming "*Guten Abend*," the escapers submitted to "the terrible torture of a cold-water shave."[12]

On the 30th, the mist hid them almost as well as the hedges they plowed through. Toward the end of the afternoon, they saw a sod cowshed. Using canvas that they found there, they fashioned a shelter and then "snuggled up together to exchange warmth."[13] Not long after, the mist began to lift, and they heard something alarming. Looking up, they saw a woman staring straight at them.

Instead of screaming and running, she slowly turned and walked toward the farmhouse, which up to then had been hidden by the mist. She signalled to others, and the two men regretted that they had not had the presence of mind to seize her. "Come on, let's beat it," said Simmons.[14] They ran toward a wood, thinking that if they had to fight it out with their bare fists, they would be better off doing so in the woods, where the search party would have to divide into smaller groups. Just as they heard men following, the rain started again, which dampened the searchers' ardour. The escapers found the wood rough going, but it provided the cover they needed.

A few passed. The rain had stopped and the sun had come out, but the air had turned cold. The land, however, was now bountiful, providing apples, turnips and, for several nights, milk, leaving Simmons to wonder if the farmers "would think the cows bewitched when they found they would give nothing [the] next morning."[15]

Near dawn on the 3rd, they gambled that the grey, misty light would hide the smoke from a fire. As the flames warmed them, dried their clothes and cooked their potatoes, Simmons enjoyed the sweet smell of fallen leaves. Hidden by the blue veil of haze and an overhang of dark green spruce, they almost forgot they "were in a world of enemies," much like the small bird Simmons saw lazily flying above, unaware that it was being hunted by a hawk.[16]

4 September 1916: Oldenburg

They "bore the farmer no ill will."[17] He was, however, different from the man they had seen on a road a few days earlier. That man was accompanied by a dog and carried a brace of birds. Despite having a hunting rifle, all he did when he saw these men with matted hair and hints of stripes on their filthy, ripped uniforms was say "*Guten Abend*" before continuing on his way.

By contrast, the burly farmer who now confronted them by the edge of the wood carried a double-barrelled shotgun and had a ferocious dog at his side. Edwards did not remember who moved first, but it didn't matter. Simmons rushed for the gun as the hunter struggled to level it at them, while the dog bit at their legs and leapt at their throats. "In those moments," Edwards later wrote, "that whole horrid film of fifteen months' torture of mind and body; the pale, blood-covered faces of our murdered comrades of the regiment, the cries of the patient Russians [tortured] behind the trees, and our own slow and deadly starvation and planned mistreatment" unspooled in their minds. To secure their passage back to the rolling beauty of Ontario's hills and hear the "good English tongue and behold 'the dear faces of our own folk,'" the farmer and his dog had to die.[18]

5 September 1916: Rennbahn

Instead of trying to get through the wire, Herbert Tustin and Gerry Burk planned to escape through the back door of the hospital and then climb over the fence behind the building. A few days earlier, Tustin had prepared the ground by going to the hospital and convincing a guard that even though he did not have a pass, he should be let in to bring books to a sick friend. On the 5th, however, another guard refused to admit them. Their appeal to an NCO who was passing by also failed, until Tustin convinced him that his sick friend might die before tomorrow.

Escaping was always a near-run thing, and their escape was timed for a few minutes before 8 p.m. Just as they were getting ready to climb out the window, the lights came on—five minutes early. Since they had already missed the evening roll call, which would require subsequent recountings, proceeding with the escape seemed as good an option as calling it off. When the sentry turned his back and started away from them, they ran past the officers' mess. No one saw them as Burk, a few strides ahead of Tustin, pulled himself over the wire using the top of the post. While Burk ran up the grassy incline that surrounded the camp, Tustin spent long moments snagged on the barbed wire, which he cleared only by a supreme effort that lacerated several fingers.

A few hours later, Tustin tripped over a signal wire strung along a train track, and as he tumbled over, many of the cans of food he and Burk had collected flew out of his pockets. Then they saw a light in a nearby cabin come on, and, cans be damned, they ran. Before dawn, they saw the lights of Münster reflected in the pale sky, and the two men looked for a place to hide.

When the sun came out after a cold, grey morning, Tustin's spirits lifted, but Burk remained discomfited. He pointed out that they would be safer in a nearby ditch covered with leaves than among some late-summer brambles. Tustin disagreed, but was silent when they heard a stick break nearby. As they pushed themselves down, they saw two sportsmen carrying rifles. With his heart sounding to him like the thumping of a dynamo, Tustin watched as the hunters' dogs stopped, their tails rose and their snouts pointed elsewhere, toward their intended prey.

Later, when Burk again suggested they move to the ditch, Tustin agreed. Not long after they had burrowed into the wet mess, they heard shouts and then the sounds of a village picnic. At one point, children searching for blueberries walked into the very brambles they had been in earlier.

That night, Burk, who had hopped trains as a teenager, suggested that they should avail themselves of the German transportation system. Tustin was less sanguine and not at all unhappy when the train they were to try to board sped by too quickly. Over the next few hours they were alarmed by barking dogs and plunged through thick hedges in order to keep their course. When it came time to hide, Tustin once again marvelled at Burk's woodcraft skills as he cut an all-but-invisible passage into a hedge, lined the watery ditch with oats and pulled "branches and other rotting material" over them.[19]

Tustin dared not suggest they move from what he feared would be a pneumonia-inducing ditch because of the sound of a mechanical reaper working nearby. Some hours later, the swish of the machine ceased, and they heard the voices of workers, who they assumed were having lunch. Neither escaper spoke German well. Both, however, understood enough German to know that the workers were talking about two escaped Englishmen.

7 September 1916: Near Holland

THE OLD SHEPHERD WEARING a velvet cloak, knee breeches and buckles on his shoes could have stepped out of the pages of "Rip Van Winkle," Washington Irving's short story that had been a staple of Canadian readers when Simmons and Edwards went to school. His air, too, "belonged to the peaceful past, and knew nothing of wars and prisoners."[20] Yet because they were still in Germany, the escapers kept themselves hidden from the first Dutchman they saw. Holland lay a few miles on the other side of the River Ems, which they reached near 3 a.m. on the 6th. After dusk the next day, to keep their clothes dry, they again built a raft, this time from a piece of fence. Had the crescent moon been waning, they might have waited a night before crossing the canal they soon came to. But even though the moon illuminated their faces, they were exhausted and hungry, so they decided they had no choice but to push on.

When he saw there was no guard, Simmons quickly undressed. As silently as he could, he slipped into the canal and waded across before throwing his clothes onto a sandbank and going back to help Edwards. However bashful either may have been before enlisting, the bathing regimen in the army—dozens of naked men soaping one another down in a large tub—ended their self-consciousness about nudity. The moment the two slipped into a nearby sandpit to get dressed, they heard footsteps. Twenty seconds later a patrol marched by.

7 September 1916: On a Field in Germany

TUSTIN AND BURK WARMED their chilled fingers on the bowls of the pipes, thinking "never did 'the fragrant weed' seem so good."[21]

Some hours later, suspecting that they were heading in the wrong direction, Tustin asked Burk to take a reading using his luminescent compass. As Burk checked pocket after pocket, Tustin felt a dull rage rise against Burk's carelessness. In sullen silence, they retraced their steps and, amazingly, found the compass. When they reached the area where Tustin had asked for the reading, he pointed to where they should be on the map and said they were miles off course.

The strain of the last few days and the time spent finding the compass almost broke their fellowship. Burk exploded: "You damned fool, you! Why the fucking hell have you got us into this mess? I left the route to you; it was your blasted job." Tustin responded, "You damned swine." Both men clenched their fists. Just as they were about to come to blows, three lights appeared, which they thought came from an organized search party. When they realized the lights came from three bicyclists, both men felt sheepish. Later, Tustin was still bothered by the thought, "[What] use would freedom have been to me, even supposing I could have won it alone, if I had, in a fit of temper, killed so fine a comrade?"[22]

9 September 1916: Holland

The ripe, juicy red apples were a treat for Simmons and Edwards after days of eating small unripe ones. And the thought that they were close to Holland heartened them even as they walked through one more dark bog, each step sinking so low into the peat that the filthy, particle-filled water flowed over the tops of their boots.

The peat, neatly cut and piled, suggested that Simmons and Edwards had passed into Holland. The sight of another canal beyond the bog confused Simmons until he realized that his map was of Germany, not Holland. Word of their escape became public with a *Globe* article published on 4 October 1916.

9–15 September 1916: Near Schöppingen, Germany

The night of the 8th started off with a scene that could have come from a London music hall review. When Burk asked Tustin if he could milk a cow, Tustin said no and Burk said, "Well, I can." Although the Port Arthur (Thunder Bay) Canadian's technique did not impress the German cow, Tustin found Burk's salty language "equal to the occasion."[23]

A few hours later, after wallowing in a clear stream, they realized that they were much farther south than they had intended to be. Their decision to take a road so as to make better time seemed a good one until, as they passed through a woodland on the beautiful moonlit night, they grew careless. They heard someone shout "*Wer da?*" (Who goes there?) and only then did they notice the sentry box on the side of a crossroads.[24] The two escapers ran, dodging through a stand of poplar trees as shots whizzed by them.

On the 9th, after a poor meal of biscuits and the last of their bully beef and only two hours' sleep, they woke to discover that they had taken shelter in thin coverage near a house. They were initially frightened by the shouts of the farmhands and momentarily terrified by the rustling of leaves just beyond them, until they realized it was only a black hen anxious to scare off another hen. Worse still, children were playing hide and seek nearby. At one point, one of the boys jumped down from a tree and landed just above Burk's head.

Traversing the deserted moor was so difficult and they were so weakened by lack of food that Burk and Tustin slept through the entirety of 11 September. At nightfall, they discussed their chances of sneaking cross the border given their appearance. Tustin's scraggly beard and his mufti—shredded trousers, Belgian forage cap and French army boots—made Burk laugh hysterically and gasp for breath. As Burk clutched his chest, he and Tustin realized that Burk, who had a weakened heart, had just suffered a heart attack. Both men knew that Burk belonged in a hospital. But to seek out one would mean becoming prisoners again. Instead, after Burk took a swig of the tonic he had prepared for just such an occasion, a potion he said "would bring a dead man back to life again," they again set out.[25]

To lessen the chances of being seen under the bright full moon, they advanced on their hands and knees. This made the going slower and more strenuous and, thus, more of a strain on Burk's heart. Tustin stopped at one point and watched as first one, then two red lights glowed ahead. Tustin wondered why he couldn't smell the burning tobacco from the cigarettes he was sure he saw not far away. Burk saw the lights, too, but to him they were green, which he pointed out to the colour-blind Tustin. Burk crawled ahead and then in stage whisper called back, "Why, they are glow-worms."[26]

* * *

ON 15 SEPTEMBER, the curtain came up on the last act of Tustin and Burk's escape. Though close to the Dutch border, Tustin and Burk knew that in order to have enough strength to continue they had to find something to eat. The turnips and potatoes they found were difficult to choke down but eased the aching void in their bellies. Near dawn, unsure if they had crossed the border, the escapers snuck into a barn and, at Burk's insistence, tunnelled into a stack of barley on an angle. Because the hand he'd lacerated on the barbed wire had become infected, Tustin could dig only with his other hand. Their spirits sank at a tattoo of rifle fire, as it suggested the rumour that Holland had entered the war on the Allied side was true and that they had travelled hundreds of miles only to find themselves in a battle zone.

The cold west wind made their burrow anything but "warm and cozy." Then a wagon rumbled up to the barn and a man shouted in German, "Here's the work!"[27] Neither escaper could quite make out what the men were working at. A dog climbed to the top of the barley pile and barked excitedly, but the men ignored it. Hours later Burk ventured out for a look and saw that the haystack that had been on the other side of the barn was gone.

The two men continued their journey, trudging through yet another bog and hiding in a copse after hearing shots. Around midnight they saw an empty sentry box. On that cold September night, the guard had left his rifle leaning against the box and was flapping his arms to keep warm. The two escaped POWs wormed their way forward through a ditch on the guard's left. A couple of hundred yards beyond the sentry's position, a hedge gave them just enough cover to climb out of the ditch onto a road running north. The paper they found on the ground that said "*Nationale Bank, Gedempte Oude, —— Haarlem*," which they read shortly after dawn on the 16th, was promising. But Burk worried that that the stiff west wind could have blown it from Holland into Germany.[28]

Not long after, a group of soldiers walked by. Their uniforms were familiar, yet even in the half-light, different from those they had seen since being captured. It took Tustin a moment to realize that instead of being by his side, Burk was surrounded by the soldiers who, importantly, had made no move to seize his unkempt and vagrant-looking companion. Accordingly, instead of making a run for it, Tustin retraced his steps and asked the men if they were German or Dutch. Long moments followed until "'*Hollander!*' they shouted in chorus."[29]

19 September 1916: The Somme, France

In the days following the Canadian triumph at Courcelette on 15 September, some two dozen men, including Private Arthur R. Wright, were captured either while on patrol or during German counterattacks. When they arrived at Dülmen and other camps, these men were able to tell their fellow Canadian (as well as British and French) POWs about the epic struggle on the Somme. British and Australian prisoners that had already arrived had shared some information, such as the slaughter on the first day of the battle (1 July), though not of course the doleful numbers. In the moments after the guns had fallen silent at H-hour, tens of thousands of British troops clambered over their parapets to the sound of whistles, followed by the ripping sound of Maxim machine guns and the screams of thousands of men. Many of those who were silent were dead before they fell on the muddy ground. In total, the British suffered 58,000 casualties, including 20,000 men killed in action.

On 5 September, during the battle for Moquette Farm, Private Edward Cunningham was captured. Cunningham had entered the battle with information unimaginable even to those who had fought at Mount Sorrel just a few months earlier. While seven more months would pass until maps were pushed down to the platoon level at Vimy, information gained from trench raids and aerial surveillance meant that the men had a much clearer idea of where they were to attack—and, equally importantly, of the layout of the trenches they had been tasked to take.

In an effort to avoid a slaughter like the one suffered on the first day of the Somme, General Sir Arthur Currie again turned to his guns. Taking a leaf from the French, the Canadians advanced over the pockmarked battlefield behind a creeping barrage, a storm of steel fired a few dozen yards in front of the men; every three minutes the barrage moved forward ninety yards. Instead of destroying trenches, the job of the creeping barrage was protecting men as they crossed a battlefield filled with the detritus of war. In the last moments of the advance, the shells fell directly on the Germans' trenches, forcing men to take shelter in the deep dugouts. Then, when the barrage passed over and began punishing those behind German lines and interdicting reserves, instead of racing across all of No Man's Land, the Canadians would be close enough, they hoped, for Lewis gunners to pour a stream of machine gun bullets into the trenches to kill the Germans rushing to man their defences. Despite these tactics, as Cunningham was marched into captivity, Moquette Farm remained in German hands. One example of Cunningham's comrades' grit was that of Acting Corporal Leo Clark, who earned a Victoria Cross for singlehandedly killing five Germans and capturing another in the narrow defile of a German trench. Sadly, Clark was killed by a stray shell a few days before his VC was printed in the *London Gazette* on 26 October 1916.

The Canadian command learned quickly. To shred the German defences even before the men went over the top, Canadian gunners fired hundreds of thousands of high explosives and shrapnel. A Bavarian *Leutnant* named Hermann Kohl on the other side of No Man's Land referred to the rain of shells as a "regimental witches' sabbat." An "unparalleled hurricane of fire blew over from the front. It was like a crushing machine, mechanical, without feelings, snuffing out the last resistance with a thousand hammers."[30] The bombardment prepared the way for Arthur Wright and thousands of other Canadians by blowing up German emplacements and obliterating the unlucky. Even in the well-built, deep bunkers, the concussions, some caused by shells weighing more than a hundred pounds, caused men to vomit and their ears to bleed. It left some shell-shocked.

In some places, the Germans were so decimated that the Canadians' advance resembled a route march. According to one Winnipeg captain, "We were only 250 yards from the trench. Our lads made the rush in fine style . . . the huns in the trenches made really little resistance."[31] In other places, such as where the 21st Battalion advanced as casualties mounted, men like Sergeant Frank Maheux found themselves unable to turn off what the future British historian called "the engine of killing."[32] When Maheux saw that one of his chums had been killed, he saw "red" and even though the Germans had put up their hands, he wrote home, "Dear wife, it was too late."[33]

The stories that fired the imagination of the newspaper readers back home and would have done the same for the prisoners were the stories of the tanks, seven of which were first used at Courcelette on the Canadians, who were attacking on a 1¼-mile front. The soldier who wrote home about seeing "land dreadnoughts" was closer than he knew; the "land cruisers," as they were still officially called, were the brainchild of the former First Lord of the Admiralty, Sir Winston Churchill.

The five-man crews in the twenty-eight-ton Mark I tank laboured in temperatures above a hundred degrees. They were immune to machine gun fire, though not, as the Germans soon learned, to shellfire. The tanks were capable of firing a thousand rounds per minute from their machine guns, and in the "male" variant, six-pound shells from two guns. The tanks' primary purpose was not to engage the enemy in gunnery duels but to crush barbed wire and roll over trenches, from which a disconcerting amount of rifle fire still came. As the tanks crossed the trenches, the machine guns swept them. Unlike the tanks commanded by generals Erwin Rommel and George Patton in the Second World War, which could travel up to thirty miles per hour, the tank that lumbered across the same No Man's Land moved at a mere four miles per hour, much slower than soldiers, even weighed down with sixty pounds of kit, could run.

The tank with its caterpillar tread that ran around the sides and its tail of two huge wheels (needed to stabilize the tank) roared from behind the shell-pocked battlefield. "Down and up the shell holes it clambered, a weird ungainly monster, moving relentlessly forward." Neither the Germans who had gone to ground to protect themselves nor the prisoners who heard about the tank for the first time needed training in the tactical doctrine that would develop to realize that the ironclad "gigantic toad" constituted a moving lee behind which soldiers "followed in the rear as if to be in on the kill."[34] From his trench, Leutnant Kohl saw the first tanks as "unearthly monsters" spewing death.[35]

Wright was one of the 294 Canadians captured on the Somme.

Late September 1916: Stendal POW Camp, Germany

AFTER THREE AND A HALF months in the hospital, Harry Laird was transferred to Stendal POW camp in central Germany. During an overnight stop in Cologne, he and other former patients were herded into the station's unlit basement. By a candle's sputtering light, Laird and the others added their names and addresses to those other POWs had left on the walls since the beginning of the war.

At Stendal, Laird was even hungrier than he had been in the hospital, where he had been able to purchase a little extra food using money his family sent him. The Germans had converted the funds to Reichsmarks after deducting one-third. In the POW camp, the only food the 320 men in his barracks usually received for breakfast was a tub of burnt-acorn *Kaffee* or thin soup and a small hunk of *Brot*. "The noon meal consisted of soup that would have turned the stomach of a buzzard . . . On Sunday evening we were always given raw fish, salted beyond recognition. We gave these to the Russians, poor devils, and they were grateful for them at that."[36] After several weeks, lack of food and sleep had undermined Laird's mental state to the point where he began to lose interest in eating. He credits his survival to two soldiers, one British and another Canadian, who together ensured that he ate the best of their food, including some from their parcels.

Laird suffered from the pain of his wounded leg and from the hunger that gnawed at his stomach, and he saw men suffering from such ailments as tuberculosis. But it was the absence of mail that was at times all but too much to bear. Mail call was at 4 p.m. "Men who had no hope of a letter or parcel would crowd around the carrier and insist that they were expecting something, that they had been overlooked and unfairly treated by the officials—anything that would serve as a pretext to bolster their longing and disappointment."[37]

In the absence of mail, a "new kind of melancholia," he recalled, "gained dominion over [his] imagination, and all that [he] could do seemed powerless to free [him] from this plague."[38] Since his wounds continued to discharge, Laird could not consider volunteering for work outside the camp; even aiding the German economy would have been better than what amounted to existential boredom. Nor were the debates his comrades staged or the concerts of the music of Liszt, Rubenstein, Mozart and (surprisingly, given his place in the pantheon of German nationalists) Wagner. Neither activity was enough to fill the empty hours.

As the end of September neared, Laird found himself slipping deeper and deeper into depression, at times even hallucinating about fine meals.

End of September: Dülmen

Though he was often hungry in the Leipzig hospital, Douglas slept on clean sheets, went to Church of England services (whose form took some getting used to for the Presbyterian) and was allowed parole walks (during which POWs promised on their officers' honour not to try to escape). He also had access to a phonograph. Douglas convinced the director of the hospital to allow him to use the phonograph to stage a concert. On the appointed day, every man in the ward who could sat upright. Douglas was not above a little sleight of hand. The guards surely noticed that one song was particularly popular. It came from a musical comedy that included a rendition of "God Save the King," but the Germans did not notice it.

At Dülmen, sports and concerts were "mere 'scraps of paper,'" which is what the Kaiser called the treaty that had guaranteed Belgium's neutrality, trotted out only when the American ambassador visited.[39] Unable to participate in recreational activities, Frank MacDonald amused himself by convincing the camp doctor that he was *krank* (sick), thus depriving the Germans of two strong hands. By holding red-hot cloth-covered stones under his arms until just before he saw the doctor, he appeared to have a deadly fever. MacDonald also kept a small flashlight under his arm to help keep the "fever" up before the French orderly, who was in on the ruse, took his temperature.

When MacDonald was still alive two weeks later, the doctor became suspicious. To avoid a punishment sentence, MacDonald pretended to make a miraculous recovery and was sent to work in a mine. As soon as he could, he joined the "Sleepers," men on the first shift who ignored the roof that threatened to collapse and bedded down while one man made himself visible as the lookout. Were the men to be caught, they knew they would face a beating. But the risks were worth it to ensure that "much less coal was being mined for Germany."[40]

Chapter Seven

October–December 1916

Early October 1916: The Somme

Private Edward P. McQuade's life almost ended on 8 October, on the left of the Canadian attack on Regina Trench, or *Staufen-Riegel*, which has the rather curious meaning of "Stuff-Stop Line."[1] This was the second attack on the Regina Trench in two weeks. That attack was summarized by a communiqué writer: "Desperate fighting occurred and our men succeeded, despite heavy machine gun fire, in penetrating into several sections of the German lines. The trench, however, was one strongly built and protected by two rows of barbed wire entanglements which our artillery had not succeeded in totally removing." By the time the "enemy counter-attacked in force and regained the whole of Regina Trench," a couple of dozen men belonging to at least five battalions had been captured, joining the two dozen captured on 26 September in the

Battle for Thiepval Ridge, the Canadians' first attempt to reach Regina Trench.[2]

As McQuade lay in a hospital bed, General der Infanterie Fritz von Below's Special Order of the Day of 12 October 1916 praised his men in terms generals like to use: "The attack was smashed to pieces against the iron wall of First Army."[3] McQuade could have no such praise for von Below's medical staff. To locate the bullet in McQuade's body, a surgeon inserted an explorer into McQuade's open wound without first anaesthetizing his patient and then, upon locating the wound, continued to probe it unnecessarily and extremely painfully.

Herr Doktor was as cruel as the one who had traumatized Arthur Gibbons and then all but ruined his leg. When McQuade jumped from the pain of the exploration and knocked over the doctor's instrument case, the German shoved the wounded man off the operating table. Nor does it appear that the mud-covered McQuade, who had lain for four days in a slimy shell hole and in his own filth, was given a tetanus shot, for he developed lockjaw. How the anti-tetanus serum was administered several days later is not recorded, but according to McQuade it was administered in a "brutal way."[4] For all his pain, McQuade was luckier than Lieutenant Arthur B. Irving. Hours after the Germans recorded his name on the list of captives on 9 October, his death certificate was filled out, giving the cause of death as *Starb an Wunden* (Died of Wounds). The same fate befell Private William Roberts, who lived for eight days after being captured on 16 October 1916.

24 October 1916: Leipzig Hospital, Germany

As he waited to be called into the examining room, Harvey Douglas was nervous, though not because he awaited word on how successful the operation to graft together two bones in his arm had been. What concerned Douglas was the calculus used by the three doctors. From the smile he saw on his friend Private James D. Barnes's face when he walked out of the examining room, Douglas knew that Barnes had just been adjudged as being of no military use.

Dr. Meyer's behaviour had always been professional, at times even friendly, but Douglas never forgot what uniform lay beneath the German's white coat. Douglas found it strange speaking to the Swiss doctor, who examined the deep gash stuffed with gauze and asked in perfect English about his arm. What struck Douglas was not that he was having a conversation with this doctor about his visit to Canada, but that he seemed to be "talking to a friendly neutral who was in a position to help."[5] Following a short consultation in German between the two doctors, during which Douglas heard Meyer mention to the Swiss doctor that Douglas's family could join him in Switzerland, Meyer escorted Douglas out of the room, whispering "Congratulations."[6]

Fall 1916: Münster, Germany

David O'Brien climbed over a fence onto the street. He planned to travel at night, trusting his civilian clothes to smooth his way past inquisitive eyes.

"Thoughts of freedom and release from the horrors of captivity" kept the "terror of expecting to be captured or shot" at bay.[7] As dawn approached on his third night after escaping, O'Brien saw a man watching him. Just as his hopes of escaping Germany faded, the man drew close enough for O'Brien to recognize his British uniform. The two escapers decided to stick together, but because of the man's uniform, they would have to avoid roads. Three nights later, as they neared the Dutch border, fearing that the Germans would search the underbrush, they slept as they had in the trenches, one man on watch at all times.

The next night, O'Brien thought of what he would do in London with the pay that had been accumulating since his capture. They passed the first of two lines of guards right before the border by timing their advance to the guards' beat. They crawled for five hundred yards and then rested. Only one last line of rifles slung over German shoulders sat between them and Holland. They froze when the guard nearest to them grasped his rifle and peered into the brush.

The guard resumed his beat, and the escapers rose to run. They had not eaten a meal or slept much in days. For these adrenalin-filled men, forty yards, perhaps fifty strides, would have taken about fifteen seconds, more than enough time for the guards to see them, yell "*Halt!*," shoulder their rifles and fire. The bright moon made them easy targets. Though the bullets missed their mark, they nonetheless accomplished the guards' main goal.

O'Brien and the British soldier were placed in a cell containing a number of recaptured, bootless Russian escapees. O'Brien was moved to pity at the sight of the rags wrapped around these men's feet. The guards brought the men green tea the next morning. A few hours later, O'Brien was taken back to Münster. For two hours each day for the next twenty-eight days, the Germans tortured

O'Brien by tying him in an upright position with a block pushing up on his jaw so that his neck was painfully extended.

October 1916: Konstanz, Germany

Harry Laird was so weakened mentally that the thought of going home and having to make decisions for himself filled him with "horror." Believing he would be a "useless burden" to his family, he did not even want to appear before the delegation of doctors coming to Stendal to determine which POWs would be eligible for medical exchanges. Even though he walked with a cane and had to hold on to a table to stand before the doctors, Laird was convinced that the committee would determine he must remain behind German barbed wire. Accordingly, he was surprised two days later when he was told that he would join a number of other men for the trip to Switzerland early the next morning.

An *Unteroffizier* charged with getting the men ready to leave the hospital almost caused a riot when he ordered those who were to be left behind to give Laird and the others their best greatcoats. As part of the propaganda war, the Germans wanted the POWs interned in Switzerland to make the best possible impression. In the end the warmest coats stayed with the prisoners in the camp. As Laird waited to hobble out of the barracks, he felt none of the elation he saw in his comrades. Instead, he sat in "gloomy silence," feeling as if he was deserting the men who had fought to keep him from "the darkest depths of despair."[8]

The train taking Laird's party across Germany was not equipped with water or cushions for the wooden seats. The trip did not, of course, give the POWs up-to-date news of the front, where the

Canadians were still fighting for Regina Trench, but they could glean much by looking through the windows. In the Frankfurt station, girls acted as guards and women carried baggage, which indicated something about Germany's manpower situation. The gangs of mainly Russian POWs fixing train tracks testified to the scarcity of German workers and the wear and tear the war had wrought on the nation's railways. As October 1916 slipped away, however, what really mattered to Laird and the men in his party was their dinner—meat, vegetables, bread and butter, as well as real coffee and tea with cream and sugar—at the small hotel they were led to in Konstanz. They even slept in beds with clean linen.

4 November 1916: Cassel POW Camp, Germany

After his three-week *Strafe* sentence, during which he lived on water and nine ounces of *Brot*, Fred McMullen was back in Cassel. On his first stint there, he and the men with him had been given two thin blankets and sent to dirty huts with leaky canvas roofs that McMullen found even worse than the trenches. At least in the trench system, there were areas where the men who survived the troglodyte world could wash and change clothes. On that first day at Cassel, their dinner was "stewed grass"; the next day, it was horse-chestnut soup, which, although tasteless, was at least hot.

To keep their "spirits up," they "just had to sing."[9] Not surprisingly, as soon as the guards heard McMullen and the others singing, they rushed into the huts with fixed bayonets and laid into the men with their rifle butts. McMullen does not say what songs were sung, but some of the more recent POWs would have known a tune that had quickly become the unofficial British anthem, "Jerusalem." The words came from a poem by William Blake, which had been set to music by Sir Herbert Parry earlier in 1916.[10]

Mercifully, this time McMullen was quartered in a barrack and had access to Red Cross parcels. The parcels allowed him and his comrades to slip food to the dragooned Belgians who refused to work. Because the Belgians were civilians, they did not receive Red Cross parcels and subsisted on two bowls of heated water with some solid matter to give it colour each day. The Belgians were forced to sleep on dirty straw and were not allowed to wash their clothes. They suffered the bites of fleas, which carried typhus, a disease that killed on average seven Belgians every day. Also painful to watch was the mistreatment of Russian POWs—as a reprisal for the Russian treatment of German POWs, the captors said.

7 November 1916: Dülmen

Frank MacDonald and Lance Corporal Wallace Nicholson planned on cutting through the wire near a sentry box. By a stroke of good luck, the workers who brought in the box had not reattached the wire. Even more fortuitous: since the next day was a public holiday, they would not be back to fix it for two days. On the intervening Wednesday, the breeze blew the smoke from the cooking fires of the French POWs across the sentry's beat, hiding the efforts of MacDonald and Nicholson as they pushed the sentry box aside and cut their way through the second and last fence.

Once beyond the fence, MacDonald and Nicholson sneaked around the coke ovens on a platform to avoid being seen by the many civilians near the main gate of the *Kokerei* compound. They slithered through a pile of bricks and dug a hole under the fence. As they drew their first breath of free air, Nicholson whispered, "Oh, God, Mac, how good it is!"[11]

The escapers had a few hours before their absence would be noticed at the evening *Appell.* They struck out toward the west, following MacDonald's compass. They soon reached a river that was too wide to swim. After hours of working their way through willows beside the river, they came upon a rail bridge. The escapers decided to climb up onto the bridge at the water's edge.

Just as they stepped out of the willows, however, they heard a shout and the shot of a rifle. The escapers turned and ran back toward the river while the guard fired a number of rounds. Nicholson ran straight into the river and wanted to try to swim it, but MacDonald pulled him out. After hiding for about an hour, they inched their way downriver, looking for another way to cross.

A few hours later, they saw an iron barge tied to a pier near a house. They slipped aboard the barge, cut its moorings and, using a long pole, pushed it into the current. Just as the barge started moving down the river, a number of men came out of the house, cursing. MacDonald and Nicholson shouted back, "Go to hell!"[12]

Fall 1916: Augustabad POW Camp, Germany

THERE WAS NEVER ENOUGH food, but when they had meat, at least it was fresh, as they were allowed to keep rabbits. And the parole walks in the fall air were pleasant. Much more important, however, was the escape plan that John Thorn had begun working on when he saw a woman wearing "widow's weeds" (mourning clothes) walking by the POW camp that before the war had been a hotel.

Thorn's first step was to ask two Belgian officers to get him the materials needed to create widow's weeds. The men began making a hat from chicken wire stolen from the rabbit hutch, an old piece of black lining and some black crêpe; the crêpe was furnished by a suborned guard who believed the Belgians' story about wanting to entertain some men at Christmas. The Belgians also made a veil from the crêpe, which had cost them a bar of soap. After their first attempt to make a coat by eye failed, they "borrowed" one from an elderly lady who worked in the laundry just long enough to sketch out its pattern on newsprint.

To ensure that Thorn looked womanly, another tamed guard provided corsets. This guard also accepted Thorn's story of wanting "to have some fun with the officers in the camp." Given the harsh penalties for such behaviour in German military law, the guard almost certainly did not suspect the request had anything to do active homosexual practice.[13] After making the skirt, Thorn turned to making a wig from a swath of hair sewn into a skullcap, procured by a Belgian orderly.

12 November 1916: The Dutch Border

For five nights, MacDonald and Nicholson—wet, cold and hungry—evaded patrols as they neared the Dutch border. Now they were only about four miles from freedom. Though each gust of cold wind sapped their strength, they knew that its chill would make the German guards take cover.

An arc light illuminated the line of sentries in the driving rain and pointed the way to a ditch that led to a field. They "wriggled along like snakes" past a light standard. Then the escapers got to their feet, pitched their faces to the wind and walked west. The men saw another line of sentries and assumed they would be Dutch, but rather than take any chances, MacDonald noted, they "decided to try to get past them and further into the country before revealing [themselves]."[14]

After making their way through a swamp, they spent long moments on their stomachs in the slimy mud. Another miserable trek through a smaller swamp ended at the outskirts of a town. The light from a window seemed just enough for MacDonald to read his map, but it had been reduced to pulp in the rain and mud. He looked up at the window and saw something he had not seen in long months—"a rather pretty girl in a lace-trimmed night-dress." When she saw the two haggard, filthy men, she screamed and drew down her blind.[15] The escapers quickly slipped into the darkness, but since they were sure they were in Holland, this time there was a bit of a spring in their step.

As dawn broke, they found themselves on the main street of a large town. Knowing how awful they looked, neither man was surprised that the (Dutch) soldiers—in dark blue uniforms decorated with two rows of brass buttons, so different from the *Feldgrauen*, the Uhlan Guards or the *Landsturm*—looked at them strangely. At a railway crossing, men the escapers took to be railway police asked them a few questions before seizing hold of them. In the guardroom of Wesel, MacDonald and Nicholson learned they had crawled into Holland—and then back into Germany.

14 November 1916: Leipzig Hospital

At 2:30 p.m. on 14 November, an orderly rushed into Douglas's ward with the order that Douglas and another nine men who were

"Unfit for Duty" be ready to leave in half an hour. They had hardly started to pack when another order arrived: send your packs downstairs to be searched. And then another: come immediately to the inspector's office.

The inspector's concern had nothing to do with contraband and everything to do with setting his account books right. Since Berlin had disallowed the pay raise he had given the POWs some weeks earlier, he would not allow any man to leave if he did not pay back the difference. Douglas had enough money to cover his and another man's debt. A few moments later, Douglas learned that he would not be able to take his steel helmet with him because it was judged "war *matériel*." Less clear was the reason he had to surrender his photographs and letters received at the hospital. Safe in his pocket, however, was the chequebook that he marvelled had not been looted from him when he was captured (and that had allowed him a few months earlier to send a cheque to England) and a little diary.

On the train later that night, Douglas was reunited with Lieutenant Adam Sime, whom he had not seen since Mount Sorrel. They and other men talked all night. Those who had travelled in Germany remarked on the castles and countryside the train chugged past. At 11 p.m., the train pulled into the station in Konstanz, Germany, where they were to wait to be exchanged for German POWs. The first person Douglas saw in his new barracks was Lieutenant Frederick Hubbs, who had been captured at Mount Sorrel a day after him. Hubbs greeted his comrade by asking what he was doing there. As it turned out, Douglas had been reported killed in action.

19 November 1916: The Somme

The 50th Battalion men captured in either Desire Trench, or in the hundred or so yards behind this last major defensive line, knew that their commander would have thought it a good exchange: six Canadians for fifty German soldiers.

Ordinary ranks such as Lance Corporal Robert Bradley and Private Henry Wood may have known less about the casualties than Canadians back home did. There, long column inches of names, some days numbering into the hundreds, documented the killed, wounded, missing and captured Canadians. But from the number of battalions that had been rotated into the battle over the previous two months, the men had a rough and ready understanding of the bloodletting. Indeed, the land told them much. Behind the lines, they camped in "Sausage Valley," so named because the ground had been so thoroughly churned up. From the trench (in the mid-right of the Canadian line) they entered on 17 November, a mere two hundred yards from Desire Trench, they could see the remnants of both the struggle for Thiepval Ridge and the previous attacks on Desire Trench.

Today, where the undulating green slopes lead to the 140-foot-high Thiepval Memorial, limestone curtains bear the names of more than 72,000 British, Anzac, South African and Canadian soldiers who died during the Battle of the Somme and have no known grave. In November 1916, Wood and his comrades saw the ragged scars in the earth that had been the muddy trenches, many all but obliterated by shell fire, skeletons from previous attacks, rats scurrying for shelter under the bombardment and uncut jumbles of barbed wire. Today there are fields of white gravestones, those belonging to Canadians signalled by a maple leaf pitched slightly

Wounded Canadians receiving medical treatment in the trenches.

Major Peter Anderson, Canada's first and highest-ranking escapee.

Private Arthur Gibbons, who was captured at Ypres, 22 April 1915.

THE AUTHOR IN THE FRONT LINE TRENCHES.
The film from which this print was taken was torn in two and concealed in his tunic. It thus travelled with him to the German Prison Camp.

Private Arthur Gibbons in the trenches.

REVERSE.

OBVERSE.

LUSITANIA MEDAL.

The Lusitania medal that was shown to Private Arthur Gibbons when he was in a Belgian hospital.

THE AUTHOR AS HE APPEARED ON HIS ARRIVAL IN ENGLAND.

Note the Crippled Right Leg.

Gibbons after his return to England. Note that a German surgeon rendered his right leg "crippled."

Lance Corporal Thomas Bromley, who was captured at Ypres.

Private Mervyn Simmons, who was also captured at Ypres.

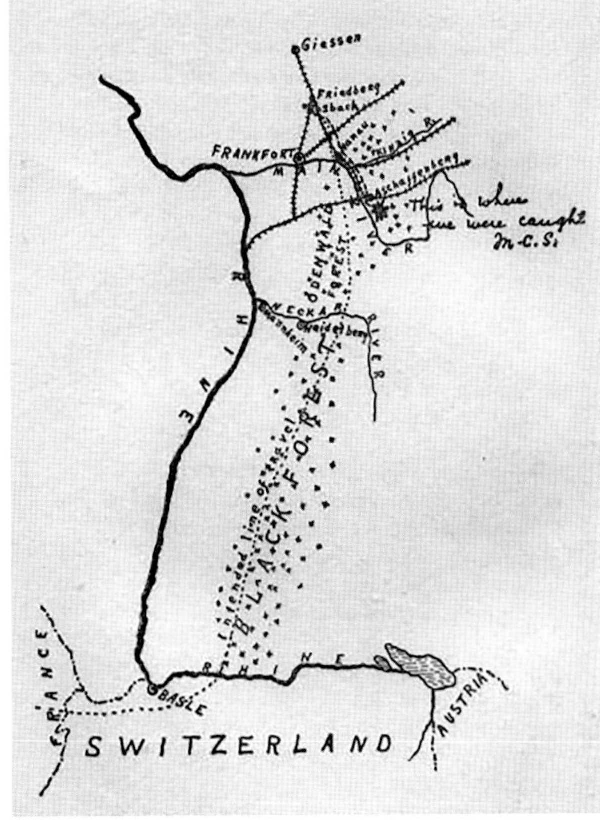

A map of the first escape attempt of Simmons and Bromley. Note how they skirted Frankfurt.

Officers' quarters in one of the POW camps where Simmons was held.

Friedrichsfeld POW camp in summer.

Lance Corporal Edward Edwards, who was captured on 8 May 1915.

Thursday 6
1916
Jan 22nd Escaped from
Vehmn-moor Lager in
company with Tom
Bromley 3rd Toronto reg.
Murvens Simmons 7th B.C.
reg. captured on the 27th

Friday 7
at the town of Latham
on the river Ems six
kilometers from Holland
spent two days in civil
jail at Meppen got
little or very little food
one days rations

Saturday 8
2 Oz. Bread 3/4 pint
coffee 1 pint gruel
returned to Vehmn-moor
on the 30th Jan after
being marched through

A page from Edwards's diary telling of his failed first escape.

A POW cemetery at Celle Lager POW camp.

Private Jack Evans, who was captured at Mount Sorrel, 3 June 1916.

AS I LOOKED WHEN I LEFT GERMANY

AS I LOOKED BEFORE I SAW GERMANY

Kriegsgefangenenlager 2, Münster i. W. (Allemagne)

Kriegsgefangenensendung

Mrs James Evans
143 Celina st
Oshawa
Ontario
Canada

Adresse exacte de l'expéditeur:
Nom et prénom:
Kriegsgefangenenlager 2, Münster i. W. (Allemagne)
Block — Chambre
Compagnie No.

Card from Private Jack Evans to his mother.

A postcard that Private Jack Evans wrote to his mother.

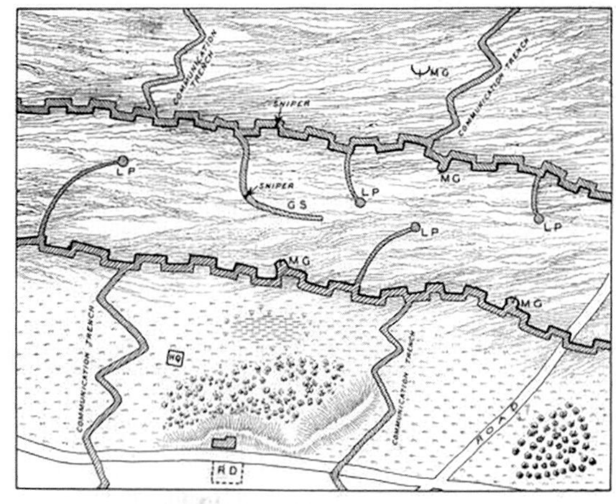

Sketch of part of Zillebeck line where McMullen was captured.

A map showing where Corporal Fred McMullen, who had been captured at Mount Sorrel on 2 June 1916, was apprehended on his first escape attempt.

A class picture showing four escaped Canadian POWs, including Private Jack Evans (*front left*) and Corporal Fred McMullen (*front right*).

Upper row—Howitt "Toby" Boyd Hockey
Lower row—Evans McMullen Masters

These men are all members of the 4th Canadian Mounted Rifles who were captured in the spring of 1916 and who escaped from German prisons within a month of each other.

This photo was taken at the request of Col. Gordon, Officer Commanding the regiment to which they belonged, and who is now in England, acting as O. C. of the 8th Reserve Depot Mounted Rifles.

O'BRIEN AND MACDONALD
Who fought their way together out of "The Black Hole" of Germany and over the Holland Border

Private Frank MacDonald and his escape partner, Lance Corporal James "Jack" O'Brien, captured at Mount Sorrel on 2 and 6 June 1916, respectively.

MacDonald as he looked when he sneaked into Holland in May 1917.

THE AUTHOR
From photograph taken in Holland three days after his escape

EVEN A LITTLE FUN AT TIMES
British soldier-prisoners taking part in a "sketch" in Münster Camp

A play put on in a POW camp. Note how the "woman" is dressed.

One side of a postal sent from Friedrichsfelde Camp

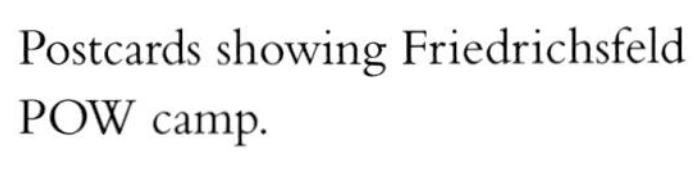

Postcards showing Friedrichsfeld POW camp.

Unloading Red Cross parcels at Friedrichsfelde Camp

toward the left. A lichen-covered German pillbox survives at the far end of the graveyard immediately in front of Thiepval; its dark, foreboding architecture suggest just how intense the battles here were.

Despite the protection the creeping barrage offered Canadians and the punishing blows of their artillery fire, the redoubtable Germans in Desire Trench fought off attacks on both 1 and 8 October. From the German point of view, on the 1st, following the "muzzle flashes of countless guns . . . The earth shook under their dreadful impact. The air was filled with bursts, crashes and claps of thunder. In no time the whole battlefield was enveloped in smoke."[16] While thousands of men from across Canada prayed, wrote a quick note in their paybook to their wives, mothers or girlfriends, or checked to be sure they had the extra rounds, Leutnant Wulf and his men—trusting to the infantryman's belief that lightning doesn't strike the same place twice—crouched in a shell hole, talking about their homes and families to take their minds off the horrors around them.

Moments after the barrage lifted, Wulf recalled, "the emptiness of the battlefield filled up as my men crawled out of the craters and holes in the ground," ready to fire on the advancing Canadians, "who went down like cornstalks before the scythe." Wulf's second hunting metaphor, which suggests that he came from a rural part of Germany—"But too many dogs means the death of the hare"—explains why, as the gaps in the Canadian line were filled, his men had to pull back.[17] Wulf knew his trade, however, and after gathering his men in a sap, he distributed grenades. As the unsuspecting Canadians entered the trench, the Germans shouted "*Hurra!*" and let loose a number of potato masher grenades, killing many of this group of Canadians.

This attack was followed by another and another. During one attack, the Canadians captured *Feldgrauen* named Olin and

Klempke, who were freed when Wulf's men counterattacked. Canadian grenades shredded Adler and wounded Schmidt, Kröning, Olin and Müller, while Wulf's efforts were so devastating that, as the battle moved back and forth in this abattoir, several times Wulf's men "came across five or six Tommies piled up on top of each other and . . . literally had to climb over the corpses."[18]

When the Canadians became more cautious and started leaping from crater to crater, a change indicative of the spread of small-unit actions (by platoons or even sections), Wulf's men reached for their Mauser 98 rifles. Vizefeldwebel Lietz helped steady the men, telling them every shot must count and then, "See that tall man there? He's mine." Lietz squeezed the trigger and "the British steel helmet described a wide arc in the air, but its wearer fell." Another Canadian had died trying to take Regina Trench.[19] Seven days later, 1,364 Canadians were killed, wounded or captured in another failed attack on the "Stuff-Stop Line."*

Late November 1916: Friedrichsfeld POW Camp, Germany

The guard charged with taking MacDonald and Nicholson to Friedrichsfeld POW camp opened the breech of his rifle and showed them the dumdum bullet in the chamber. Because of the terrible injuries their soft lead cone caused, such bullets had been banned by the Hague Treaty. The Germans had accused the Canadians of using them at Ypres, which they had not.

After serving a ten-day "Black Punishment" sentence in a three-

* On 11 November, the Canadians took Regina Trench in a stunning eight-minute dash. Several days later, they used Regina Trench as a springboard to capture Desire Trench.

by-six-foot darkened cell, MacDonald was again assigned to the mine, where he rejoined the Sleepers. The following day, a German entered their gallery and examined the broken timbers. Through the weak light of a pit lamp, MacDonald saw the man's eyes widen before he left without saying a word. The following day, worried that the Germans were going to seek some sort of revenge, MacDonald went to another gallery. Later, he heard about the melee that started when more than a hundred German civilians, armed with sticks and cable wires, entered the gallery containing the Sleepers.

MacDonald was banished to a *Kokerei* for having been a Sleeper. The conditions in the prison coke plant undermined MacDonald's faith that he was living in a "civilized age."[20] For twelve hours a day, without any protection, amid clouds of chokingly hot and poisonous gases spewing from the glowing coke and ovens, prisoners loaded brands of red-hot coke onto carts. Once each cart was loaded with eight tons of coke, the prisoner would push it to the edge of the platform and dump the brands into a railcar below. Each push across the broken plates of the platform required an even deeper breath of the stygian smoke that burnt their eyes, faces and throats. Every second Sunday the prisoners were forced to work a double shift, and the foreman would check off that they had loaded, pushed and dumped sixty-four tons of coke into the Kaiser's war machine.

If a guard saw that a man had stopped working, he "would grab a shovel or an iron bar off the front of the oven and hammer" him. But the guards could not see everything. At the risk of being charged with mutiny and long *Strafe* sentences, MacDonald and the others adopted the tactics of American slaves in the antebellum South: working inefficiently and, when possible, breaking tools. They infected scratches that otherwise would have healed quickly by rubbing dirt into them. Men sacrificed fingers, arms and legs "for the cause just as truly as if [they] had been shot off in Flanders."[21]

Late November 1916: Augustabad

THORN'S ESCAPE BEGAN WELL. First, a Belgian with a wheelbarrow transported a French POW to a disused icehouse outside the camp. The POW was to help fill out the ruse by acting as the widow Thorn's "hunchbacked son." Then the Belgian took Thorn to the icehouse, where he changed into his widow's weeds. At the local train station, Thorn purchased two tickets to Berlin and played the part of a German widow so well that an officer stood and offered "her" a seat in the station.

The plan began to come apart a few moments later when Thorn's "son" returned. (He had left the station to avoid attracting attention.) The ticket agent who had sold Thorn his tickets noticed the hunchback and alerted the stationmaster that something seemed amiss. As the Germans seized the hunchback, Thorn made a quick exit. Soldiers caught up to him a short distance from the station and, politely, took the widow back to the stationmaster's office. The stationmaster questioned Thorn and accused "her" of wanting to get out of the country with an escaped French POW.

Dissatisfied with Thorn's answers, the stationmaster brought in two women to search the mysterious widow. This was enough for Thorn, who threw up his hands and exclaimed, in broken German, "*Ich bin ein Englander offizier, nicht ein Frau*" (I am an English officer, not a woman), adding with a tone of mortification, "For God's sake don't let those women search me."[22]

The guards showed a grudging respect for Thorn by offering

him a cigar. Word of the Englishman's attempt to escape dressed as a woman changed into a story of Thorn being a spy. That story spread so quickly that when he was marched through the town on his way back to Augustabad, hundreds of people lined the streets yelling at him, calling him a spy.

Early December 1916: Konstanz

The conditions were better at the hospital in Konstanz than at the one in Leipzig. Here, Douglas could bathe, and he had access to a canteen where he could buy canned sardines and other food to supplement the German rations, which included real coffee and rolls made from white flour for breakfast. The men could play cards, bridge and chess, and smoke while sitting in comfortable chairs. An English officer's canary was the mascot in the barracks where Douglas lived, and it was not considered a potential source of food. Still, they were prisoners and patients far from home, and because they had had to surrender their letters, they were cut off from the words of their loved ones. Without these talismans of home, the mystic chords of memory stretched almost to the breaking point. Their feeling of being "absolutely cut off from the world" ended when a batch of letters arrived.[23]

Over the course of several days, Douglas was examined by a number of Red Cross and Swiss doctors. On some days, an *Unteroffizier* appeared and read off the names of six men who had failed their medieval examinations and would not be exchanged because they could be of no use to the British or Canadian armies, not even as clerks. At the end of the second week of December, Douglas and more than 430 other POWs boarded the first-class carriage of a train. Within moments of leaving the station, they were in Switzerland. Women and children lined the tracks, waving handkerchiefs while standing in the snow, cheering the Allied troops with shouts of "*Vive l'Angleterre!*"

15 December 1916: Fort Rastatt, Germany

INSTEAD OF CONTINUING ON to internment in Switzerland as Douglas had, Laird and the fifty men with him were now quartered in a long, damp tunnel he likened to a sewer. With them were several men with tuberculosis whose coughing grew worse as they lay on the floor without even straw to insulate them from the cold and damp. Breathing was a trial for the other men because of the odours that emanated from the damp and the scores of unwashed men, many, like Laird, with festering wounds.

After the fine food they had eaten in the hotel in Konstanz, the dirty water with (if they were lucky) mouldy vegetable pieces that passed for soup was a special trial—as was the barley in which bugs and worms were intermixed. The strain of living in darkness—for they were not allowed candles—increased their feelings of hopelessness. They became sullen and despondent, and at times even feared one another. "There were no serious quarrels, although there was wrangling and unpleasantness most of the time, and an undercurrent of menacing personal antipathy that we were all afraid of. Each one of us had reached a stage mentally where we could no longer trust ourselves, and it was this distressing lack of confidence that made us suspicious of others," recalled Laird."[24]

But the men did not break. Laird's health was worse than at Stendal and his stomach emptier, but his depression began to lift. Others too, he noticed, plumbed some inner depth and, like drowning men, bobbed to the surface intent on gulping air and living. Resisting the Germans by holding off the black night of despair and coping with hunger pangs became a source of strength.

This newfound strength did not last from day to day, but rather, had to be found anew each day. It had to be found in the darkness, through the miasma they breathed and with the ever-present gnawing hunger calling each man back to his own all-too-human body and its unfulfilled needs. For these men, the simple act of living, of keeping some Germans tied down by watching them, was a victorious act of war.

Ten days before Christmas, Laird and some of the men were put on a train that took them back to Konstanz, where they ate good, filling soup provided by the Red Cross. An elegant Swiss Red Cross train that would take them out of Germany awaited them.

Late December 1916: Dortmund, Germany

Jack Evans did not put much stock in the judge who told the Canadian private that he "would be justly treated."[25] Evans stood charged with giving as good as he got after three foremen started beating him with sticks when he was caught sleeping in a mine.

One foreman told the court that Evans had started the brawl by "striking him with the lamp in the jaw."[26] Evans, whose Attestation Papers listed his calling as "Auto-Tire Builder," showed a natural legal mind when he ended his statement by pointing out that had he hit the *Steiger* as alleged, he would have a scar from the wound. Evans was exonerated, and the judge fined the foremen RM 100 for bringing a false charge. Equally appreciated by the POW was the schnapps that the guard bought the *Schweinehund* in a tavern they stopped at before going to the train station.

Christmas 1916: Germany

HARRY HOWLAND WAS THANKFUL for the effect the cigars and oranges had on the guards in Cassel. These gifts from the "All Highest" (Kaiser Wilhelm) may have been meant to prove to his soldiers that the stories of the breaking of the Royal Navy's blockade were true. In the camp, however, these Christmas presents put the guards in such good humour that they excused the POWs from work on the morning of Christ's nativity.

At Augustabad, by contrast, Christmastide, as many of the Catholic POWs called the period, was especially painful. Since no one had confessed to helping Thorn escape, the *Kommandant* had restricted the POWs to their rooms and suspended parole walks.

For his part, Thorn was not surprised by his *Strafe* sentence. "Life in a fortress was as you made it," he said. "If you sat down and moped, then it went hard with you, but if you tried to occupy your time, even if it was digging a tunnel or bribing the sentries, the time did not hang so heavily on one's hands."[27]

Some of his friends elsewhere in the prison had managed to sneak him a can of Maconochie, a canned stew of sliced turnips, carrots and potatoes in a thin soup, for Christmas dinner. Yet with the sound of German guards drinking and singing "*Die Wacht am Rhein*" (The Watch on the Rhine), Thorn did not find it festive to sit in his cell eating cold stew "with no light save the faint glow of a candle . . . stuck in an empty bottle, the place bare of any furniture except a wooden bed and chair."[28] After his dinner on his second Christmas in Germany, he crawled into bed, knowing that his family at home in Vancouver would be thinking of him with the same sentiment a little girl in Rockland, Ontario, felt when she added this P.S. to her letter to Santa Claus: "And please don't forget Cousin Dick that is a prisoner of war in Germany."[29]

At Dülmen camp, MacDonald's *Strafe* sentence ran through Christmas. He had only a couple of candles, which provided enough light for him to write a poem about Ypres. But flickering light was not much compared to the warmth and light from a fireplace log in the home of his youth in Rainy River, in the southwest corner of northern Ontario, near the border of Manitoba and Minnesota.

MacDonald bribed a guard to provide him with something of a Christmas dinner. Hidden in the food was something the guard believed was even more important: a batch of letters that McMullen was anxious to read. Yet once he struck a match and looked at the envelopes, he "found to [his] disgust that they were all six or seven months old."[30]

Chapter Eight

January–March 1917

Early January 1917: Canada and Friedrichsfeld

Released a few minutes before "Auld Lang Syne" was played in ballrooms and on pianos across the country, the last casualty list of 1916 brought deep sorrow to eighty-two families, including that of Private Charles Barnes. The private, captured on the Somme, was now listed as "Died a Prisoner of War." Privates Joseph Gorst's and Walter Cann's families started the year with new hope, for, missing since the Somme, these soldiers were now officially "Prisoners of War."[1]

The first part of the Canadian Red Cross's press release of 5 January was hopeful. While signalling that the Red Cross would soon be asking for more donations, it said that the 2,196 Canadian POWs in Germany were "not threatened with any shortage of food."[2] Although most readers may have taken the words for mere information, the implications of the second part of the release—"caring for them is made very difficult by the

German practice of shifting prisoners from place to place"—were much darker.

The ever-tightening blockade caused German-supplied rations to drop further. And a change in how Red Cross tins were doled out lessened their effectiveness. Previously, each can had been marked with a man's name and then placed in a central store, from whence it could be retrieved unopened. Now, POWs had to go to the storeroom with a basin into which the food was dumped, often mixing meat, cheese and jam together, and it could not be saved for escapes. The cold and the heavy snow that fell on Friedrichsfeld early in January reminded Canadians of home, but it strained relations with the French in Fred McMullen's hut. Despite the stench from dozens of unwashed bodies, each time a Canadian opened the hut's window, a Frenchman ran over to close it.

Less Chaplinesque was the march Harry Howland endured one frigid early January morning during which he and other men who had missed the latrine call suffered the indignity of wetting themselves as they were forced to march to a work camp. It is unclear whether Howland's fellow Bokelah mutineer, Private Clifford Sherwood, was on this march, but on 1 January, Canadians learned that he had been sentenced to "twelve years' imprisonment for refusing to assist in making ammunition in Germany."[3]

5 January 1917: Arbeitskommando 47

PRIVATE FRANK MACDONALD AND a soldier he called "W. H." marched on the blind side of the guard closest to them on their way to the *Kokerei*. Then, as the civilians returned from their day shift, a few of the POWs' comrades whisked off MacDonald's and W. H.'s coats. Now sporting passable civilian clothes without the telltale prisoner stripes, the two escapers wheeled around and joined the exiting workers. A few moments later, when MacDonald saw that the plant's manager and three foremen were directly in front of them, his heart leapt into his throat, but none of them noticed two more shabbily dressed men.

Since anyone walking through the gate risked an identity check, the escapers slipped behind a pile of bricks near the fence and tunnelled beneath it. Twenty minutes later, as they scraped off the muck from the marsh they had just waded through, they heard the alarm ring at the *Kokerei*. Late that night, they saw a horseman a few fields away advancing toward them. MacDonald and W. H. dropped into a nearby ditch.

The River Lippe presented the first natural obstacle for the two men. They jury-rigged a raft by lashing a couple of doors they had found in a barn to two railway ties. MacDonald and W. H. were up to their waists in freezing water before the raft achieved buoyancy. Later, to avoid stepping in the frigid water under the ice in the fields, the men had to risk walking on the road. As day approached, MacDonald dug out a shallow shelter in the snow, where they huddled together for warmth and away from prying eyes.

Early January 1917: Fort Zorndorf

AFTER TEN DAYS IN solitary confinement, John Thorn was allowed an hour's walk in the courtyard each day. On New Year's Day, his door swung open and two actual widows and a couple of drunk guards came to view the soldier who had dressed as a "*Witwe*" (widow). During the second week of January, eight parcels addressed to Thorn that had been at Augustabad were forwarded to Fort Zorndorf. Among them was one from Captain Scudamore, who, after missing out on being interned in Switzerland in late 1915 because the German exchange party was smaller than the British, was interned there in late 1916. Scudamore's package contained a cake, which was smuggled into Thorn's dreary cell.

9 January 1917: Friedrichsfeld

For a few moments at the Oberhausen train station, McMullen and more than two hundred other POWs thought they were about to be fed. Then, someone realized that the soldiers standing on the platform were singing "The Maple Leaf Forever." In a trice, the wine and beer that had shimmered on tables a short distance away vanished, replaced by a number of military police who tried to stop the men's singing.

The guards at Friedrichsfeld clubbed the men, who were so enfeebled by the day spent without food or water, they fell down on the march from the train station to the camp. The guards' cruelty was systemic; McMullen realized this a few days later when he saw German officers beat and kick their own men. It was a measure of the Germans' ferocity that McMullen—who belonged to an army that still practised Field Punishment Number 1 (tying a man with his legs together and his arms outstretched on a gun wheel, known to the men as "crucifixion")—wrote that if their officers treated Canadian troops as German officers do theirs, "there'd be a mutiny in a minute."[4]

12 January 1917: The Dutch Border and the Kokerei

MacDonald's weak German was strong enough to pass muster when he grunted *Guten Morgen* or *Guten Tag* to the people he and W. H. met on the roads. It was not, he knew, good enough to order food, which the hungry escapers needed, in the shops in Ramsdorf. Nevertheless, because the road went through Ramsdorf, the escapers had no choice but to risk going there—and hence expose themselves to more prying eyes. Once back in the countryside, MacDonald and W. H. took shelter among four snow-covered, scrubby pines at the top of a hill, where, for the first time in days, they found enough dry wood to build a fire.

At 2 p.m., through heavy sleet, they saw "a long line of Germans armed with sticks, pans, horns" coming toward them.[5] As the men neared the POWs, they saw that they carried shotguns, and soon realized that the Germans were hunting rabbits. Not long after, an old couple trudging up the hill came near them. Bent over with the weight of a sack of potatoes, the man stopped and, apparently guessing the unkempt men were escapers, said something that sounded to MacDonald like "Legoff." Taking it to mean "good luck," he repeated the word as the couple walked on into the storm.

The arrival of a warm front turned the roads slushy, slowing the escapers' advance, but they were heartened by signs saying "It is forbidden to pass this way," which indicated they were close to the Dutch border. An old windmill, beyond which other would-be escapers had told them the patrols thickened, provided the fillip that the men needed. Their luck ended when, as they stood on the road arguing about whether to follow it or, as MacDonald urged, keep to the fields, a German patrol surrounded them.

* * *

MACDONALD AND W. H. WERE treated fairly in the days following their capture. The guards had received a bounty for capturing the escapers a half-mile from the Dutch border. Though no longer free, the escapers had decent food, water and mattresses to sleep on.

One of the guards had learned English in the United States. He was friendly, and the men assumed this was because he had been conscripted into the Kaiser's army at the outbreak of the war while visiting his family.

British POWs at Münster convinced the *Kommandant* to let them share the largesse contained in the Christmas parcels that had arrived late. This allowed MacDonald to give several guards small pieces of cake, which put the lie to the claims made in the German newspapers that Britain was starving. The cake loosened their tongues enough for them to tell him of the struggles at Verdun and on the Somme; where, the guards said, the Canadians were highly regarded as "shock troops."

The bitter black bread and bowl of ersatz coffee a nurse at a station gave MacDonald was a foretaste of what was to come, however. In the middle of the coldest winter in a century, MacDonald was shoved naked into a dark, stinking cell with no furniture and no source of heat. As he shivered, he heard the bolt of W. H.'s cell being opened. "In a moment there was a sharp cry of pain and the sound of a body falling heavily." The moans of his escape partner were interspersed by the sounds of kicking and pounding, and stopped only after "unconsciousness had mercifully come to [W. H.'s] help."[6]

Realizing that even if he managed to push past the guards now coming toward his cell, he'd likely be shot before he reached the yard, MacDonald readied himself to fight by hiding in the darkest corner of the cell. The guards entered. "Every once in a while from the grunts and cries," MacDonald knew he'd landed a punch or a kick, at the price of being badly cut up. Finally, the guards withdrew, leaving the bloodied Canadian awake on a night so cold that he felt freezing to death would "have been a merciful release."[7]

Morning brought neither food nor water. Instead, the two beaten and freezing prisoners were made to stand at attention in the snow. When W. H. collapsed, the guards let the unconscious man lie in the snow for a while before ordering other prisoners to take him to the hospital. Not until 4 p.m. was MacDonald allowed to go into a barracks, where other POWs gave him what hot food they could. Not long after, a senior camp official ordered MacDonald to appear before him in his office, where he was harangued. "You are always running away and will not take our warning. We punish you but it is no use and now we will kill you with work. Work, work, you must always, ever work."[8]

In an effort to prevent MacDonald from even trying to escape, he was ordered to hand over his boots and was given wooden clogs that chafed his feet. For five days, he loaded thirty-two tons of coke per day into cars—all the while breathing scalding, gas-filled air. In those few moments when he let up, guards pounced on him or kicked him. Rank with sweat, MacDonald pushed through this steady grind in "that earthly branch of hell," a phrase that for men who were regular churchgoers was more than a rhetorical flourish.[9]

After six days, MacDonald moved to save himself. Deliverance did not come without pain, as he poured boiling water over his left hand until it blistered, ostensibly from a burn at the *Kokerei*. Even after seeing the badly burnt hand, the doctor resisted taking him off his stint at the *Kokerei*, but finally acquiesced. On the next morning's sick call, the doctor got his revenge when he ripped off the dressing with such violence that "he took [off] all the skin and most of the flesh from the hand, so that the cords and bones were almost bare."[10] Then, he told MacDonald he would almost certainly lose the hand, an exchange the carpenter was willing to make if it got him out of the *Kokerei*.

Winter 1916/17: Dortmund

REDUCED TO NINETY POUNDS and subsisting on one bowl of watery soup, three potatoes and a small piece of *Brot* a day, David O'Brien joined hundreds of other POWs digging out coal in the mine at Dortmund, one thousand feet below the pleasant hills of Westphalia. The air was so foul in the galleries, barely held up by what to a Canadian used to seeing stout two-by-fours seemed like scantling, that O'Brien schemed to be sent to the same sort of coke ovens that had almost broken MacDonald.

The heat of the coke ovens blistered his hands. O'Brien's task was to spray the coke with water until it was cool enough for the POWs to break it into small pieces with their bare, festering hands. After two months of heavy labour, O'Brien was so ill with fever that he was sent to the hospital. Three weeks later, he was shipped to the Holzminden POW camp.

O'Brien was at Holzminden for only a month before being sent to the POW camp at Hamm. There he was again forced to work.

To the tattoo of truncheons and pieces of coal thrown by civilians, he loaded heavy sacks of cement onto barges bound for Holland. When a civilian threw coal at him, O'Brien defended himself by smashing a heavy stone over the man's head. A few moments later, the nearby guards beat O'Brien, who was later smashed with a heavy stone over the head in return. O'Brien was then transferred to the Krupp Munitions Works in Essen.

When O'Brien and the POWs with him refused to work, an officer ordered the guards to attack the POWs with rifle butts and their hobnailed boots. When they again refused to work, the officer ordered them to be taken to a steel trestle where cord was tied around their thumbs and little fingers. Their arms were hoisted up and the cords thrown over a steel beam; the cord was then drawn tight.

After two hours of this torture, the POWs still refused to work, so the Germans chose two exemplary victims, an Australian and O'Brien. Moments after O'Brien witnessed the Australian being held down by a number of guards while another used a pen to tattoo his face, leaving it torn and bleeding, he felt the point of a knife cut into his neck just above his spine. The pain, mercifully, was short-lived, for O'Brien collapsed into unconsciousness. When he came to in a stable, a Russian POW was washing his face. O'Brien was partially paralyzed.

Mid-February 1917: Fort 9 POW Camp, Germany

Thorn was not a logistics officer. He was, however, enough of a military man to know that despite what the leaflet said about the large number of ships Germany's U-boats had sunk, Britain still commanded the seas. The parcels that continued arriving from Canada showed that Britain was far from "throw[ing] in the sponge."[11] Indeed, from what he gleaned when he saw what he estimated to be a line of eight hundred women in Berlin, each holding her family's weekly milk ticket, and from what a loquacious guard told him about the rationing of food, he knew it was Germany's economy that was under severe stress.

Built in 1866, Fort 9 was surrounded by a fifteen-foot-wide moat. The rooms built into the ramparts were cold and damp, and the Germans supplied only two hours' worth of coal or wood each day. The cold also made using the lavatory a trial, and Thorn found the lack of partitions, which had been burnt for heat, violated his sense of decorum.

Despite *Strafe* sentences imposed for the slightest infraction, Thorn and the others planned their escape. He teamed up with a Royal Flying Corps officer named Wilkin a few weeks after nine French officers "ran like hares" once they were outside the gates, ostensibly to refill their mattresses with straw.[12] Thorn and Wilkin found a way to open two heavy doors before reaching a storeroom, where they hoped to climb out a window. They cut out panels that allowed them to reach the bolt and handle, respectively. Concerned that Feldwebel Fabel would see the pins that held the cardboard over the hole in the second door, Thorn returned to the door to push the pins in. Inadvertently, he rubbed off the paint he had mixed to cover the pins; they were soon seen by the Germans.

Mid-February 1917: Recklinghausen POW Camp, Germany

IN THE MONTHS SINCE being captured at Mount Sorrel, Jack Evans and William Raeside did double duty. Under the watchful eyes of a foreman, they dug away at the anthracite. At night, using a small shovel smuggled out of the mine, they pried up a few floor boards and then started digging, hiding the spoil under their bunks.

The digging went surprisingly well until they hit a stone wall. Evans said that getting through it "was no pink-tea job."[13] His words hardly reflected the hours they spent naked so the Germans would not see the dust caused by hammering away at the concrete in a tunnel barely wide enough for their bodies; the innumerable times their faces were stung by concrete chips; the burning of their eyes from the dust; or the fright that followed the thought that the sound of this strike might reach a guard's ears. After three weeks, the tunnel ran beyond the last sentry's beat outside the last barbed wire fence.

Raeside and Evans opened the tunnel at midnight on a dry February night and made their way down a road to the River Lippe. As Evans later admitted, they erred by not discussing their plans with more seasoned escapers, for as soon as they reached the river, they made a rookie mistake and attempted to cross a railway bridge. They had not realized it was guarded, and they were captured and unceremoniously marched back to camp by guards with fixed bayonets.

Winter 1917: Friedrichsfeld

THE GUARD IN THE SHABBY, mismatched uniform didn't mince words. "The war is no good. The Kaiser is crazy." Nor did the guards who were willing to do much for a pair of socks to replace the rags wound round their feet. After hearing McMullen say that there was "lots of soap in England," the guard said in a disgusted tone, "No soap in Germany. Everything all gone. No meat. No bread. No potatoes."[14]

Had it not been for the food parcels, McMullen would have starved on the six ounces of *Brot*, now augmented with sawdust, and the bowl of thin mangel soup (made from beets grown as fodder) the Germans provided on most days. McMullen knew that even the army was suffering in what the Germans called the Turnip Winter. One day while working outside the camp, he saw the soldiers' rations: about half a pound of black bread, a bowl of soup at noon, burnt-acorn coffee and a small herring for dinner. Canadian soldiers, he believed, would never have obeyed the regulation that stated "it was a crime to eat all the bread ration at once."[15]

Early March 1917: Canada

TWO YEARS EARLIER, CANADIANS had been urged to adopt POWs and send them parcels. By early 1917, with more than two thousand Canadians behind German barbed wire, the shipping system could no longer handle personal parcels as well as those sent by official organizations, such as Vancouver's Prisoner of War Committee. Accordingly, the government decided in February that personal parcels could no longer be sent.

The regulations that came into force on 1 March did not, however, transfer the funding of the parcels to the government. The fundraising by the Patriotic Funds in British Columbia in February alone totalled $1,598,223.66 ($26.9 million). On 3 March,

Revelstoke's Prisoner of War Committee received donations from a number of small British Columbia towns. The list of individual donations, some as humble as fifty cents, was extensive, the amounts mattering less than the link the act of giving represented between individual Canadians and the nation's POWs. Some adopters, who now could only exchange mail with their POWs, developed what can only be called a bantering relationship with them. For example, here is one response sent back to Canada: "You asked me in your last letter if I have a wife or a sweetheart. Well, I can tell you that Cupid has not come down my street yet—me and him are not the best of friends."[16]

4 March 1917: Queenston, Ontario

Isaac Field, Private Walter Field's father, was not the only one in the village of Queenston, Ontario, celebrating on the night of 4 March. With the Niagara Township Fruit-Grower's Band supplying the music, most of Queenston's villagers turned out to welcome Walter home. The "stalwart villagers" carried the soldier captured at Mount Sorrel (who had been repatriated because one leg was so badly damaged it had to be amputated) to Laura Secord Hall, where many Queenstonians waited to shake Walter's hand.[17]

By calling him "the Queenston hero," the anonymous *Globe* author deftly linked Field—and by extension every other POW—with the two most potent stories in Canadian military history. The first is Laura Secord's famous walk, on the night of 21 June 1812, to warn Lieutenant James FitzGibbon of an impending (surprise) American attack. The second was memorialized by the 56-metre-high column visible from every point of the village Field had grown up in. The villagers who interrupted Field's tale of battle and survival in the POW camp, and the readers of the *Globe*, knew that "the hero of Queenston," Sir Isaac Brock, had been mortally wounded while commanding the forces defending Queenston Heights on 13 October 1812.

Even before Field was "Struck Off Strength" on 30 June 1917, his name was entered on the rolls of the Military Hospital and Convalescent Commission and soon would be on the list of the Board of Pension Commissioners. The "Table of Incapacities" dictated that Field merited a disability pension of 60 percent because of the loss of his leg; the era's understanding of manliness set the same rate for a man's loss of his genitals. The algebraic clarity of the table, which was borrowed from the French, did not, however, factor in inflation, which by 1917 was some 30 percent, while soldiers' pay remained frozen, with predictable results of the likelihood of a returned soldier sliding into poverty.

Mid-March 1917: France and Canada

For weeks the news concerning POWs had been worrisome. In early January, the French and German governments were engaged in a war of words and threats about forcing POWs to work within thirty kilometres of the front lines. In fact, both countries made extensive use of forced labour in the battle zone. Conditions on both sides were terrible; POWs were not issued gas masks, with sadly predictable results. Nor were they given warm clothing or hip waders, so many saw their frostbitten toes turn black. "In addition," one German soldier reported once he had been exchanged in Switzerland, forced labourers "were eaten all over their body by vermin and as most were suffering from diarrhoea, they soiled themselves over and over again with their own faeces."[18] The Germans, for their part, had provided such poor rations that French POWs were forced to eat grass. And thousands were made to work within sight of French lines, where they were sometimes trapped—and killed—by French shellfire.

On 11 March, following the British refusal to limit their use of forced labour to farther than thirty kilometres from the front, the German High Command ordered that new British POWs could work within an equal distance as the German POWs. This was not reported in Canada, though it was in the *London Times*. Ironically, this meant that some of the sixty men captured at Vimy might have known about this policy. What these men would have said had they known that Field Marshal Douglas Haig, the general commanding the British army to which the Canadian Corps belonged, had declared that forced labour was so important to the BEF that he refused to limit where POWs could be used, can be surmised. Letters from POWs forced to labour near the front to the Red Cross, the high commissions of both Australia and Canada, and the Vatican blamed the British. That they did so was, no doubt, the reason German censors allowed these letters to stray from the censorship rules that forbade discussion of the war or politics. One British soldier wrote: "I am working behind the line through our government keeping the German prisoners behind our lines. We are getting bad treatment until justice is done to their men, they say, so the sooner our officials takes it into consideration [*sic*] the better it will be for us, so no more."[19]

Then, on 13 March, in an article titled "Germans May Starve British Prisoners," the *Globe* pointed out a hitherto unrealized consequence of the American decision to break relations with

Germany in early February. That decision had been prompted by Germany's resumption of restricted submarine warfare and the publication of the Zimmermann Telegram, which promised Mexico financial support and the recovery of "lost territory in New Mexico, Texas and Arizona" if it allied with Germany. It meant that, with the departure of U.S. Ambassador Gerard from Berlin, the POWs' protecting power had vanished. The news on the 26th that, having worked out legal technicalities, Berlin would allow the International YMCA to oversee the distribution of food parcels was a great relief to the families of the POWs and the two most recently freed Canadians, privates William Thurgood and Sam Gordon (both captured at Second Ypres). They told the press how the parcels had kept men from starving. No doubt for morale-boosting reasons, the 9 March story that told of their escape elided the fear of being captured and the battle against the cold by falling back on a comforting Canadian hunting image: "there was not much difficulty in escaping, as the rivers were frozen."[20]

If Mrs. C. Brooke, who had been keeping vigil for her son, Billy, captured at Second Ypres, walked the few blocks from the Ottawa home where William had grown up, to the stately stone Dominion Chalmers Presbyterian Church two blocks away, to thank God for the parcels that would feed her son, she needn't have bothered. For the better part of two weeks, the private's remains had lain in a grave in Südfriedhof, the largest cemetery in Leipzig.

Since Harry Howland's memoir was not published until the 1970s, Mrs. Brooke likely never learned that the *Strafe* sentence in the dark, dank and damp cell in which Brooke contracted the pneumonia that killed him was punishment for ending a letter to her in which he praised the conditions at Cologne prison with the sentence, "You know, Mother, I am not like George Washington." Upper Canada families like Brooke's could still view the American revolutionaries through a Loyalist lens. But Parson Weems's mythology of young George Washington and the cherry tree was well known, so these last words of Brooke's actually told his mother not to believe a word of what he had just written. Unfortunately, the German corporal who censored the letter had worked as a salesman in the United States. Before ordering the *Strafe* sentence, *he* told Brooke, "Your excellent knowledge of American history will cost you three days."[21]

Howland could not attend Brooke's funeral because he was fighting for his life against double pneumonia. Like his fellow mutineers, however, he contributed money so that Brooke's body could be embalmed in the hope that "Billy could go home after the war." Although some bodies were taken back to Britain, the sheer number of British and Commonwealth dead prompted the decision to establish cemeteries in France and Belgium, making these patches of ground, as Rupert Brook wrote, "forever England," a metonymy for the Empire to which Canadians like Brooke proudly belonged.

19 March 1917: Stadtvogtei Prison, Berlin

THE *GLOBE* REPORTED TWICE in the previous year that Canadian member of Parliament Dr. Henri Béland had been freed, the last time being on 21 June 1916, when it reported he had been allowed to join his ailing wife in Holland. Then, on 12 August, came the report that he was still a prisoner and that both Canada and Britain were doing their utmost to have him released.

Mr. C. Mellor, a British subject who was interned with Béland, overstated things by saying that the MP was "herded with common criminals." Béland's fellow inmates at Berlin's Stadtvogtei included political prisoners and British internees who had been recaptured after escaping from Ruhleben Internment Camp.[22] Mellor was surprisingly candid about Béland's depression, caused by years of imprisonment in an eight-by-ten-foot cell "devoid of furniture, save for the wire mattress bed and bedding and a wooden stool," and by the Germans' refusal to allow Béland to attend his dying wife's bedside.

Béland's depression did not, however, break his will. Neither did the number of times he had been told he was about to be released. One time, with his bags packed, he was summoned to the *Kommandant's* office to be told that the commander had just received word that Béland was not to be released. Indeed, as a kindly German doctor discovered, these mistreatments seemed to strengthen Béland, who told him "that after being treated in such an inhumane manner . . . it is quite impossible, while I maintain my self-respect, to ask for any favor from the German Government. I was refused justice when I entreated for what was just. I have nothing to demand now."[23]

Spring 1917: Arbeitskommando 529, Near Essen, Germany

McMullen was planning on escaping again. He had hidden a compass and a map of northern Germany while being transferred to a farm near Essen. The items had cost him only a single pot of jam, which indicated just how much the German food supplies had dwindled.

The food situation was so dire in Germany that McMullen was

amused to see Herr Becker on the floor of the barn picking up a few grains of sugar that had fallen out of one of McMullen's parcels. He also appreciated Frau Becker's wails and the wringing of her hands when the voracious German army seized the forty loads of turnips the Beckers had hoped would feed their family and cattle until the fall harvest. Herr Becker had to get permission from the village gendarme to slaughter one of his twenty-two pigs. Moved by the Germans' plight, McMullen and the other POWs would break off a little of the chocolate they received in their parcels to give to the local children. "It used to break our hearts to see these little children suffering so with hunger and we gave them what we could, but that was mighty little."[24]

Chapter Nine

April–June 1917

8 April 1917, Vimy Ridge, France

George Scott had been busy for weeks after noticing that the bars on his cell were screwed into the wooden sash. As tens of thousands of General Arthur Currie's troops practised for their attack on Vimy Ridge on realistic models, Scott filed down a piece of metal to make a screwdriver. On the night of 8 April, two days after the United States entered the war, as the German defenders on Vimy Ridge endured another night of heavy shelling that blasted trenches, destroyed gun emplacements, shredded bunkers and deafened and killed men, Scott unscrewed the bars and climbed out of his cell.

What Scott puckishly called a "great adventure" got off to a slow start.[1] Just moments after climbing out the window, he realized he had forgotten his water bottle. In a stage whisper that he hoped was loud enough to waken a soldier named Murphy—but not a nearby guard sleeping off his Easter revels—Scott called for the bottle. Long seconds later, Murphy appeared and threw down the bottle, allowing Scott and Arthur Corker, who had been captured at Ypres, to start running toward a road.

After several nights on the run together, Corker knew the sounds Scott made while climbing out of a ditch, which explained why he noticed an unfamiliar rustle. "Watch out, Scotty," Corker whispered before sliding a finger forward and turning on a flashlight they had stolen from a farm. The light illuminated the faces of the two escapers. Corker spotted two women and quickly shut off the flashlight as the women ran, calling out words referring to generations-old folktales that meant "the Goblin man."[2]

12 April 1917: Vimy Ridge

FOR A WHILE ON 11 and 12 April, the most important former Canadian POW was Lance Sergeant Clement N. Malmloff, who on 10 April was one of the sixty-seven Canadians captured during the attack on Vimy Ridge.

More than half of the men came from 75th Battalion, part of the second wave, tasked with following the 87th Battalion between strong points on Hill 145 and the fortified village of Givenchy-en-Gohelle (on the centre let of the attack line), while another large number came from the 54th Battalion fighting in the same sector. None of these men emerged from the subways, the tunnels cut into the chalk leading from the Canadian lines into No Man's Land so that thousands of attackers could appear on the battlefield hundreds of yards closer to the German defensive line. It was hoped that these men would reach the German trench before the enemy emerged from their deep dugouts to man the machine guns. As the *Woche des*

Leidens (Week of Suffering)—which included being heavily shelled and drenched in poison gas—reached its crescendo, one anonymous Canadian newspaper correspondent was moved close to poetry, writing that the artillery explosions "made a continuous play like that of the northern lights in this Dominion or distant sheet lightning."[3]

Poetry, however, was not part of Private William Coveyduck's or Corporal Donald Sutherland's stories. Intelligence believed that this small stretch of trench was unoccupied and could be used by the Canadians for their command centre during the advance, so the artillery kept a respectful distance. As they waited in the trenches, the men of the 87th Battalion could see new barbed wire had been strung across the trench a little more than a hundred yards away. But even though the Canadian army had pushed much responsibility down to the platoon level, like the men immortalized in Alfred Lord Tennyson's poem "The Charge of the Light Brigade," these men knew "theirs [was still] not to reason why." During their charge toward a trench that was not only fully manned but had been augmented with *Feldgrauen* who had fled the bombardment, "Theirs [was] but to do and die." Within a few yards of the top, 60 percent of the battalion lay dead, dying or wounded.

Knowing the circumstances of their capture, Sutherland, Coveyduck and the other thirty-two men could easily surmise something they would not want to tell. As one historian noted in gentle words, the carnage on the battlefield "so unnerved" the men of the 75th Battalion who were tasked with following the first wave that "most did not leave their trenches."[4] Instead, small clots of men advanced where they could. Some three dozen broke into the German lines only to be captured. Some who went to ground in front or to the right of the German line were captured, likely by a certain Unteroffizier Kremer's 1st Company (belonging to the Reserve Infantry Regiment 261), which had extreme difficulty moving them back to more secure German lines. The position the Germans had defended was now a small salient that they assumed would be pinched off the next day. Of the fifty-nine men reported missing, thirty-four ended up in the bag.

Sometime on the 11th, the number of 5th Battalion men captured (on the far right side of the attack line) dropped by half. Exactly how Lance Sergeant Clement N. Malmloff escaped is unknown. But slip the Germans he did, and he made it back to his comrades, who now looked down upon the unspoiled landscape of the Douai Plain. Malmloff brought with him the kind of information about German positions and the *Feldgrauen*'s morale that intelligence officers craved.

11 April 1917: New York City, USA

THE AUGUST BALLROOM OF the luxurious Biltmore Hotel, across from Grand Central Station in Manhattan, had never been the site of such a speech. Beneath the four-level chandeliers, more than 1,500 (mostly Canadian) diners sat at tables with crisply ironed white tablecloths, waiting to hear James Gerard. The men, in starched white shirts and pressed black dinner jackets, and the women, in costly evening gowns, bursting with pride at the praise lavished in the *New York Times* on the Canadian victory at Vimy, had come to hear the former U.S. ambassador to Germany speak about the treatment of the POWs for whom he had acted as the Protecting Power for almost three years. Knowing how unpalatable the words he would soon speak were, Gerard began with a lesser violation of international law. The Kaiser's government, he joked, was so fond of him that it "kept me a week after I had said I wanted to go home" following the rupture of relations between the two countries in early February.[5]

To do what he could for the POWs, the ambassador had routinely issued statements using the most diplomatic language; now he dropped all pretense. The well-heeled audience—the very sort of people expected to purchase war bonds—heard how German authorities had imprisoned German civilians who sought to give starving POWs on trains food and drink. Men and women who could effortlessly negotiate a fifteen-piece cutlery service heard that "small German boys were allowed to shoot arrows tipped with nails into the bodies of prisoners."[6]

"You sitting here in the Biltmore," Gerard continued, "cannot imagine the horror of living two and half years in a German prison camp."[7] Even though New York had been free from typhus for seventy years, it lived on in popular memory (partially by being confused with the epidemics caused by Mary Mallon, "Typhoid Mary," the last of which occurred in 1913). Thus the diners were horrified hearing that French, English and Canadian troops had been purposely exposed to the typhus that had broken out in one camp's Russian compound. As the competition between British and German steamship companies for the Blue Riband (symbolizing the fastest Atlantic crossing) indicated, the pre-war business class was international. More than a few of the men and women who heard that the Germans had unleashed dogs on prisoners would have laid bets at Berlin's Ruhleben Racetrack. None could have imagined that within a few years, the stalls there would house up to six prisoners each, that they would be significantly underfed, and that some would become so despondent that they lost their minds.

Mid-April 1917: Friedrichsfeld

A DOZEN DAYS OF *STRAFE* had done nothing to dissuade Jack Evans from organizing the digging of a tunnel. Both the digging and the spiriting away of cans of food went unnoticed. On the appointed night, a POW named Nicholson led the group into the tunnel. Just as he was about to dig upwards to make the exit, a sentry's boot broke through the earth above him. [Later they learned that the sentry's beat had been altered earlier in the day.] The sentry was startled, and Nicholson, Evans and the other POWs were able to scramble back to their bunks. They put on a bravura performance, denying all knowledge of the tunnel.

The next morning, when they heard the order for all British POWs to parade, Evans and the others realized trouble was coming. The Germans "threatened that they would punish the whole bunch if the guilty ones were not given up." While their comrades licked their wounds from Vimy, three of Evans's 4th Canadian Mounted Rifles comrades gave themselves up for "seven days 'black' [punishment]."[8]

Early to mid-May 1917: Münster Camp

THE HOSPITAL CAMP AT MÜNSTER was much better than the one Harvey Douglas had been in in 1916. Thanks to the British Prisoners of War Book Scheme (BPWBS), there was a good library. Whether the books had been sent by friends or family, the Red

Cross, or the London-based camp's library or the BPWBS, they could be censored. In one camp, Dickens was seized, while books on such subjects as Judaism, military history and, ironically, modern tunnel practice were approved. The yellowed advertisements in the pre-war British newspapers for Cadbury chocolate and Marmite, not to mention women's fashions and automobiles, made for odd reading. Every Sunday, the POWs could play football and mount concerts. More complicated were the vaudeville-like sketches they put on, because of the props required and the need to make up men and costume them like women. In the half-light of a prison camp room that doubled as a theatre, one of the prisoners' own appeared in a wig, wearing a skirt, his lips and cheeks rouged, his stomach pushed in by a girdle and with bulging "breasts."[9]

Münster was also a theatre of cruelty, where to "get everything out of them" the Germans worked the Russian POWs until all but the strongest died. Had it not been for MacDonald and other POWs who, after receiving Red Cross parcels, gave the Russians their German rations, more would have died. Even with these rations, the Russians "seemed to have no flesh at all on their bodies and the skin hung down over the bones in horrible yellow wrinkles" that were bruised and scarred from beatings and kicks.[10] The wanton beatings of the starving French and Belgian civilians, who, after seeing the Canadian and British prisoners eating food from their parcels, broke the windows of the hut and with bleeding hands and bodies "begged and cried out most piteously for food," pushed Frank MacDonald to write:

> May God punish us adequately if we ever forget the cruelty, bestiality, unfaithfulness and murdering spirit of this nation,

which has sent thousands of our men and women to the bottom of the sea and gloated over it, which has forgotten all the instincts of decency and humanity, and has murdered, raped, mutilated, enslaved and committed every other crime in the category. When the time comes, they will try to whitewash themselves and blame their leader, who, guilty though he may be, could never have provided for such horrible conditions of affairs had not the German people themselves been united in a mad lust for blood, conquest, and the ultimate subjection of the world.[11]

* * *

MACDONALD SPENT A WEEK as a labourer at a factory connected to Hiltrup POW camp, which gave him insight (which he might well have preferred to live without) into the rations the Germans provided. He saw huge loads of carrots, potatoes, turnips and beets pitched into a big chopper. Since the vegetables were not washed and rotten pieces were not removed, the strips that came out of the chopper contained rotten vegetable matter, roots, worms, peelings and earth. "This mess was then shovelled into vats and dried until it was shrivelled up like shavings," which were packed into sacks and shipped to *Arbeitskommandos*, where they formed the basis of the vile soup.[12]

On his last day at Hiltrup, MacDonald knew that when he returned to the *Kokerei* he would be bound for the *Strafe* cell because of the self-inflicted scalding wound. Before being shipped back, however, he and another prisoner sneaked into the boiler room and smashed grease and oil cups, steam gauges, the boiler's water glass and a water pump. Knowing that the damage would soon be discovered, the two men (along with a third, who volunteered to stand by them) concocted a story they stuck to, despite being held for days in "black cells" and being fed only *Brot*. Over the next two months, during which the authorities "moved heaven and earth to find a morsel of evidence on which to convict" them, MacDonald and others remained at Münster, with the threat of a minimum two-year sentence at hard labour hanging over their heads.

The policy of moving men from camp to camp bred horror stories. There was a rumor that at the POW camp in Wittenberg, plague-stricken prisoners had been left to die within sight of the cathedral where Martin Luther posted the Ninety-Five Theses that touched off the Protestant Reformation four hundred years earlier. Those "who let their minds dwell on this sort of thing and on their own misfortunes, could not be roused out of their despondency [and] gradually lost their reason."[13] MacDonald and his conspirators kept the prison camp version of what in the next world war would be called the thousand-yard stare at bay by taking turns keeping one another cheerful.

23 May 1917: Near Recklinghausen

Fred McMullen had sprained his ankle three nights earlier dropping from a window, but that had not stopped him and Private Thomas Hart from making a bid for freedom. Fuelled by two tins of bully beef, some biscuits and chocolate, they walked for three nights toward the Dutch border. On the next day, after getting lost, they found themselves near Recklinghausen and were so tired and thirsty that they chanced going into the town to buy food and get water.

None of the soldiers they passed as they headed for the fountain in the centre of the town noticed the prisoner stripes on their clothing. Neither did the patrons or the bartender at the *Biergarten*. Their German was good enough that they ordered beer without incident. Neither had the civilian card they needed to buy food.

Later, McMullen sensed that their luck was fast running out when a man passing them on the road looked at them "rather queerly but said nothing."[14] Once he was out of sight, the two escapers walked as quickly as McMullen's ankle would allow. A few minutes later, they saw two Russian wolfhounds gaining on them. Before they could find a place to hide or a tree to climb, one hound sank its teeth into Hart's leg. As soon as Hart stopped struggling and McMullen stood still, the hound let go, and the two attack dogs circled the two escapers until a gendarme arrived on a bicycle a few minutes later. Before being searched, McMullen had time to slip their map into his sock and ram his compass into his anus.

26 May 1917: Friedrichsfeld

WEARING BELTS STUFFED WITH ten pounds of French biscuits, Private Jack Evans and a POW he identified as Nick may have looked a little portly as they walked away from the mine. And, while a few of the civilians did look at them oddly, none said anything as they walked to the time clock, picked up their cards, punched them and walked out of the camp. So as to hide in plain sight instead of making a run for it, once beyond the gate, they followed the other miners to a lemonade stand. Evans, who had survived shot and shell at Mount Sorrel, recalled "quaking all the time" as they stood drinking lemonade.[15]

As they walked down the street (which because of double daylight saving time was still bright at 10:15 p.m.), Evans and Nick revelled in the freedom. Once outside of town, they turned toward the River Lippe. They swam across the river, pushing a jury-rigged raft on which they floated their biscuits to keep them dry. Nick was a soldier who had seen battle and survived German POW camps, but it wasn't until Evans saw him naked and shivering but "with his eyes skinned, looking for trouble" that he realized the mettle of the man. Near dawn, they crawled into a newly green clump of bushes in the middle of an acre of scrub.[16]

It didn't take long for the mosquitoes to find them. About half a dozen times over the next few hours they thought of making a run for it but were dissuaded by what the morning's light revealed: a farmhouse a hundred yards away. Later, children played for several hours about twenty yards away from the increasingly itchy escapers.[17]

Late May: Münster

Given his weak command of English, the officer charged with conducting Jack O'Brien and his escape partners to their *Strafe* cells did not realize he was aping the Commandments brought down from Mount Sinai: "You shall be in a dungeon for ten days. You shall see no daylight. You shall have no blankets. You shall not take your coats. You shall live on bread and water. If you try to get away you shall have to die."[18] Nor did he care that in the six-by-three-foot cells POWs slept on cold, damp, filthy floors.

O'Brien and his three escape partners had been on the run for five days. The barbed wire entanglement on the disused bridge spanning the Lippe tore at their clothes, but also proved a welcome sight to men who had survived the trenches, as it told them that the bridge was unguarded. While hiding each day in a forest or in the mouldy hay in haylofts, two men slept while two kept watch. On their third night, they waded through a swamp, numbed by the cold water. The escapers were frozen in somewhat ridiculous poses when they were spotted by a military policemen and captured.

The next morning, two camp guards transported the escapers back to Münster. Once back in their hut, they were made to stand at attention for seven hours, every twitch bringing a heavy kick by a hobnailed German boot. At their trial the following day, the Germans kept asking why O'Brien and the others "wanted to escape," which prompted a man named Sammy to say they "wanted a change, that was all."[19] During their ten days on bread and water, the escapers mocked the hunger that left them so weak they were almost unable to walk out of their cells by planning elaborate dinner menus and yelling them out to one another.

29 May 1917: On a Field Near the River Lippe

Evans knew enough German to respond to the people he and Nick met on the road. The moments of concern after they heard gunshots one morning gave way to relief when they realized a man was shooting crows in a nearby field. They slaked their thirst, which had prevented them from eating their dry biscuits, by ignoring a lecture from training camp and kneeling on the ground to drink from a muddy puddle.

On the night of the 28th, Evans assumed that their unshaved faces and "cadaverous" look had alarmed the two farmgirls they passed enough for them to alert the authorities. Not long after the girls had run away, the escapers were fleeing what Evans likened to a posse. As "men who knew the country like a book" searched for them, the Canadians staggered through the bushes fattened by new growth.[20] After two hours, the searchers gave up.

Late May 1917: Near the Dutch Border

The green forest was enchanting. Beneath towering trees that made Scott think this patch of Germany was a natural church, he and Corker walked mile after mile on deserted roads leading toward freedom. At one point, they heard something crashing through the branches. A moment later, wild boars broke from the trees, freezing the two escapers in their tracks. The boars stood "higher on their legs than the domestic pig and their tusks give them an indescribably horrible appearance, horrible and disgusting." Moments later, they disappeared into the forest.[21]

For a short time after leaving the forest, Scott and Corker were in a lonely valley. Lonely, but not deserted, as they discovered on their fourteenth night on the run when under a viaduct they ran into a German guard, whom they could not bribe, and were recaptured.

After being transported to Giessen, they were locked in a stifling room and made to stand at attention for long hours. At night, they were given a thin blanket and made to sleep on bare wooden bunks. The misery the Germans inflicted on Scott made him think often "of the square deal a German prisoner would get as punishment for doing a soldier's duty" and escaping in Canada.[22]

30 May 1917: Near the Dutch Border

AS DUSK FELL, the women who had been hoeing the turnip field a hundred yards away from where Evans and Nick were hiding in a hole left for the day. Before they could stretch out their cramped limbs, the men heard someone coming through the patch and crawled back into the hole, but did not have time to pull decayed leaves over themselves. Evans credited their ability to lie still and not be noticed to their training for night raids through No Man's Land: it is "mighty hard to spot anything when it doesn't move."[23]

By about 2 a.m., the two men were so weary and hungry that they could barely walk. But the knowledge that they were only a few miles from Holland kept them walking as straight as they could on roads they could not avoid and through swamps that at least offered some protection. Evans's hopes soared when they came to a signpost that, according to the map, was on the border; one arrow pointed northwest into Holland while the other pointed to a German town more than two miles back. Nick was less sanguine, so they continued to move down the road cautiously. Just as Evans was ready to start whooping it up in victory, "three sentries with fixed bayonets stepped out from behind the bushes not three yards away."[24] They were only two hundred yards from Holland.

Early June 1917: Canada

THE NEWS THAT CAME on 4 June that Britain and Germany had agreed that prisoners were to be kept a minimum of thirty kilometres from the firing lines on both the western and eastern fronts put an end to at least one worry for the families of the almost three thousand POWs. The relief, however, was short-lived. Two days later, the *Globe* reported Sergeant Forrest G. Hammersley's story of his treatment in the years after he was captured at Ypres.

Once again, Canadians read about how the Germans kicked and used rifle butts on unarmed men. Word that POWs had also been flogged was especially distressing, as was Hammersley's story of the forced march that was punishment for his and another POW's refusal to work.

Mid-June 1917: Friedrichsfeld

McMullen and Hart thought the court might go easy on them for escaping from Herr Becker's farm. Instead, they received a twenty-one-day *Strafe*. Even worse than the diet of a mere eight ounces of *Brot* each day (which cost the already slight McMullen a pound a day) and sleeping on the cold, damp floor was the "enforced silence," which gave rise to "helpless feelings" that McMullen could not find words to describe.[25]

The guards who searched him before leading him to his cell missed the tobacco sewn into the lining of his coat and the pipe hidden in a fold of his cap. Thanks to the matches a pliant sentry provided, McMullen was able to smoke his pipe.

Chapter Ten

July–September 1917

Summer 1917: Cologne

David O'Brien's speech, which had been badly affected by the dropped jaw caused by nerve damage suffered when he was stabbed in the neck, had improved. And after a number of operations, he was well enough to sweep the street in front of the hospital in Cologne. The day a nurse called him a *Schweinehund*, the broom in his hand became a weapon—until a group of guards who saw him lift the broom ran over and beat the recovering POW bloody. The cell in the prison in Cologne in which he served a forty-day punishment sentence was a "big damp hole" with only a bare stone floor and no blankets. Once a day, the trap door in the ceiling opened and a small piece of black bread and some water were lowered. Alone, depressed, hungry, pained by his suppurating, open wound and dismayed by his unwashed, increasingly reeking body, O'Brien could do little but "sit on the floor, sing, cry and curse the Germans."[1]

22 July 1917: Near Dülmen Camp

THE SAFETY OF FRANK MACDONALD and Jack O'Brien on the roads of Germany depended largely on how well they had sewn covers over the prison stripes on their trousers. They escaped by following a sentry on the *Kokerei* platform just closely enough that when he turned a corner they could drop to the ground. Then they ran the two hundred yards to the cover offered by some empty boxcars, and from there another two hundred yards to several bushes, sprinkling pepper behind them to put the bloodhounds they knew would be following off their scent. They hugged the ground to avoid detection.

Since the wire entanglements on the disused bridge crossing the River Lippe were not guarded, O'Brien and MacDonald pushed past them easily. Though cold and hard—and difficult to choke down—the young beets and seed potatoes they dug up from gardens were like manna from heaven. Before dawn, the escapers took shelter in a wood, only to discover with the morning light that it was rather small and next to a farmhouse. Fortunately, no one was about and they were able to crawl some distance to a low, vine-covered bush.

Summer 1917: Near Friedrichsfeld and the Dutch Border

HERR BECKER ASKED that Fred McMullen and Thomas Hart be returned to his farm. Before they left Friedrichsfeld, a guard sold them a compass for a few pieces of soap. McMullen smuggled it out of the camp by hiding it in his mouth. His map was secreted between the glass and the backing of Hart's "old cracked looking-glass." These words suggest that it resembled the kind of mirror McMullen's grandmother would have had on her dresser.[2]

After the starvation rations of the *Strafe* sentence, both Canadians were pleased to be on the farm, for even with the army's requisitions, food was plentiful enough that they could steal some in expectation of their next escape.

23 July 1917: On a Road Near Dülmen

Their stomachs warmed by a few potatoes baked in the embers of a small fire, MacDonald and O'Brien were able to start out early, since heavy cloud cover made the evening dark. Not long after, they saw a few cows in a field. Over the next few minutes, they reprised the roles of privates Gerry Burk and Herbert Tustin as dairy farmers. Only after MacDonald had petted one cow as O'Brien pulled on her teats did they hear the sound of milk splashing into the pail. Later that night, satiated from still more milk, O'Brien wondered if they looked as swollen as "observation balloons."[3]

Sometime during the day, while they were bedded down, the men awakened at the sound of something rushing toward them. Each grasped his heavy walking stick and waited. Just as their nerves were about to break, they saw two bright eyes and realized their imagined attacker was a hedgehog. MacDonald stayed O'Brien's hand, saying, "No, let the little devil alone; it's a sign of good luck."[4] Their luck held. At 1 a.m., when MacDonald turned on a light to check their compass, a man saw them and started firing at the light. Before he could come any closer, the two escapers managed to climb down a grade and hide in the undergrowth.

Four days later, although buoyed by the knowledge that they

were close to the Dutch border, MacDonald and O'Brien knew they were weakening quickly. A failed escaper had told them that in an effort to catch deserters more than escapers, patrols had been thickened in the months since MacDonald had crawled into and out of Holland. On the next-to-last line, guards stood two hundred yards apart; at the final line, guards with bloodhounds walked a quarter-mile beat each.

To the escapers' surprise, the road that served as the third-last line was white, presumably so that guards could better see men trying to cross it. After waiting a few minutes in the darkness of the wood that ran by the road, MacDonald whispered "Now, Jack," and the two dashed as quickly as they could across the road. Shortly after, they found themselves looking down the barrels of three German rifles.

As they threw up their hands, the escapers grunted something disarming and the guards lowered their rifles. The Canadians may have been haggard and tired, but they were trained infantrymen and, more to the point, close to freedom. In the heat of the moment, they cared nothing for the dictum that escapers should refrain from violence (so as to protect future escapers from being shot on sight). Accordingly, "instead of finding two helpless prisoners," the guards "were met by good hard blows delivered in true British fashion." The prisoners then ran toward a field of slough grass that led to a swamp, where they hid.[5]

Late July 1917: Germany

Rumours ran rampant at the front and in POW camps. Unlike the papers back in Canada, which breathlessly announced in twelve-point type the next "Big Push" or (again) the impending defeat of the U-boats, the soldiers (including the POWs) had a finely developed ear for bullshit. They refused to follow orders to refrain from spreading what they might believe to be baseless rumours. Like office gossip, which acts both to define the in-group and to let off a certain amount of steam, repeating rumours, even patently false ones, is a bonding mechanism. According to the *Listening Post*, the Canadian trench newspaper cognate to the better known *Wipers Times*, rumours normally broke down under their own weight. At the same time, the paper noted the reason why rumours were, for lack of a better word, "fun": they were "sufficiently highly coloured to appeal to troops whose one and everlasting hope is change."[6]

Almost all the soldiers had heard the rumour about the men who had simply given up and now lived in or beneath No Man's Land. The English writer Osbert Sitwell may not have believed such communities existed, but he nonetheless wrote, "They would issue forth . . . from their secret lairs, after each of the interminable checkmate battles, to rob the dying of their few possessions"; they may have lived in squalor and dressed in rags, but "at least they *lived*."[7] Another rumour (planted by the British army) concerned the making of soap from rendered soldiers' bodies.

In the POW camps, rumours abounded about the impending arrival of mail and food parcels. Other rumours told of battles lost and won. Most turned out to be false. One rumour that turned out to be true was that Harry Howland and the Fannigans were about to be released from punishment prisons. It had taken months of hard bargaining, but Britain and Germany had agreed that punishment for attempted escapes would not exceed fourteen days, or two months for "aggravated offences," and that prisoners "now doing punishment for such offences shall be restored to ordinary captivity at the latest by the first of August."[8] On that day, 1 August, Howland and the others were sent to the POW camp at Cologne.

28 July 1917: The Dutch Border

THE WORRYING SOUNDS OF movements through the tall grass in which MacDonald and O'Brien hid were soon accompanied by the voices of girls. The girls were searching for firewood, and were so busy talking that they didn't notice the two men. After the girls had left, around 4 p.m., MacDonald turned his hand to another outdoorsman's task, fashioning moccasins from pieces of their overalls, which he and O'Brien hoped would allow them to slip noiselessly across the border.

Shortly after midnight, the escapers were convinced they saw a figure in the darkness. They laughed when they realized it was, in fact, a stack of peat. But then they heard the bark of an attack dog. In an effort to confuse the dog, MacDonald started to sprinkle pepper on the ground. He needn't have bothered. Before the barking dogs got much closer, a sentry saw the escapers and shouted at them to halt.

Faced with being recaptured, the two men called on their last reserves of strength. As they heard the guard call out again and fire into the darkness, they ran "for [their] lives, or what was dearer still—liberty."[9] Their training camp sergeant-majors would have been pleased to note that as they threw themselves to the ground, they remembered to turn so that they could see if they were being followed.

At dawn, the escapers neared a town that was not on their map. Concerned about being so close to a town during the day, they flipped a coin to decide which way to go. After swimming a canal, they saw a signpost whose lettering was too worn to read but looked to MacDonald like "Neda." A paper they found on the ground with the name of the Dutch town recalled as "Haakshergen" was not considered conclusive. Neither was a half-remembered *Daily Mirror* picture showing Dutch soldiers wearing pillbox caps enough to override the escapers' reticence when they saw a mounted troop that was otherwise dressed as German soldiers. This caused the escapers to step into the shadows. At about 9 a.m., they saw a fat man spreading gravel on the road. Knowing that even in their exhausted state they could still outrun him, they stepped out from some bushes and asked the startled man if they were in Germany or Holland. A moment later, a "broad smile slowly spread over his good natured face."[10]

Mid-August 1917: Canada

Privates Harold Henderson and Ralph Dusenbury made their escape from Münster POW camp sound almost like a weekend camping trip in Ontario's Prince Edward County, where Henderson had grown up. The hardest part of the escape, they said, was resisting eating all the food in their Red Cross parcels so they could accumulate an escape cache. For the escapers to say, "Hiding the stuff about the camp when we went on work parties" made secreting contraband, such as unopened cans of bully beef—an act that merited *Strafe* in darkened cells without bunks—sound like a lark played by schoolboys.[11]

Henderson's assertion that they had "met nobody that asked them any questions" could have been true; like other escapers, they travelled at night. And while they could have "slipped off, with no alarm," once their crew was back in camp and had been counted, the alarm would have gone up, and they would have been close enough to the camp to feel the kind of fright other escapers did. Foraging, too, sounded easy: "Once we found a friendly chicken who went the rest of the journey inside us." By ending the story of their escape with the words "It was good fun, the weather being fine," Henderson provided Canadian readers with an upbeat *Boy's Own Annual*–like story of an escape that bore little resemblance to the travails escapers routinely faced. But, no doubt, it buoyed home-front morale.

15 August 1917: Hill 70, Near Lens, France

As the Germans on Hill 70 north of the city of Lens were being systematically blasted apart, Britain rejected Pope Benedict XV's latest peace proposal—restoration of all occupied territories and recognition of freedom of the seas—as having a "German flavour" (because of the lack of reparations). In what would become the "Canadian way of war," Canadian generals bet their men's lives on machine gun bullets, poisoned gas and the explosive force of hundreds of thousands of shells—aimed directly at German fortifications, behind them and in creeping barrages. In this battle alone, gunners wearing their small-box respirators (to protect them against gas shells used in counterbattery fire) fired more than eight thousand gas shells. In an effort to lessen the tension felt by the men of the 23rd Battery, a box gramophone was rotated among the battery's six gun pits, prompting Driver Frank Hazelwood to write, "With 'Carry Me Back to Old Virginny' on the machine, I felt right at home."[12]

The attack, protected by a creeping barrage (one gun for every sixty feet of the front), was augmented by a new weapon: the Livens projector, essentially a large mortar capable of firing canisters of poison gas or flammable liquid more than 1,600 yards on a trajectory that landed them in German trenches. When firing flammable liquid, the Livens projector turned swaths of earth into infernos, immolating men and, equally importantly, interdicting the movement of reinforcements. Unlike the men seventy miles north struggling through the mud of Passchendaele, where, despite a month of triumphal headlines, the British had made precious little progress, men like Private Ernie Lambert of the 10th Battalion advanced over dry, though broken, ground.

Despite the heavy bombardment and gas, enough machine gunners and artilleryman survived that Lambert found himself advancing through a heavy barrage. A red-hot fragment from one shell bashed the button on his tunic, cutting the webbing of his equipment, while another splinter sliced deeply into his arm. At the dressing station he crawled to after a stretcher-bearer bandaged his arm, Lambert marvelled at another fragment of German steel that had cut into his left pocket and scraped along the top of his prayerbook, making him one of many who credited their survival to the *mysterium* of fate and an almost talismanic belief in the physical presence of the New Testament. Lambert's comrades had seized their objective a little under two hours after they had gone over the top.

The triumphal headline "Canadians Mow Down Prussians by Thousands" in the *Winnipeg Tribune* on 17 August overstates the case. The headlines and communiqués announcing the capture of Hill 70 were accurate, but as always, words like "Our troops have carried the German front lines of defense and are making satisfactory progress" obscure as much as they reveal.[13] The article's tone is the one mocked by a "Teech Bomas" article in the trench newspaper the *Wipers Times,* published two days earlier:

> All was still as the first flush of dawn lit the sky. Then suddenly the atmosphere was riven by the crescendo chorus which leapt to meet the light as a bridegroom to his bride. The delicate mauve and claret of the dawning day was displaced by the frothy and furious fandango of fire. The giant troloythic ichnyosarus crept forward from their lairs, and gamboled their way to the line.[14]

Blanched from the newspaper's account is the terror of rushing across broken ground thumping with the explosions of both your own and German artillery. Absent are the curses that German machine gunners had survived and the wonder—if that is the word for what was both a half-formed thought and an emotion—that somehow those hundreds of bullets scything through the air are missing you. Nowhere are there words about the tremors caused by both fear and adrenalin coursing through his veins when a soldier mounts a parapet and jumps into a German trench, not knowing if he will be through, and find heaps of German dead or men raising their arms. Undiscussed is the frantic spade work of reversing a parapet so that the expected German counterattack could be, as it was on the 17th, broken up. Also unmentioned is the terrible thirst suffered by men who breathed cordite-filled air.

A few inches down from the stories that told of the futile German assaults was a short article about Private Agie Nelson. The carpenter from the postage-stamp-sized town of Erinview, Manitoba, which boasted a one-room schoolhouse with eight glass windows, was the

882nd man to enlist. An original member of the same "Little Black Devils" (8th Battalion) that suffered four hundred casualties in the battle of Hill 70, Nelson was captured at Ypres and became the ninetieth Canadian to escape from Germany.

Like Henderson, Nelson escaped from a work detail outside Münster POW camp. With two British soldiers, he travelled the eighty miles to Holland. Many "times German women working in the fields passed so close [to where the escapers were hiding] we could hear their talk." Unlike Mervyn Simmons, Nelson and his comrades did not have a compass, nor does it appear they were trained in celestial navigation, because they "had to guess the direction" they were going in. Luck was with them, however, even on the night when a dog threatened to reveal their whereabouts, for one of them had a wooden stake.

26 August 1917: Freiburg, Germany

LIEUTENANT FRANK LAWSON SURVIVED those horrifying moments on 8 May when, after hearing the gas alarm, he reached into the haversack on his chest, pulled out his rubberized face mask and then pulled it over his head. He had also survived heavy bombardment when his 19th Battalion attacked trenches in the T 24 C sector—only to face four months of near starvation, lack of exercise and the monotony of prison life.

Now, however, the Torontonian fairly revelled in the weekly walk from camp to a local bathhouse, where he and other officers from the Freiburg POW camp cavorted almost like children. On the walk there he saw several denizens of Freiburg, who were more friendly than the people in Cologne, where Harvey Douglas had been in the hospital. Lawson was comforted by the beautiful treelined streets that dated back to when the "Free City's" (*Frei-Burg*) university was founded three decades before Columbus sailed from Spain. Part of the walk to the bathhouse followed the riverbank. After the path turned into a woods, it passed a seventy-five-foot waterfall Lawson glimpsed through the gaps of the trees, making the scene even more picturesque.

Lawson's diary is unique among writings by Canadian First World War POWs. Its closest equivalent is *The Prisoners of Mainz*, written by Alec Waugh (brother of novelist Evelyn). Like Waugh's, Lawson's mental equilibrium depended not just on reading but on understanding how reading *in extremis* differed from the normal practice. For Waugh, the "insidious germ" of despondency generated by life in a POW camp "perverted the author's meaning." Upon reaching the scene in *La Débâcle*, Émile Zola's novel about the Franco-Prussian War, when the French emperor, Louis Napoleon, is alone in his room surrounded by scrumptious and untouched food, Waugh's hunger spoiled the author's intended effect. "Here is this appalling ass . . . surrounded with meats, fish, entrées and omelettes and the fool does not eat them." Waugh added acidly, "If only they had given me a chance!"[15]

Lawson's experience was more positive. Books as different as *The Journals of Gordon* (Major General Charles Gordon, who had died at the siege of Khartoum in 1885) and *Sesame and Lilies* (a collection of essays on education and human behaviour by the Victorian art critic and aesthete John Ruskin) moved the Canadian. He was especially impressed by Ruskin's demonstration of how the "English language can be perfectly formed," which signals something more than Lawson's own taste for prolix prose. While not surprising given his education the Great Tradition of English letters, in the context of being in a German POW camp, Lawson's praise of the English tongue was a decidedly political, albeit secret, act.

Lawson was at one with Waugh on how reading opened a person's mind by, paradoxically, leading him "into the heart of the writer and feeling with him as he writes."[16] Ruskin's judgment against what he saw as decadent—the late Victorian architecture of department stores and railway stations—or nothing more than "mere money making undertakings" might seem a world away from the concerns of recovering from the shock of capture and coping with hunger pangs. Yet for Lawson, such notions are intimately linked to his and his comrades' present status. Though POWs, they were still men who had the desire for truth and beauty and, thus, in Ruskin's terms, would profit emotionally and soul-wise from "proper housing and pleasant surroundings." Indeed, just as Shakespeare's exaltation of England stands as a counterpoint to the Germans' view of the country as lacking *Kultur* (some Germans even claimed that despite writing in English, Shakespeare was a "German" author), Lawson's discussion of Ruskin's belief that it is a sacred duty to "properly clothe, house and feed the people" in his secret diary is a thin gloss on the German treatment of POWs.[17]

Mid-Summer 1917: A Punishment Camp on the Kiel Canal, Germany

Shovelling coal for the *Kaiserliche Marine* was not what Howland expected to be doing when he and the Fannigans had been transferred from the punishment camp to a camp near the Kiel Canal. The work left them covered with a black, oily sheen that was more smudged than removed by the rough German soap and water. The fine coal dust turned cuts and deep scratches into jagged tattoos. Yet shovelling coal was a better fate than what Howland had feared when he and the others were shipped north: execution on a remote Baltic island.[18]

The Fannigans knew that filling the holds of a German cruiser that would go to sea to challenge the Royal or American navies was far safer than being in the trenches. But, Howland averred, being a prisoner was a "constant pain." Unlike the men at the front, who after six days were rotated back to support trenches and then to the rear, there was "no let up . . . they live a merry-go-round of trouble and hunger." According to Howland, "if given a choice," the prisoners would choose active service.[19] The pain caused by knowing that their forced labour violated the Hague Treaty by aiding the German war effort was partially offset by the pleasure of stealing some food and of seeing the defaced posters of Field Marshall Paul von Hindenburg, who, together with General Erich Ludendorff, essentially governed Germany as military dictators.

18 September 1917: Holzminden, Germany

Karl Niemeyer, the *Kommandant* at Holzminden, had lived in Milwaukee for seventeen years before the war, but that had not left him with much fellow feeling for his North American prisoners. Indeed, the bullying *Kommandant* revelled in telling John Thorn that because of what he had learned escaping from the United States (where he had been when the war broke out), escaping from his camp was impossible. Niemeyer had even picked up a certain American swagger, wearing pearl-handled revolvers on each side of his belt, as General George S. Patton would in the next war.

Neither Niemeyer's harangue nor Thorn's recent four-month punishment stint at Fort Zorndorf dissuaded the Canadian, now reunited with Lieutenant Edward Bellew (whom Lawson had not seen since his escape as a widow) from planning another escape. Niemeyer's boasts notwithstanding, Thorn quickly spotted several weak points at the camp, including a promising lower panel of the heavy door that divided the POWs' section from the guards' sleeping quarters. It took Thorn and Royal Flying Corps officer Wilkin a couple of hours to remove the panel, only to discover wooden planks had been nailed to the other side of the door. The nails, however, were no match for the wire cutters another POW had stolen.

18 September 1917: Near Haltern, Germany

JACK EVANS CUT THE NEEDLE for the homemade compass from a Gillette razor blade that had been heated over a candle to take out its temper. He then held it near a magnet before again placing it over a flame to retemper it. Evans and another soldier named Nick had saved food from their parcels and stolen a rope from the mine. To cover the noise as he loosened the bars on the window, Evans hummed "It's a Long Way to Tipperary" loudly. Shortly before the day of their planned escape, fearing that he and Evans were being too closely watched, Nick bowed out and was replaced by Private William Masters, who had also been captured at Mount Sorrel.

Evans and Masters had little trouble getting through the camp's wire fences. After a few anxious moments on the main road to Haltern, they entered a swamp. Over the next two hours, as they waded up to their necks through cold, slimy water, at times floundering in the dark, they experienced something of what the British were then suffering in the bottomless ooze of Passchendaele. As dawn approached, the escapers took cover beside a river that blocked their way.

19 September 1917: Holzminden

After the evening *Appell*, Thorn expected to be tossed into a punishment cell. That morning, after Niemeyer had refused to give him a receipt for the francs a guard had confiscated, the Canadian told the *Kommandant* exactly what he thought of a soldier who "deliberately took money out of our pockets."[20] Later that day, a guard told the *kanadischer Schweinehund* that in the morning he was to go to Niemeyer's office to get a receipt for the money.

Thorn had no intention of keeping the appointment. Instead, that evening he and Major Gaskell, from the Indian Army, dressed in fair approximations of (increasingly motley) German uniforms, crawled through the hole in the door and walked unmolested through the German quarters. Niemeyer, whom they passed at the bottom of the stairs, didn't notice anything amiss when he saw two "guards," each carrying two water jugs: one of each man's jugs held his civilian clothes while the other contained a stash of food. As they walked through the gate, Thorn could not help thinking that this "was one of the easiest escapes [he] had yet made in Germany."[21]

As Polaris became fainter in the coming morning light, the escapers took refuge in a forest, where they found a stream that allowed them to fill their water bottles and boil up a "delicious drink of beef tea" in their Tommy cooker.[22] Though the edges of the wood were posted with signs forbidding entry, they flipped a coin to see who would stand sentry for two hours while the other slept. Thorn lost.

21 September 1917: Weser River, Germany

Thorn was not the only Canadian who crossed the Weser River on the night of 19 September. Evans and Masters did so as well, aboard an unguarded scow.

The following night, as they passed a small hotel near the village of Kleinereichen, a policeman eyed them but did nothing. When the POWs stole into a potato patch, the farmers guarding it fired a few shots at what they probably thought were hungry Germans stealing potatoes in the dark of night. Twice over the next two days, the escapers heard the crack of bullets. Those that "skip[ped] through the brush," they assumed were fired by hunters. Since the shots they heard around 1:30 a.m., while they were resting by the side of a road, were followed by the barks of dogs and the sweep of a flashlight beam, the escapers assumed the bullets were meant to flush them out. Cloaked by the darkness, they managed to outrun a dog even as a bullet zipped uncomfortably close to Evans's head.

The escapers' relief at finding good cover for a day gave way that night to the realization, when they crossed a railway that was not on the map, that they were lost. Since they could see the North Star, they knew they were heading west. They saw a couple of full milk bottles sitting by a farmhouse. Since there was decent cover nearby, the hungry escapers risked the ire of the farm dog to get them. The milk did more than remind them of home; it gave them new life.

Not long after, the terrain began to seem familiar, which accorded with Evans's plan to try the border in the same area he had before. They spent the daylight hours of the 21st hiding near Weseke, two miles from the Dutch border.

21 September 1917: Near Horn, Germany

The years of enforced idleness and his thirty-five years of age had started to weigh on Thorn, who found wading through streams, digging himself out of bogs, climbing steep hills, pushing through dense underbrush, scaling walls and running from dogs—all on little sleep and even less food—increasingly difficult. Keeping "in communication" with his escape partner was also a challenge in the dark of night. Had it not been for the glow from Gaskell's wristwatch, Thorn might have never found him after they became separated in a field near 3 a.m.

The forest they hid in on their third day on the run was much less accommodating than the one they had slept in a few days earlier. But they were so hungry that they relished the Oxo broth made from stagnant water.

On the fourth night on the run, they saw a sign saying "Horn—5 Kilometres," which confirmed that they were 50 miles from Holzminden. They survived two close calls that night. The first occurred around 2 a.m. when, despite using sticks to feel the ground in front of them, Thorn fell twenty feet into a pit and was lucky not to break any bones. A few hours later, while following a railway line, they suddenly found themselves in the centre of a town where the streets were rapidly filling with workers. Though sporting several days' worth of beard and significantly less clean than the famously tidy Germans, Thorn and Gaskell attracted little attention, perhaps because their homemade "civilian clothes" blended in with those worn by the crowd in a land where economic dislocation meant that many wore patched or hand-me-down clothing.

21 September 1917: The Dutch Border

Given their narrow escapes over the past few days, Evans and Masters did not find the presence of farm workers cutting grass on the next field too worrisome. They did, however, wait until 9 p.m. to crawl out of the ditch by the side of the road in which they had lain like logs for several hours.

Their nerves were "stretched some," Evans wrote with considerable understatement, when, lacking the stamina to swim or wade, they risked crawling across a bridge that spanned two creeks. A short while later, while again crawling, Evans motioned his comrades toward a plowed field. Even though moving through it would be more difficult and take longer, Evans could not continue on the road, for they were now in the "fearsome spot" where he had been recaptured on his previous escape attempt.[23]

They crawled like caterpillars toward the border, silently cursing each rock or stick that hurt their knobby knees, and passing several sentries. At one point, Evans figured that the sentry he was looking at was the last before "the Promised Land." When the sentry finished his beat and turned to walk away, none of the escapers was hampered by exhaustion as they "scooted over [the road] like a pair of scared rabbits."[24] Evans believed they were in Holland but was still fearful. He insisted they keep to the fields, where they could hide.

A short time later, Evans's heart sank. Off on the other side of the field was what looked like a white sheet stretched across the road. To his rifleman's eye, it looked like a screen set up on the frontier against which it would be easier for guards to see—and shoot—would-be escapers. Then the screen dissolved into two girls dressed in white along with a man. With their hearts in their mouths, the escapers waited. When the man came near, Evans asked if they were in Holland. He did not understand the man's answer. The Canadian then pointed to the ground and said, "Holland?" and the man quickly answered "*Ja! Ja!*"[25]

25 September 1917: Near Bielefeld, Germany

The night before, Thorn and Gaskell had passed through a village because they had gotten lost. Now, at 8 p.m. on the 25th, they had no choice but to walk through another village and risk being seen. Mercifully, the villagers ignored the unshaven, mud-covered "veritable scarecrows" carrying unusually heavy walking sticks.[26]

The sound of gunfire near midnight suggested to their overwrought minds that a local garrison had been organized to find them, and they ran toward the foothills in the distance. The tension ebbed only when they reached a lonely moor that, as Thorn's map indicated, they could skirt by keeping to the foothills. By daybreak, they faced a new danger, thirst, which they only partially slaked by sucking the dew off the leaves of bushes and drinking beef tea made with murky water.

Two nights later, as they neared the manufacturing town of Bielefeld, a moment of frisson gave way to laughter when, instead of being arrested by what they feared was a gendarme on a bicycle, they watched the man "peddling for dear life, dropping things as he went in his hurry" to get away from what he believed, Thorn guessed, were robbers.[27] A few hours later, they found themselves in orchard country. The apples and other fruits that soon filled their pockets were almost as welcome as a signpost that allowed

Thorn to determine they were 142 miles from Holzminden and only three days from the Dutch border. In celebration, they dipped into their supply of tobacco.

Late Summer 1917: Freiburg

Lawson was an officer. In the world of the POW camp, however, the niceties of rank and the Hague Treaty mattered less than the fact that, since their care parcels had not yet arrived, Lawson had only German rations to eat. To augment his earnings and avoid a starvation diet, Lawson stooped to doing orderly work.

Toward late summer, amid rumours of peace and stories of failed escapes, conditions at Freiburg improved. Parcels and mail arrived regularly. The prospect of parole walks, billiard games and baseball-like rounders comforted Lawson, as did his continued reading.[28]

Whether Lawson was interested in the life of the prophet Mohammad because of General Edmund Allenby's advance toward Jerusalem or because the biography was the only book available at the time, he again used reading to create a personal space untouched by the barbed wire surrounding him. "I knew practically nil about him," wrote Lawson. "[Mohammad] came from a proud, free people—the Arabs." What would Lawson's co-workers at Toronto's YMCA office have made of his characterization of Mohammad's ideas as logical and of his followers as "disciples," or of Lawson's contention that the "new religion Mahomet [as he indifferently spelled the Prophet's name] was promulgating had so much good in it"? When he wrote that the Koran "was and is a collection of some of the best of Christian writings, but in addition points on daily life were added so that the followers of Mohoumet found many of his life questions settled," Lawson all but shed his denominational background, for evangelical Protestants believe the Bible is "inerrant," meaning that it does not contain errors and cannot be added to.[29]

28 September: Twenty-Five Miles from the Dutch Border

AS THEY CRAWLED INTO the sparse clump of bushes at dawn on their eighth day on the run, Thorn and Gaskell were so exhausted that "the danger of being found did not worry [them] much."[30] The good sleep they had had and the stolen fruit that filled their stomachs had restored their spirits and readied them for what Thorn's map promised would be their last night in the Reich.

After walking twenty miles, Thorn talked of ordering "a thick steak, under-done, with French fried potatoes." Just as Gaskell got to the crowning glory of his meal, a whisky and soda, the escapers were startled by a guttural cry Thorn recorded as "*Halte! Hocher der Hands!*"[31] In their reverie, they had not noticed that they had walked up to a guarded level railway crossing.

Thorn thought of trying to snatch one of the men's rifles and "fight for [their] liberty," but common sense won out. The next morning, after being taken to a barber for a shave, Thorn was questioned by an officer who was impressed that the escapers had crossed so much of Germany. According to Thorn, he simply could not understand, however, their desire to "escape and return to our country and fight again, when we could be safe in Germany until the end of the war."[32]

Chapter Eleven

October–December 1917

2 October 1917: Near Stockum, Germany

Fred McMullen and Thomas Hart were now working for another farmer, Herr Speck, and not serving a *Strafe* sentence, even though McMullen had menaced Herr Becker with a pitchfork. The guard that Becker had complained to believed McMullen's claim that the farmer's alcohol-fuelled, foul temper had returned and that the POW had only been defending himself against Becker's whip.

When not eating hearty meals of vegetables at Speck's table or working his fields, the Canadians surreptitiously emptied sawdust from a shaft they had discovered beneath a forgotten trapdoor. This shaft connected to another that led to a room where the bars of the window were screwed in.

On the night of 2 October, they took off their boots so they could glide by two sleeping sentries and stepped softly so that the floorboards wouldn't creak. The slam of the trap door that Hart let drop may have sounded to McMullen "like the explosion of a sixty-pounder," but it did not wake the guards.[1] Soon, the Canadians had slipped through the barbed wire. As other escapers had discovered, daylight revealed that they had misjudged the size of the bush they had crawled under, heralding a day of heart-thumping close calls.

Near 3 a.m. the next day, they reached the River Lippe. Since Hart could not swim, they looked for a bridge. A few hours later, they employed their infantry skills, long unused but second nature nonetheless. They advanced to the bridge behind the lee of three large steamrollers parked before it, climbed onto the span and then dashed across the bridge under the noses of three watchmen. Around midnight, they reversed course when Hart recognized a number of landmarks and they discovered, to their horror, that the rail tracks they'd been following led toward Dülmen camp.

As dawn rose, they unexpectedly found themselves in the outskirts of a city. Since turning around would draw unwanted attention, "There was nothing to do but pike along." The road soon led to a well-lit trolley station. McMullen's mind alternated between dread of the forbidding *Strafe* cell at Friedrichsfeld and wonder that no one had understood the meaning of the stripes on their pants. The escapers shoved their way through the knot of people waiting for the trolley, only to find themselves uncomfortably close to a policeman. The sentry, who was marking a beat in front of a POW camp in the centre of the town, "*seemed* to eye us up and down," recalled McMullen.[2] But when he did nothing, McMullen realized that the shadows created by the harsh glow of the arc light illuminating the area made the escapers rather indistinct.

Before they could find a place to hide on the other side of the town, Hart noticed that a boy was following them. To avoid arousing his suspicions, they kept going, resisting as much as possible the urge to turn around. Shortly after the boy turned into a side alley, they began looking for cover and found a shallow ditch just behind an embankment that shielded them from the road, but not from the heavy rain that soon fell.

After a day holding on to the bottom of the ditch so that they wouldn't be carried downstream into the open, they "were in splendid shape . . . *Aber nicht*" (but not).[3] These words conveyed to those who had lived through the trenches not only the discomfort of their sopping uniforms and muddy hair but also the understanding that, immersed for hours in cold water, they had been forced to urinate on themselves. After they climbed out of the ditch, with each step they could feel filthy water oozing in their boots.

The two men saw some people on the veranda of what appeared to be a hotel, but they inexplicably did nothing when they saw two mud-covered men trudging along the road in the middle of a dark, heavily clouded night. McMullen was still fearful, however, and decided not to light a match to check their compass and map. When they felt safe enough to do so, they discovered that they had walked twelve miles deeper into Germany. But the picturesque town, recalled as Hayden, with its old-fashioned gabled houses, the wagons lined up in front of barns and the lowing of cattle lifted their spirits. Later, they were surprised by the peal of the bell of a village church in the middle of the night. McMullen, who had grown up near St. Andrew's Church in Toronto, found the four chimes "beautiful."

It is a measure of their humanity that a day after eating the last of their biscuits and bully beef, and after eighteen months being fed putrid rations, when they saw an old woman carrying an armful of wood, McMullen said to Hart, "I suppose her sons are all off to the war and she has to chop up that wood herself."[4]

Early October 1917: Osnabrück POW Camp, Germany

JOHN THORN WAS SURPRISED both by the German guards' contemptuous view of the British and Canadian armies, and by the military prison forty miles from Osnabrück, where he and Major Gaskell had been sent after being captured near the railway crossing.

After three years of war, the German guards still believed that the British (and by extension the Canadians) were unwilling to fight. Confused about the pre-war professional British army and ignorant of the New Armies that numbered in the millions (Canada alone had raised more than 600,000 men), one guard told Thorn that "a nation that has not drilled for years could not be made soldiers." He went on to say that the British (and presumably, the Canadians) were not "animated by the same martial spirit as the Germans," which the bloodletting on the Somme should have put paid to.[5]

Despite the fact that more than two months earlier the British and the Germans had agreed to annul punishment sentences and send all POWs to regular prison camps, Osnabrück camp held nine thousand POWs in canvas-roofed huts. At the other camps, *Appell* was at 6 a.m.; here it was at 4:30 a.m. Any man found in bed after 4:15 a.m. was beaten. After cleaning their huts, POWs—officers included—were forced to work either as batmen for the sentries, in mines or on farms. Breakfast consisted of burnt-acorn coffee and bread that "possessed the characteristics of ancient cheese."[6] To avoid working in the dangerous salt mines, some men ran rusty nails into their feet or cut their own arteries.

6 October 1917: Near the Dutch Border

SHORTLY AFTER WONDERING ABOUT the old woman's sons, McMullen realized that while the little patch of scrub trees he and Hart had taken shelter in might hide them from the children playing nearby, it was too thin to hide them from adults. Accordingly, during a few moments when the children were playing elsewhere, McMullen and Hart did what no escaper wanted to do in the light of day. They ran fifty yards across frequently used paths to a thicker copse, which hid them but did nothing to protect them from the pouring rain that afternoon.

Later, McMullen would note that the "regular hurricane" had the virtue of turning the night of 6 October into "the very best kind of night for us to travel." Even though there were hours of dark left, near midnight, the soaking, dispirited men snuck into a shed, where they found a few small potatoes and two piles of straw. The escapers were quickly disabused of the idea that the straw they burrowed into would keep them warm. The cold and damp registered with McMullen's wounded arm. A smoke would lessen the pain, he told Hart, prompting the admonition, "For God's sake, don't. You'll set the place on fire or someone will be sure to see the light."[7] McMullen complied with Hart's wishes until the pain mounted. Then, with his coat over his head, he lit a match and then his pipe. The relief was almost instantaneous.

In the morning, a farmer led a Russian POW into the shed and showed him how to make sheaves from the straw. As the Russian started to climb the pile of straw in which they were hiding, the escapers readied themselves to throttle him, not thinking that doing so would immediately reveal them to the German farmer. Midway up the pile, "for some reason we could never understand, he turned back and climbed up into the other mow."[8]

A day later, shots in the distance "sounded like old time[s], just like coming up into the communication trenches," the very sort of thing their comrades in the 4th Canadian Mounted Rifles would be doing two weeks later as they entered the trenches at Passchendaele.[9] The barking police dogs were another matter. They prompted McMullen and Hart to run as fast as they could across a field. A ditch that led behind a patch of trees prevented the escapers from being seen by two soldiers whose bicycles were equipped with strong searchlights.

Five miles of fields and bush stood between the escapers and Holland. Moments after McMullen stepped out of a bush he heard something, and the POWs dropped silently to the ground. Mercifully, the two sentries were looking in the other direction as they passed the men lying on open ground, scarcely breathing.

"Surely we ought to be out now. Let's take another chance," McMullen said to Hart after they had been following a small river for some time. Not long after, the scene shifted as they began seeing signposts that were red, white and blue, instead of red, white and black. The houses were in better shape, the "trees were pruned and there were occasional hedges." McMullen felt so confident that he took out his pipe and began to light up, but he stopped abruptly when he saw change in the ambient light. Hart, who was walking a few steps ahead, had apparently not noticed the light. The glow of an arc light came into view around the bend, lighting up "a guardhouse with a couple of sentries on a beat across a spot where the road was fenced off." McMullen grabbed Hart and yanked him back into the shadows.[10]

Prudence dictated that they hide in the gully that seemed to lead toward Holland and try again the following day. But after days of eating only a few uncooked potatoes and drinking only a little water, and being soaked and chilled, they were so exhausted that they did not see how they could last another day. Accordingly, they crawled down the gully, being careful not to slosh their way through the six inches of water at its bottom, for three-quarters of a mile, after which they dared to climb out and begin to walk. Soon they saw a letterbox that "bore a lion instead of an eagle," which, McMullen noted, was "always placed on the German boxes."[11]

15 October 1917: Freiburg

FRANK LAWSON'S EXPERIENCE WITH the YMCA put him in a better position than most to consider a question religious soldiers asked, "Why has God allowed the slaughter to continue?" Volunteer soldiers who had served in the trenches were less likely to be moved by sermons about fiery furnaces and glory than editorial writers and ministers like Rev. Dr. Thomas Eakin. In February 1917, the pastor of St. Andrew's Presbyterian Church in Toronto made a rather significant change to the Beatitudes. In place of "Blessed are the peacemakers," he intoned, "Blessed are ye armed, booted, equipped for slaughter."[12]

Soldiers appreciated padres like Canon Scott, who braved the same dangers, ate the same cold food and knew the slipperiness and weight of the same mud as the soldiers. But as Sergeant Ralf Sheldon-Williams, who at forty was one of the older men to take the King's shilling, wrote, the conditions they lived in and "the possibility of death at any moment . . . bred in us a kind of medieval paganism which substituted picturesque symbols or legends, partly of our own creating" for what was learned at church. The belief that a shell hole was probably safe owed something to the adage that lightning never strikes the same place twice, something to the physics of gunfire (each time a gun fires, its barrel becomes worn, and each shell travels through a different set of turbulents, which together alter the flight of the shell) and something to what Sheldon-Williams called "a sneaking regard for the miraculous."[13] The belief that you were safe from any shell or bullet that did not have your number on it was shared by all and was linked to the more orthodox notion that God will call you home in his time, not yours.

Lawson's minister back home would have been less than pleased when the soldier wrote in his diary that he "venture[d] to think that no woman character in the Bible can surpass Joan of Arc from any standpoint," for she was a Catholic saint. A German censor, however, would have been more interested in Lawson's praise of Joan of Arc for saving France's "patriotism [when it] was at its lowest ebb," and his opinion that England "had possession of the whole land" because of the obvious parallels to the German occupation of much of France and Belgium. Lawson crediting Joan of Arc's actions to the "'voices' that told that she was to be the means of saving France" was as theologically far from Evangelical thought as it was a muted clarion call to resist the Germans. No censor could have missed the import of the entry's penultimate sentence: "She resisted him [the Inquisitor] to the end and remained true to her faith in God and the King."[14]

Some weeks afterwards, late on a bitterly cold early November night, Lawson lay awake, barely warmed by a thin blanket and a weak fire in a stove a few feet away. The sound of an aircraft engine in the distance failed to push aside his thoughts about the men who were to leave for Switzerland in the morning, but the bark of the anti-aircraft guns that soon filled the night did. Even as he hoped that the "machines," as they were then called, had got away, with a note of sadness Lawson could not help but "imagine the townspeople scrambling out of bed and running into the[ir] cellars."[15]

Late October 1917: Schende POW Camp, Germany

Sergeant William Alldritt, who had been captured at Ypres, lay insensible on the ground of Schende POW camp after a vicious beating meted out for his escape in early October. When he came to, he was returned to the salt mines, where he worked until December.

The conditions at the camp rivalled those in the trenches. The stench of the bucket that served as latrine, and the urinal—a cut in some bricks that drained onto the ground—formed a miasma in the hut crammed with six hundred men. "The smell of the wash house and latrine is unbearable in the building, and even if you stand at the far end of the building the smell is perfectly disgusting." Even worse were the conditions in the mine, which regularly trembled with explosions, leaving piles of salt rocks with serrated edges that ripped open unprotected hands. Small punctures in the prisoners' skin caused by the jagged-edged salt led to boils; the camp doctor lanced some of these for his pleasure and a guard burst others with his club. These wounds often became infected. Alldritt recalled how he and eighteen British prisoners had suffered while working for the Reich that in the early years of the century had become one of the first countries in the world to mandate protection for miners. "Practically everyone suffered a great deal from boils—I was forced to work when I was covered with masses of them. I have worked when I couldn't lower either of my arms, and when I got working, matter would be running from the boils in both armpits."[16]

26 October–11 November 1917: Passchendaele, Belgium

At 2 a.m. on 6 November, a runner brought a message to Leutnant Jürgens of the 7th Company Fusiliers, Regiment 38, who were then holding positions a couple of hundred yards north of the ruins of the village of Passchendaele. The word was that a Canadian had been captured. The exact circumstances of his capture were unclear, but the only Canadian taken on 6 November was Private Matthew F. Percy of the 102nd Battalion. It was also unclear what condition Percy was in, but according to German records, their prisoner "said that the Canadians planned to conduct an attack on Passchendaele in the morning."[17]

Forewarned, Jürgens placed his depleted machine gun crews on his flanks. He needn't have bothered. As had happened on 26 October, on 30 October, and on 1 November, Canadian gunners loosed another devastating bombardment: "Splinters whined through the air and great clods of earth rained down."[18] The air was filled with smoke and shrapnel caused heavy casualties. As dawn broke, Jürgens saw the first wave of Canadians two hundred metres away. One of Jürgens's machine guns killed a number of Canadians, but the bombardment had broken Jürgens's right flank. A shell then wounded the German subaltern. Moments later, a wave of Canadians stormed through his trench and onto the road to Passchendaele, before being held up for a short while by fire from what Jürgens believed to be his regiment's 8th Company. As the Canadians consolidated, Jürgens awaited in hope for counterattack. To his acute disappointment, the only troops funnelled into this small swath of Belgium wore Canadian brassards. At mid-day, he was taken prisoner.

The Canadian who told of the coming attack was not doing something unexpected. Indeed, on the 26th, hours after the Canadians went over the top into the waterlogged moonscape in which men drowned in the dark waters of shell holes "for want of strength to pull themselves out," the *Globe* published a short article with information every Canadian soldier knew. If taken prisoner, they had been "warned about talking." General Currie's officers had told their men that even a stray word could "assist a wily enemy in ascertaining the disposition of the British forces." The admonition that men should be wary about talking with other POWs about their battle while in their barracks—because the Huns had established "listening posts" in them—both hints at the intelligence gathering going on in POW camps in Britain and at the reality that soldiers tell other soldiers their war stories.

By the time the four men belonging to the 46th Battalion who had been captured on the 26th reached POW camps, the Germans knew that Passchendaele had been lost in four "set piece" battles. Their own records told them of the effectiveness of the Canadian bombardments, of how the creeping barrage had seemed slower than at Vimy (to account for the difficulty of the mud, it moved forward fifty metres every four minutes) and of how the Canadians now advanced in small groups; several records speak admiringly of their abilities to infiltrate and move past strong points that were later mopped up. The Germans did not know it, but men such as Private William Sullivan, captured on the 26th, and Private Ernest R. Cobb, captured on the 30th, knew that part of the Canadian Corps' battle doctrine could be summated as "every Officer, NCO, and man was on his own," as one soldier put it.[19] Across the battlefield, "infantry sections diverted German machine-gun fire with rifle-grenades and Lewis guns, while small parties made their way around to the blind side of the enemy positions and threw bombs," notes historian Bill Rawling.[20]

Thanks to barracks gossip, some of the men captured with and after Cobb knew at least the outline of how Lieutenant Robert Shankland, a thirty-year old from Winnipeg, had earned a Victoria Cross. Late on the 26th, he and twenty survivors of his company had found themselves isolated in a stretch of trench just ahead of the Germans' second line, near Bellevue Spur. The German strategy to fall back from their forward trenches and then counterattack in force collided with the Canadian's "bite and hold" strategy. In order to convince the Germans that his command was larger than it was, Shankland ordered his men to fire at the German positions—just at the moment the Germans came over the top. Still, his depleted group could not hold its patch of Bellevue Spur for long.

The rather bloodless prose of Shankland's Victoria Cross citation—

> Having gained a position at Passchendaele on 26th October 1917, Lieutenant Shankland organised the remnants of his own platoon and other men from various companies to command the foreground where they inflicted heavy casualties on the retreating Germans. He later dissipated a

> counter-attack, allowing for the arrival of support troops. He then communicated to his HQ a detailed evaluation of the brigade frontage. On its completion, he rejoined his command, carrying on until relieved. His courage and his example undoubtedly saved a critical situation.

—hardly captures the drama played out in those desperate minutes when the battle hung in the balance.

At the Somme, Shankland had earned a Distinguished Conduct Medal for helping stretcher-bearers evacuate the wounded under fire. Perhaps that experience helped him notice that the German shells were not falling on the left side of the spur, allowing a path by which he could, and did, run down the slight hill. From there, he made his way through the muck and the mire to the 43rd Battalion's headquarters, where he informed his commander that his men held part of the spur but couldn't do so for long without reinforcements. Accounts differ as to whether Shankland led the reserves up the hill or Captain Christopher Kelly did after Shankland had left to rejoin his men. Whatever the case, the Winnipeggers used their rifle grenades and Lewis guns to break up an attack on Shankland's flank and, afterwards, to suppress fire from pillboxes while other men circled round them so they could toss in grenades. Once this threat had been neutralized, Shankland led his men in a charge that cleared Bellevue Spur.

This charge was one of the few in this part of the battle that was fought on something other than boggy ground. Here at least, a man hit by a German bullet did not face imminent drowning—and, if he survived, almost certain deadly infection from gas gangrene or a staph infection.

The Canadian high command needn't have worried that privates Elvy Baker, William Wilson, Duncan Johnston and Alexander McVicar might reveal, say, the capabilities of the Livens projector or how long their box respirators could provide breathable air. These grievously wounded men captured at Passchendaele died on 30 October; 1, 2 and 4 November 1917, respectively.

Mid-November 1917: Münster

BY THE END OF the *Strafe* David O'Brien served in Cologne, he had been in the dark so long he was almost blind. For forty days in a damp, dark cell, the wound in his neck had been discharging, and he had nothing to clean it with. The suppurating wound was so bad that he was placed in the hospital as soon as he arrived at Münster.

The operation that saved his life was almost medieval. O'Brien's arms and legs were strapped to the operating table so tightly he could not move. Without anything to deaden the pain, O'Brien "just had to take it" as the doctor cut deep into his neck.[21]

O'Brien's racist statements about a French-African soldier who was in the hospital with him and who he called a "vicious looking chap" make for grim reading. O'Brien's claim that he had been told that "he had fourteen pairs of ears on a cord around his neck when he was captured" plays on stereotypes common in Germany and in Canada (as well as Britain and the United States) through such works as John Buchan's bestselling 1910 novel *Prester John*.[22] The Canadian premier of *Birth of a Nation*, D. W. Griffith's film that glorifies the Ku Klux Klan, had been a major social event in O'Brien's hometown of Ottawa in August 1915.

Late November 1917: Ströhen POW Camp, Germany

After a stint in the *Strafe* cells in Holzminden, Thorn was transferred to Ströhen POW camp. Until his parcels caught up with him, the officers in his hut shared food from their parcels. He contributed to the fund to buy wood—at ten times the price in town—to augment the little fuel the Germans gave them.

A week after arriving at Ströhen, the two men Thorn had teamed up with surmounted the camp's wire, using a ladder that the three had carried undetected on a foggy night. By the time it was Thorn's turn, a guard had already fired a warning shot, causing the prisoner to beat a hasty retreat. A week later, using wire cutters that had arrived from England hidden in a can containing bacon, he cut the wire in preparation for a breakout. He abandoned that plan the following morning in favour of another scheme.

This plan involved picking the lock to the laundry room, emptying the baskets, climbing into them and drawing them closed. The plan appeared to be working when the basket containing Thorn's escape partner was duly placed in the laundry truck. Because the basket containing the British major was missing a handle, the Germans lifted it and by chance placed it upside down in the truck. Though uncomfortably on his head, the British officer in the basket waited until the truck began moving before trying to change into a more comfortable position. When he did so, the basket fell from the truck, "the lid breaking open and a real live British officer being disclosed to the view of the sentry at the gate," who immediately raised the alarm. Hoping that he might still escape as the guards searched the other baskets, Thorn pulled down on the lid of his basket until it occurred to him that the Germans might resort to using their bayonets. Then he let go and "bobb[ed] up like a jack in the box."[23]

Early Winter 1917: Giessen

AFTER WEEKS OF WORKING out how to send a message home that would reveal the way he and other POWs were being treated, George Scott hit on the idea of sending letters from different barracks. One detailed how well he was being treated, while another expressed sympathy for a certain Drillio and disapproval of the way the government was treating conscripts.[24] "Drillio" was his middle name, so Scott knew his parents would pick up on the hidden message that he was being mistreated.

The first inkling that the plan had misfired came from a suborned guard. Later, when Scott was berated by a captain, he threw himself on the mercy of the court. The *Hauptmann,* who, by coincidence, had censored each of the three letters, smelled a rat. He demanded to know who "Drillio" was. Scott replied that he was a conscientious objector. He got partway into his speech about how poorly the government had treated Drillio before the German stopped him with words that surprised him. "But you can't tell me that. I've been in Canada. I lived in Montreal for ten years and they do not do such things there as you say they do."[25] (Scott's excuse, incidentally, indicates that at least some POWs had a working knowledge of the Conscription Crisis then gripping Canada.)

Scott's attempt to convince the captain that "Canada at War was very different to [*sic*] the Canada as he knew it, with conscription and rationing in force" got him nowhere, since the *Hauptmann* believed that Scott was writing about someone in Germany, not about "Drillio."[26] The censor decreed that until Scott could produce a letter from his cousin Drillio, he could not write back to Canada.

Early December 1917: Near Vimy

Unlike most of the other prisoners captured at Vimy, who were quickly sent to the POW camp at Wahn, Donald Sutherland was sent to a hospital in Lille, France, because of a serious injury. Perhaps because Lille was close to the German line, once Sutherland recovered from his wound, he was sent to an *Arbeitskommando* near Vimy. This violated the agreement between Britain and Germany, signed a month before Vimy, that POWs were not to be used close to the battlefield.

At the *Arbeitskommando*, Sutherland and a number of Australian POWs were forced to do labour that violated the Hague Treaty's prohibition on doing war work, including digging gun pits and carrying ammunition. The POWs were given only starvation rations and beaten when they did not work fast enough for their German masters. Worse still was the fact that they were forced to work under shellfire—from British guns. The chauffeur from Port Hope, Ontario, escaped this hell in early December when he was sent to a regular POW camp.

6 December 1917: Giessen

The SS Mont-Blanc, laden with tons of TNT, picric acid, high-octane airplane fuel and gun cotton, collided with the SS *Imo* on the morning of 6 December, 1917, in the Bedford Basin off Halifax, setting off the largest non-nuclear man-made explosion in history. What became known as the Halifax Explosion was reported in papers like *Frankfurter Zeitung* with a certain *schadenfreude*. The *Kölnische Zeitung* shed crocodile tears for the "hard-hit Canadian town" where some two thousand men, women and children had been killed or badly wounded, before asking, "Is it not better that these munitions should not have reached . . . the trenches, there to be used against our people in its hard struggle for freedom and independence—our people which did not seek the war, and also did not produce these munitions, which have now struck those who wanted to trouble us with them?"[27]

The story of the explosion, however, provided Scott with the cover he needed to gain back his postal privileges, the denial of which violated the Hague Treaty. Using another Canadian POW as the recipient, Scott forged a letter ostensibly from Canada in which the writer laments "Drillio's" horrible death in the explosion. With no way of checking names, the Germans accepted the story and restored Scott's postal privileges.

Winter 1917: Castrop POW Camp, Germany

THE GERMAN NEED FOR labour meant that even weakened POWs such as David O'Brien were sent to work in coal mines. Taking advantage of his job as a cleaner, O'Brien secreted away food for another escape. Unlike most POW camps, Castrop was not surrounded by barbed wire. Instead, the authorities trusted the prominence of the stripes on the uniforms of the POWs to prevent escapes. For their part, one night as they walked through the town, O'Brien and his partners trusted that standing in the large doorways of the houses and the gathering dusk of a Ruhr Valley night would hide the stripes from prying eyes.

Just before the men entered a rail yard, where they planned to hop a freight train, a civilian spotted them and they were captured. The civilian earned himself a hefty reward. The guards who soon arrived brought the escapers to an officer who wasted little time in demonstrating the power of his boots. In stereotypical Prussian fashion, the *Kommandant* slapped O'Brien across the face before handing down a sentence of thirty days in solitary confinement for the short escape.

Given the terrible food situation at the camp—guards augmented their own rations by stealing food parcels and entertained themselves by watching famished POWs scramble through the garbage for potato peelings—O'Brien was not surprised that his rations consisted of watery soup and all but indigestible *Brot* every third day. To his surprise, after a couple of days the door to his cell opened a little and a bottle of tea and a sandwich were pushed through. Another POW had paid for this food at the cost of a small piece of soap. A few weeks later, a bar of Castile soap bought O'Brien a gold crown for a tooth and something that would have shocked Major (Rev.) Charles Gordon. Not long before, when asked about the army's traditional rum ration, Gordon, an ardent supporter of prohibition, told the *Ottawa Journal* that "the boys don't like it."[28] O'Brien's soap also bought him a much-appreciated bottle of brandy.

Christmas 1917: Ströhen

The change that Thorn had noticed earlier in the month in the guards enforcing his *Strafe* sentence (for trying to escape) did not affect the camp's *Kommandant*. In early December, after more than a week of boasting on the part of the Germans about their country's military and technological prowess, all of a sudden "it was evident from the looks of the officers and soldiers that something had happened."[29] Likely, what Thorn had seen etched on their faces was the accumulated strain of the losses of at least 300,000 men at Passchendaele, including 24,000 captured, as well as another 45,000 casualties at Cambrai (20 November–7 December).

Six days before Christmas, Thorn wrote the *Kommandant* asking if he could be allowed to join the Canadian officers for Christmas dinner. Though Thorn promised on his officer's honour not to try to escape, the *Kommandant* not only refused the request, but also ordered that Thorn survive on German food alone.

With visions of ham, Christmas pudding and tins of fruit dancing in his head, Thorn was not to be denied. The day after receiving the *Kommandant*'s refusal, Thorn wrote a letter to a POW named Baker, asking him to smuggle him an iron bar that he could use to loosen the bars to his cell. Thorn got the letter to Baker via another POW, acting as an orderly, who came to sweep out the cell. The orderly knew to pick up the letter from under Thorn's bed because Thorn began singing a popular tune with somewhat altered words: "Under the bed you will find a note, take it in to Baker, take it in to Baker, take it in to Baker . . ." The orderly soon joined in, "I have found the note, sir, I have found the note, sir," as the uncomprehending sentry looked on.[30]

Thorn's plan for him and other prisoners to attend the Christmas dinner involved loosening the bars on their cells' windows and making dummies for their beds. The torso for the fake "Thorn" was made up of an old sweater stuffed with straw; rolled blankets became legs and his head was a bump under another blanket. The plan also relied on the guards drinking more than their ordinary amount of beer.

Thorn and the two other men who were sprung for Christmas dinner were shocked that their comrades had decorated the walls of their barracks with coloured paper. The branches they had collected on a parole walk added to the festive mood. The "glorious feed" of tinned chicken, bully beef, canned potatoes and canned corn was washed down with the contents of bottles bearing the label "Canadian Malt Vinegar"; in reality, Canadian rye whisky.

Harry Howland's Christmas was also devoid of religious activity. The guards provided some mirth, however, when they brought in a tub filled with sawdust and told each prisoner to reach into the tub and pull out a present. Howland pulled out a "china ornament in the shape of two pigs supporting a matchbox on a tray." Letters around the bottom said "Two little Englanders." With the funereal, monument-like ornament in his hand, Howland said, "Who said Fritz has no sense of humor? This proves he really thinks we are swine."[31]

At Freiburg, Christmas was observed by a few officers putting on their cleanest uniforms, by a boxing match and by skating. Lawson ended his entry for Christmas by speculating in his diary whether the friends and families of the POWs back in Canada had any idea how hard it was for the POWs to write home, since they could say so little.

Late December 1917: Ströhen

Thorn and the other men who had broken out of their cells for Christmas dinner were relieved. For days, they had been expecting to be hit with an even tougher *Strafe* sentence.

The Germans had not realized that the men had escaped from

their cells, but found out the ruse on their return. Thorn made a ruckus when his addled comrades pushed him through the window with such force that he fell, landing on his head, and knocked things down. As he heard the guards rushing toward his cell, Thorn had enough time to hide the dummy and be ready to demand an immediate trip to the lavatory. Just as Thorn was returning to his cell, the wooden fence Baker had to stand on to help Blake back into his cell collapsed. Baker and Blake somehow managed to get into their cells. As the guards with bayonets at the ready ran outside, Gardner tried to climb through the window; they found him with his head and shoulders inside but his legs dangling out the (debarred) window.

The irate *Kommandant*, who had been called away from his Christmas dinner, ignored Thorn's polite welcome and called him a number of choice names. However, seeing that his prisoner was in bed and not halfway through the window as Gardner had been, the *Kommandant* did not think that Thorn had gone to Christmas dinner on "French leave." That is, until the morning, when the *Unteroffizier* saw the men's paths in the light snow, which prompted him to rush into Thorn's cell, yelling, "*Mein Gott, Hauptmann Thorn, wieder!*" (My God, Captain Thorn, again!) at the Canadian's gall.[32]

According to the camp's grapevine, Thorn and the others had escaped punishment when threatened with *Strafe* because the *Kommandant* "was afraid that if he reported the affair to [a] higher authority, he would get into trouble himself for not having had a better guard on us."[33]

Chapter Twelve

January–June 1918

Early January 1918: Canada

On 5 January 1918, while people across Europe and Britain's Allies considered the full meaning of Lloyd George's rejection of the latest German peace plan, which included a demand for democratizing Germany, the Prisoners of War Committee in London, the Patriotic Workers of Port Coquitlam (PWPC), the Crofton House School in Vancouver and the Kamloops Red Cross had other concerns. Since their "adopted prisoners," privates William Bailey and Roy Stamps, and Captain Frank Smith, were now in Switzerland and no longer needed their patronage, the organizations sought to help other prisoners of war. The PWPC had already received a thank-you letter from Bailey, who told of how "what the Germans call soup is nothing but water, often dirty" and that he had brought out of Germany a sample of a day's bread ration "to show what way they fed their prisoners."[1]

On the 14th, the *Globe* reported a speech by Dr. Henry Van Dyke, the former American ambassador to Holland, who had facilitated many prisoner exchanges. The prisoners held in England who had been returned to Germany appeared "well cared for and well fed." By contrast, he told a packed meeting in New York's Carnegie Hall, among the prisoners coming from Germany there were many "with tuberculosis, or otherwise crippled by the hardships they had endured." Some had been driven "insane" by "indescribably, inexcusably, vindictively bad" conditions. Given what Van Dyke had said, the news that another group of Canadians was about to be exchanged could only cause their fellow countrymen to worry about what the POWs' condition would be when they passed into freedom.

29 January 1918: Freiburg

THE SNOW THAT CARPETED the POW camps in late January reminded the Canadians of home. Red Cross–supplied skates allowed them to play shinny and relive dreams of Stanley Cup glory. As important as these diversions were for the POWs, though he mocked bookworms like himself, Frank Lawson continued to read avidly.

Toward the end of January, Lawson found himself in the midst of an eight-hundred-page book on the history of the Church of England, much of which was unknown to the Baptist. His observation that when compared to the deity, whose plans "go on & on & on," an individual's decisions do not count for much would not have alarmed his minister, the Archbishop of Canterbury or a German censor. Had he seen Lawson's writing, the censor would, however, have poured acid on the sentence "England has had its life ebb and flow and yet gone on to a newer and better existence."[2]

Lawson could have reasonably assumed that a censor would care little about what he wrote under the heading "English Humorists of the 18th Century," although Jonathan Swift's *Gulliver's Travels* was a much more political book than was normally recognized. Likewise, Joseph Addison's play about the last days of Marcus Cato has as its theme opposition to the tyranny of Julius Caesar and could easily be read allegorically in the Kaiser's Germany. Lawson didn't think it was worth trying to hide his praise for Lord Thomas Macaulay, whose five-volume *History of England* was a ringing endorsement of parliamentary government.

Late January 1918: Clausthal POW Camp, Germany

FOR THE FIRST FEW moments after the *Kommandant* entered the guard house, John Thorn thought he would soon be trudging his way back to the train station to be sent to still another camp, for before him stood Kommandant Niemeyer. Back at Holzminden, Niemeyer had warned Thorn that because of all the trouble he had caused, Niemeyer did not want to see him again in his camp. Since Niemeyer knew Thorn well, the Canadian was confused when the *Hauptmann* commanding the camp asked his name. Thorn soon learned this *Kommandant* was Karl Niemeyer's twin brother, Heinrich, who like Karl, spoke English with a Milwaukee accent.

This Niemeyer then watched his guards strip-search Thorn and find two gold sovereigns that he had managed to hide through two years of searches. At the end of another speech forbidding escape, Niemeyer mocked Thorn by saying that the only reason the Canadian had escaped was that he did not have comfortable quarters; accordingly, the *Kommandant* was giving him "luxurious quarters."[3]

Niemeyer quickly added that if Thorn tried to escape again, he would suffer the worst punishment the *Kommandant* could order. A few minutes later, Thorn and Blake found themselves in a small room in a pre-war health resort looking at two beds with real mattresses and clean sheets.

1 February 1918: Limburg POW Camp, Germany

MISS ALMA RUSSELL, British Columbia's provincial archivist, carried on a correspondence with at least ten POWs, including Harvey Douglas, and sent them parcels as often as she could. On 17 November 1917, Russell wrote a long letter to Lance Corporal Percy J. Tappin, who had been captured at Mount Sorrel, that arrived in Limburg POW camp on 31 January 1918. Although Tappin's answer was twice as long as the two pages stipulated by regulations, the censor did not return it to him.

Tappin's letter shows the limits of what POWs could say. Thanking Russell for both letters and parcels was permitted, as was writing about his wife and "two dear little children." The censor allowed Tappin to say that he knew Russell was no longer allowed to send parcels, and that he was writing "now to tell you how we or I pass the long dreary days away [from home]." Perhaps this last comment had slipped through as a reference to the early February weather as seen by a POW who was "working with a gardener," and not as a comment about the lack of activity the camp provided the POWs.[4]

As most letters written by POWs, Tappin's establishes its own temporal scheme. Memories of his wife and his children, whom he had not seen since he went overseas years earlier, crowded out the present. The ache he felt when he recalled "childrens [*sic*] loving little ways" might have been "more than words can tell," but paradoxically, it provided Tappin with a private place beyond the wire. The "long lane that has no turning" ended, he must have believed, with a return to such familial moments that he could not help but imagine without his children and wife having aged. The memory of the Red Cross–supplied Christmas pudding also altered the normal flow of time. The words returned Tappin to an evening a few weeks earlier redolent with memories of Christmas with his wife and children, of his own youth and the future outside a POW camp.

How much of this the censor caught is unknown. There is no doubt, however, that something on the first page caught his attention. For three lines between "I am not much good at writing letters" and "hope some day I shall have the pleasure of seeing & thanking you personally" were destroyed by acid paint.

Early March 1918: Clausthal

THORN HAD NOT SEEN Major D. Rykert McCuaig since before the gas attack at Ypres almost three years earlier, so it was with great pleasure that he caught up with McCuaig, who had been wounded and captured. For his part, McCuaig thrilled to Thorn's stories of carrying on the fight behind enemy lines.

Despite the barbed wire ringing the camp and Niemeyer's bluster, Clausthal kept something of the air of its pre-war status as a health resort. The barbed wire, for example, was strung sufficiently away from the building that officers could walk around and get exercise. In contrast to the men labouring in *Arbeitskommandos*, Thorn had access to a library. Niemeyer's sticky fingers meant that the camp's canteen sold items such as tins of sardines at a significant markup; when a guard heard the POWs gripe about paying five marks for a can of sardines, he told them that they were cheaper than in Berlin. Niemeyer allowed lectures, and several days each week some twenty-five officers were marched to a disused mine so they could shower.

Niemeyer's strategy of smothering his charges with the POW camp equivalent of cotton candy failed. While enjoying all the privileges they could, Thorn and Blake set up their room as the headquarters for the POWs' "Spring Offensive," preparing maps and making compass needles from Gillette razor blades and spindles from gramophone needles. So that escapers could use the compasses in the dark, pieces of luminescent material taken from watches were affixed to the points of the needles. A tamed guard provided the camera that allowed them to photograph maps.

The Spring Offensive was almost undone by Niemeyer's chance entry into Thorn's room while he was finishing a compass. The general search that followed turned up a few more compasses and several photographic plates. (Others had been hidden away.) Thorn assumed that Niemeyer did not bother with another *Strafe* because the paperwork required to order one wasn't worth it. Instead, the *Kommandant* contented himself with repeating his threat that if he found Thorn preparing to escape, he would be sent to a punishment camp. Two weeks later, two prisoners wearing what Thorn judged to be poor imitations of officers' uniforms simply walked out of the camp, carrying in a kit a map and a compass Thorn had made for them.

13 March 1918: Freiburg

AFTER TEN MONTHS living as a POW, Lawson found that time was speeding up. In part, this was because the rate of repatriations had increased. The latest soldier to leave Freiburg was Major Robert McKessock. When McKessock heard that he was going to Baden, Switzerland, Lawson noted that ten years seemed to melt away from the major who had been captured at Ypres.

Lawson passed many hours reading. He was especially taken with a biography of Sir John A. Macdonald that celebrated Confederation, the building of the Canadian Pacific Railway, education policies and his willingness to have the "best men in the cabinet." Lawson praised Macdonald as "an Imperialist bred in Canada," which would have been one way of characterizing Prime Minister Sir Robert Borden, who a few months later would attend the Imperial War Cabinet. After hearing from General Sir Arthur Currie about the conditions the Canadians had fought in at Passchendaele and about the general's less-than-charitable view of the British commanders, the Canadian prime minister shocked the British high command with his criticism; Borden had received some encouragement from Lloyd George to question Field Marshal General Douglas Haig's competence. Borden's support for the war, however, never wavered. Nor, as historian Tim Cook has noted, did Borden have any answers to the strategic problems on the Western Front.[5]

Late March 1918: Clausthal

THORN AND MCCUAIG WERE TORN. Over the past few weeks, they had bid goodbye to sick and wounded men being interned in Holland.

Both felt that if they were interned, they would lose the chance "of getting back to the firing line and be able to have a little revenge for the treatment they had received at the hands of the Germans."[6] Accordingly, they resolved that if they were included in a party to be exchanged, they would violate its parole-like terms and try to escape.

Their plan started with tranquilizing the guards on the train. Thorn had experience with ad hoc pharmacology. During his second stint at Fort Zorndorf, he had tried to extract opium from poppies. After soaking tobacco in the liquid that oozed from incisions made in the poppies, Thorn slid the tobacco back into the cigarette paper. He tested the augmented cigarette on an unlikable Russian officer. His passion for English cigarettes was so great that he apparently failed to notice that after a few puffs the cigarette's paper turned black as charcoal. Then, "all at once his face turned various colors, and he was so sick that we had to call in the German doctor," recalled Thorn, who destroyed the remaining part of the cigarette so that the Germans would not know what the POWs were up to.[7]

Thorn and McCuaig's plan was less sophisticated but more likely to succeed. With the aid of a number of men who suddenly reported insomnia to the camp doctor, Thorn acquired a stock of sleeping pills. On the day they left camp, Thorn dissolved the pills in some wine in his Thermos flask, but did not end up drugging the guards.

Thorn and his party left Clausthal toward the end of March. His observation that, but for "lick[ing] the boots of the German working man" the Kaiser had lost his hold on the people, indicates that they were in transit before the 22nd.[8] That day, news broke of the massive success the Germans had had in the first days of the Michael Offensive, Germany's attempt to split the Allied armies that had advanced to within fifty miles of Paris. Lawson heard about it in mid-April, after the arrival in Freiburg of several Canadians captured in the first days of the battle.* (By then, however, the offensive had stalled, and British and American armies were driving the Germans back.) These Canadians also brought word of the enfranchisement of women and overseas soldiers, and of the re-election of Sir Robert Borden's government the previous December, as well as the implementation of conscription.

Early Spring 1918: Recklinghausen

FOR THIRTY PFENNIG, the equivalent of six Canadian cents (81 cents) a day, David O'Brien was working at a factory turning out wheels. The civilian foremen did not care that the seventy-pound Canadian with a discharging wound could not keep up the pace, which they enforced with a billy club. When a German officer intervened, O'Brien was sent back to the POW camp at Senne.

O'Brien's passable French, German and Russian won him the job of the doctor's translator. His knowledge of French also meant that he understood when female Belgian and French internees cried out as German soldiers raped them. More than once, he heard the "beasts that were committing this outrage . . . [say] they were just showing what our people were doing to interned Germans in our countries . . . [and] prisoners faint with rage at having to witness such crime and being helpless to do anything about it."[9]

* Harry Howland also recorded hearing of the Michael Offensive, though not until several British POWs arrived at Vehnemoor in late July.

Early April 1918: Aachen, Germany

THE USUAL NOTICES saying "*Verboten*" seemed oddly out of place in a room with freshly painted walls and beds with sheets, blankets, and pyjamas neatly folded on the tables. And the officers and NCOs who dealt with Thorn and the other POWs didn't treat them as might have been expected in a POW camp within sight of the fortress from which Charlemagne and Frederick Barbarossa had ruled the first German Reich. Even more wondrous than the tablecloth covering the table on which the prisoners ate their first breakfast in Aachen were the pieces of sausage that accompanied the fresh white bread and, for the first time in years, the coffee made from the *Coffea arabica* plant.

After a week of sharing their experiences with other POWs who had been in a number of camps, Thorn and McCuaig got down to the business of escaping. On the appointed day, they slipped unseen into a bathroom and then hid behind a curtain. As night fell, just as they readied to climb out the bathroom window, a guard came into the bathroom and lit several gas stoves to heat water but did not see the POWs.

After the guard left the bathroom, the two Canadians quickly turned off the lights. But several Germans came in just as they were about to exit the room. With the spectre of being sent back to a punishment camp for breaking the rules against escaping before them, Thorn and McCuaig explained their unexpected presence by saying that they, too, needed to bathe. The Germans bought their story but sent the men back to their room unwashed. Their failure to escape and, more importantly, their brush with another *Strafe* sentence tipped the balance for both men. Despite their soldierly pride, they could not face the risk of being sent back into a POW camp. A few days later, they joined a party heading for Holland.

Mid-Spring 1918: Sieburg Brick Factory, Germany

THE GUARDS BEAT DAVID O'BRIEN for refusing to load more than fifteen bricks in his wheelbarrows. One day, an officer went further, ordering the recalcitrant POWs to stand while facing the red-hot brick oven as he walked behind them whipping their buttocks with a rubber hose so hard that the men soon felt blood trickling down their legs. Repeatedly, he ordered the lot of them to work faster before switching tactics and yelling at each man individually.

When the German demanded of a POW named Morgan if he would work, Morgan refused. As Morgan moved to protect himself from a blow, the "officer stepped back, drew his revolver and shot Morgan through the head."[10] Seeing Morgan's body slump forward, a woman in the factory fainted, and another guard ordered O'Brien and the other POWs to move to a different area, where they were locked up. O'Brien assumed that Morgan's death would be reported as an accident.

During the two days they were locked up, O'Brien and the other POWs kept their council for fear of German plants "who had been in our countries and knew our habits and languages."[11] When they were returned to the brick factory, the orders were to move twenty, not forty, bricks. Because of his weakened state, O'Brien could manage only twelve. A couple of days later, the few potatoes they had been given each day and even the weak soup vanished, leaving them with inedible tainted canned sauerkraut and a small piece of *Brot*.

O'Brien and the others again refused to work, due to these scant rations. The senior officer called in guards to beat the famished prisoners. Private Wallace G. Winslow, who had been captured at Mount Sorrel, had his nose and arm broken, while four other men were beaten unconscious. O'Brien got off relatively lightly, suffering only a blow with an iron rod to his chin. It was administered by a civilian who had joined in beating the rebellious prisoners, who were then locked up for two days without food, water or medical care.

14 May 1918: Ottawa

The cheers and chorus of "For He's a Jolly Good Fellow" that filled the House of Commons were for one of their own. The four words "I am released: writing" in a cable to the Speaker of the House announced that Dr. Henri Béland had been freed after almost four years of captivity.

Four weeks earlier, Béland had been summoned to the *Kommandant*'s office and told he would be freed the following week. Having been burnt before, he asked, "Is this certain?" The *Kommandant* took proper Prussian umbrage, "Do you doubt my word?" Béland replied, "Well, I recall the fact that two years ago you communicated to me . . . news identical to this announcement . . . Nevertheless, I am still your boarder." Somewhat bemused, the *Kommandant* said, "Well, on this occasion you may rely upon what I tell you."[12] Béland later found out that he was being exchanged for a specific German prisoner.

The *Kommandant* told him that any papers he wanted to take with him had first to be submitted to a censor in Berlin. Two days later, Leutnant Block told Béland that Berlin would allow him to pass through Belgium on his way to Holland "in order that you may have the opportunity and pleasure of visiting your children in Antwerp." Three days later, Block told Béland that he had been chosen to accompany him to Brussels and then to the Dutch border. One week passed into a second and Block brought the doleful news that while Béland was still to be released, he would not be allowed to go to see his children. Béland, who thought in terms of a parliamentary government, the trappings of which Germany still had, asked, "Then what authority is it that is so highly situated it can override a decision taken by the Government?" Block replied simply, "It is the military authority!"[13]

A few days later, at the temporary station near the Dutch border, an officious inspector tried to seize Béland's *Tagebuch*. When the Canadian protested that the diary was empty, the inspector replied that his orders were to prevent all "printed matter" from leaving the Reich. Béland replied that he might as well confiscate his shirts, collars and cuffs. Concerned that he had missed something, the inspector asked "Why?" Béland's answer belies the national stereotype of the courteous Canadian: "And, what is more serious, instead of the printing being in German, which you understand, the names printed on the shirts, collars and cuffs are those of English and American firms, which you might not understand."[14] The inspector got a certain revenge by seizing a number of photographs that had previously been approved by Berlin before allowing Béland to reboard the train that a little more than an hour later brought him to freedom in Holland.

Mid-June 1918: Hamburg, Germany

THOUGH NAVAL EXPERTS DOUBTED IT, the story told by Second-Lieutenant Herman Hadler, who had deserted from the German navy, was published in the *Winnipeg Tribune* on 15 June 1918, on page eight. According to Hadler, between the Battle of Jutland in mid-1916 and the entry of the United States into the war, the Kaiser's navy had been preparing for "*Der Tag*," the day when the High Seas Fleet would again engage the Royal Navy, while 200 naval transports bearing 400,000 men with light equipment and machine guns dashed for the English coast. "It was reckoned that if even half of these transports reached their objective and successfully landed an army of 200,000," it would reach London in five days. The entry of the United States into the war required the Germans to plan for the High Seas Fleet to defeat first the RN and then the American navy. Hadler cautioned against complacency in naval intelligence by saying that for three years the high command had renamed ships a number of times, sometimes giving the same name to five different types of ships in order to confuse the Allies.

Hadler's rather fantastical tale would, however, have been believed by the one Canadian POW who at this point in the war was in the hands of the German navy, David O'Brien. Nothing he and the twelve POWs transported with him to a U-boat in Hamburg harbour had seen indicated that naval morale was cracking. The boat's commander warned them that if they caused any trouble he would make them wish they had never been born. It says something for the narrowness of the U-boat that these veterans of the trenches found the passageways claustrophobia inducing. Fear of being underwater was so great that they walked the passageways with greater care than they had walked the trench duckboards, so as not to touch the valves on the piping running through the passageways.

After surrendering their matches, personal effects and boots, the prisoners were taken to a bare compartment. Each was placed before fifty pounds of sand and ordered to "build it up like a pyramid and when this was done . . . rub it all flat again and repeat the same thing over and over." O'Brien's memory of how the sand rubbed his hands raw was still strong long after the war. Two days later, the captain told the men, who had not had anything to eat or drink since boarding the submarine, that if they were caught sleeping or resting and not building the sand up and rubbing it down, "the sub would go down deep and [they] would be drowned as the compartment . . . was used for water ballast when they submerged." [15]

Over the next four days, O'Brien and the others managed to steal a few hours of sleep. However, they were at the Germans' mercy for food and water, which amounted to a small dried fish, a biscuit and a small bowl of water each day; a few ratings snuck them cigarettes out of pity. While none of the ratings mistreated them physically, some delighted in the psychological torture of taking prisoners to the main deck (because U-boats were not true submarines and travelled most of the time on the surface), from where they showed the prisoners the minefields sewn to sink Allied ships.

The conditions in the prison camp at Libau, Latvia, where the prisoners were next taken, were the worst O'Brien had experienced. Here, far from civilian oversight, the army treated the prisoners, the majority of whom were Russian, as "*Untermenschen*," to use a term made notorious in the next war.[16] The Germans allowed O'Brien and the others to become, as the Russians were, infested with lice. Food consisted of a mash of mangles and potatoes, and a minuscule piece of *Brot*, which provided nowhere near the four thousand calories the POWs needed to perform the hard labour of carrying rail ties. O'Brien cringed when a woman who stabbed a guard who had been mistreating her was stripped to the waist and shot three times, while guards held her up to make a better target.

The punishment meted out to a British sailor caught stealing a piece of bread hearkened back to the Days of Sail: "he was tied to a post and lashed across the bare back with a piece of rope" until he bled profusely.[17] Mercifully, when O'Brien collapsed from a combination of exhaustion, the discharging wound in his neck, and what appeared to have been malaria, the Canadian found kindness. His bed may have been only straw on the floor, but the doctor gave him a pillow and three blankets. For several weeks, two or three times a day, he provided the delirious O'Brien with canned milk, water and lifesaving quinine.

Chapter Thirteen

July–November 1918

17 July 1918: Freiburg

In counterpoint to the world inside the wire, games represented a "reality" to the POWs where relationships were governed by strict rules. The rules of each game, whether cards, checkers or sports, were beyond the guards' power and reached back to the time before the prisoners' capture. Thus, games were not unlike religious services in the sense that they were among the few activities that the men could be sure unfolded for them as they did for their loved ones. Furthermore, phrases like "British fair play" and words like "sporting" rang in Frank Lawson and his comrades' ears without the irony heard today. The words invoked something of the famed "playing fields of Eton," where following the rules fulfilled an essential part of their culture's view of manliness.

Were a German censor to have known the debt English Puritans owed to Martin Luther, he likely would have smiled at the beginning of Lawson's diary entry after he read John Bunyan's *Pilgrim's Progress* (1678). Were he to have known, however, that Bunyan spent twelve years (1659–1671) in Bedford County Gaol for abjuring the Church of England and the restoration of the monarchy under Charles II, he might have had another view entirely, for reading *The Pilgrim's Progress* politically required no great interpretive skill.

Lawson would have had no trouble seeing Bunyan's telling of the Man in the Iron Cage as something more than the story of the sin of despair. Or to be more precise, as how even as the sin of despair cuts the soul off from the "goodness of God," in his context, despair would cut the POW off from participating fully in the hope for his deliverance. Just as it was Bunyan's avatar, a Christian's duty to live the life of the Christian man, it is the POW's duty to remain true to his faith as Bunyan did as a prisoner, in the righteousness of the Canadian soldier's cause, which many considered a crusade.

Mid-July 1918: Vehnemoor

HARRY HOWLAND FOUND HIMSELF both shocked at and frankly a little disappointed in the guards' deportment. After years of following the lead of martinet officers, the guards taking him to Vehnemoor were notable for their "slackness." Some could even be heard "telling the *Feldwebel* where to go." As they waited at the Oldenburg train station, a Fannigan cheekily asked a guard for a coffee, and he went to get him a cup. The over-aged guards, too, were different from those who had tormented Howland during his last stint at the camp. One sergeant, who had avoided being transferred into the army, was "easygoing and anything but a bully."[1]

The prisoners were still made to cut peat, haul boats and dig ditches, but there were no beatings. Under these changed circumstance, when hauling a canal boat loaded with bricks one day, Howland was struck by something he had never noticed in Wilhelm's Germany: the beauty of Lower Saxony.

For a few moments, Howland enjoyed the reverie of "peaceful scenes so far removed from war." Walking along the Thames where it flows through Oxfordshire, other men, he imagined, were "walk[ing] sweethearts along towpaths, [making] love or propos[ing] marriage at stiles like these." Even after all they had been through, as they came to a town's ancient cobbled streets and saw the rows of neat houses, Howland thought, "Will this war ever end? Others will pollute the air with remarks concerning everything connected with it."[2]

23 July 1918: Holzminden

THANKS TO CANADIAN CAPTAIN WILLIAM COLQUHOUN, the eighty-six men in faux civilian clothes or German uniforms, carrying identity cards lithely lifted from civilian workers in the camp, readied themselves to climb into a tunnel dug from *Kaserne* B. Since being captured near dawn on 28 February 1915 while making a reconnaissance after a trench raid at St. Eloi, Colquhoun had escaped a number of times but had been recaptured. At Holzminden, Colquhoun accepted the challenge contained in Kommandant Karl Niemeyer's boast that he "had never had an escape." Colquhoun's plan was to "drive a tunnel under the wire."[3]

The tunnel was well beyond the wire. The first man to break through the sod discovered that it was some yards short of the rye field that the men had hoped would cover their escape. As the Great Escapers in 1944, the men seeking to escape Holzminden decided to go ahead. The third man out of the tunnel was Lieutenant Andrew Clousten of the Royal Newfoundland Regiment. Twenty-nine men escaped, but Colquhoun was not one of them. After the thirtieth man became stuck in the exit, further escapes were called off. Ten men made it out of Germany.

30 July 1918: Toronto

After 676 days in the King's army, three and a half years as a POW, twenty-one days on the run and three weeks after the *Ottawa Journal* had reported that he had arrived in Canada, Private Arthur Corker was "Struck Off" the 7th Battalion's rolls. Responsibility for the newest veteran of the CEF now rested with the Board of Pension Commissioners.

Corker and his two partners had little trouble escaping from a workhouse: a picked lock, a silent walk to a window and a careful climb down a telephone pole close to the building put them on an unguarded street in Giessen sometime after 1 a.m. They travelled only at night, spending the warm summer days sleeping in ditches and copses. When they reached the Rhine, Corker felt much at home, for he had been at the same spot on two other escape attempts. The first time, he had stolen a boat and rowed across the river at the heart of much of Germany's mythology. The second time, he swam to the same boat, then moored in the river, and rowed across but was soon recaptured. On this, his seventh escape attempt, Corker again swam to the boat and, since it did not have oars, ripped out a seat to use as a paddle. Proving that there was honour among thieves, he "left a small amount of Germany money to cover the damages."[4]

While Corker and another man were sleeping on their fourth day on the run, the French POW with them decided to strike out on his own, but before doing so, he rifled through Corker's and the other man's packs and took their supply of biscuit. The hunger that Corker felt over the next seventeen days reduced the five-foot, nine-inch Canadian to 120 pounds.

Germany's manpower problems and some good luck explain why Corker and his escape partner did not encounter any guards. They could not, however, avoid two deep streams and the damage to their feet from wet socks and boots. Luckily, the day the blisters became too painful, they were able to hide in a large stand of trees that was open to the sun in the middle, so they could dry their socks and boots. Corker's war had started at Ypres, where men had survived by breathing through urine-soaked handkerchiefs. Later he had seen labourers hasten the healing of their blistered feet by urinating on them. Now, he and his partner urinated in their boots to help soften them and ease the pain on their blistered feet.[5]

On at least one of his earlier six escape attempts, Corker had been close enough to the border to see one of the effects of Germany's collapsing economy. Pushed by the food crisis gripping the Reich, people had the verge between the fences marking the German and the Dutch side planted with turnip plants that were high enough to hide the prisoners as they crawled unobserved into Holland.

Summer 1918: Frauenstein, Germany

GEORGE SCOTT SEEMED NOT to have known the irony embedded in the story he told about his time working in a vineyard in Frauenstein, Germany. The beauty of the country and the scenic hills running down to the Rhine contrasted not only with his life as a POW but also with the way his *Meister*, a certain "Delyghty," treated his wife.

One day, after finishing moving some logs, Delyghty was upset that their dinner was not ready. His wife noted that it was only 11:30 a.m.; dinner was usually eaten an hour later, and she had just put the potatoes on to boil. Delyghty flew into a rage that lasted well into the night, when Scott heard him tell his wife that she was "shiftless, crazy-headed and could not even get a hardworking man something to eat."[6] Scott pitied the woman he had found to be kind and intelligent, and who lived in the village of Frauenstein, named for the nearby ruin of a keep. The word translates as "Woman's stone."

Early October 1918: Amiens, France

THE AUTUMN RAINS and the early chill foretold another winter as a prisoner. So, too, did the schedule of classes Lawson could choose from: English, German, accounting, mathematics, religion, bookkeeping, shorthand, history and even Hindu.

Lawson's diary is silent on what the POWs knew about the Allies' advance over the past few weeks. From German papers he would have known the broad outlines of the battles the Canadians had liberated at Amiens (8–14 August), and the breakthrough of the defensive positions known collectively as the Hindenburg Line

(27 August–1 September) and then the Drocourt-Quéant Line in early September. A British tank corpsman captured on 8 August brought Lawson's camp first-hand knowledge of the attack that had smashed the German lines at Amiens.

The message "KEEP YOUR MOUTH SHUT," pasted in the back of soldiers' paybooks, testified to General Currie's concern with security before Amiens.[7] But it hardly mattered after the more than 130 Canadians captured at Amiens arrived in the POW camps. By then, the Germans had already analyzed the tactics that had caused their defeat and resulted in more than five thousand Germans being sent off to British POW camps. Central to the victory were the 430 tanks that had rumbled across the battlefield and over trenches, machine-gunning hundreds and crushing many, helping to clear the way for the four-mile advance. Also essential was the bombardment, which differed from the one at Passchendaele. Instead of days of bombarding the Germans, at 4:20 a.m. on 8 April, shortly before the men climbed out of their trenches, two thousand guns opened up, their collective flashes making a man in the middle of the line think, "You could read a newspaper whichever way you looked."[8] The fusillade devastated the shallow German defences, in some cases destroying entire companies before they could figure out that an attack was underway.

As the few German guns that survived the Canadians' counter-battery work replied, thousands of Canadians (supported by Australians on their left and British on their right) had crossed No Man's Land, protected by a creeping barrage that advanced four times faster than at Passchendaele. Battle doctrine now had men filtering around strong points and, if that were not possible, employing fire and movement in what would have seemed to men like Lawson, captured only a year earlier, like something out of a silent movie: "Half the men would rush forward with their Lewis guns firing from the hip, while the light machine gun of the other half of the platoon would provide covering fire along with their rifle grenades."[9]

Still, even with all these innovations, cork bridges that made spanning creeks easier, and pilots spotting for artillery and raking the ground with machine guns, trenches were taken by men. Private Stanley Carr's recollection of his 10th Battalion platoon crossing the battle field so quickly while the fog was lifting that "in no time at all we were right out in a nice pleasant countryside, the scene we'd always talked about and dreamed of" was different from what the 13th Battalion faced on the right side of the two-thousand-yard assault frontage. There, "heavy resistance was encountered from Croates Trench, where a large party of Huns held out, using Rifle Grenades and bomb [grenades] effectively. Our men were at a disadvantage, as they were but poorly equipped with grenades and bombs, but Lieutenant Greene of the Trench Mortars, hurrying up with his two guns, turned the tables and assisted in quickly reducing the garrison who put up white flags."[10] These men joined three others who surrendered to one Canadian; when he first saw them lying in a shell hole he thought they had been killed by a blast wave. This Canadian's concern with ensuring that they would not be harmed (the Canadian Corps had a reputation for not taking prisoners) was much more in keeping with the cross on his collar than the words "Glory be to God for this barrage!" yelled by Canon Scott when the sky glowed red moments after the morning's fusillade hit a German ammunition dump.[11]

Judging what the guards knew is difficult; though censored, the press could not hide major defeats for long, however much they were dressed up as strategic retreats or "straightening out the defensive line." More influential was the soldiers' grapevine. The details of the Canadians' innovative night attack at 3 a.m. on 26 August that had caught the Germans by surprise might be garbled. So, too, might the stories of how the Canadians had broken the Drocourt-Quéant Line, which did not live up to its billing "as one of the strongest fortifications constructed in any war," falling as it did in a few hours of intense combat.[12] The crossing of the Canal du Nord on 27 September would have also been known. Perhaps no guard (and few of the longer-term POWs) could have explained how, after unleashing a bombardment that a noted historian, borrowing a term from a more recent war, called "shock and awe," they then hitched their guns to limbers so that the artillery could follow the men who had "bounced the canal," a term the men used that utterly fails to capture the grit needed and blood spilled to cross it. Had they known of it, however, the Canadian POWs would have appreciated the despair felt by a German POW who was sent back to his command post with the message "'English' [Canadians] were over the Canal and all his comrades killed."[13] The guards could have no doubt, however, that the once-mighty German army had abandoned *Stellung* after *Stellung*.

Early Fall 1918: Minden POW Camp, Germany

The destroyer David O'Brien was on was delayed due to course changes made to avoid the Royal Navy, and it took three weeks for the desperately ill man to be delivered to Hamburg. O'Brien, who now weighed less than seventy pounds, was immediately placed in a naval hospital, where a two-week diet of fresh milk, rice pudding and vegetables made him strong enough to be sent back to a POW camp. From there, he was again sent to work at the shoe factory from which he had escaped.

The *Fräulein* O'Brien had sweet-talked into bringing him civilian clothes and food was still there, and she was once again receptive to his blandishments. This time, however, she was too frightened to bring him clothes. But she was willing to bring him extra food.

The conditions at Minden were significantly worse than those at Lawson's camp. Instead of classes and games of rugger and basketball, O'Brien had to settle for amusements devised by the Russians who were still prisoners, despite the Treaty of Brest-Litovsk, by which the new Soviet government of Vladimir Lenin took Russia out of the war. One entertainment involved placing lice "in the centre of a plate, then bet[ting] a piece of bread or something on which cootie would reach the rim first."[14]

12 October 1918: Freiburg

ON 12 OCTOBER, LAWSON was uncharacteristically forthright in his diary. He knew that Bulgaria had "thrown in the sponge" (30 September) and that politics "was already in a topsy turvy state," with the democrats clamouring for power. Lawson had got the date wrong—Hindenburg had told the Reichstag that Germany must seek a negotiated peace on 2 October, not 30 September—but that is a detail.

What Lawson called the Kaiser's Constitutional Act was the appointment of Prince Max Baden as chancellor of Germany and the announcement of a return to parliamentary government. Lawson would have known that the British were by then in possession of Lens and Cambrai.

8 November 1918: Freiburg

For Lawson the immediate impact of the change of government that brought Georg Friedrich Graf von Hertling to power on 1 November was the sudden ending of censorship of the newspapers. Like his mother in Toronto, Lawson could watch (in what for the era was "real time") the German government angling for the best terms it could from President Woodrow Wilson. On 6 November the *Toronto Globe* reported that German reparations was a non-negotiable demand. Two days later, the paper reported "The World Waits News of What Is Happening When Huns Meet Foch" (General Ferdinand Foch was Supreme Commander of the Allied Forces), along with news of mutinies in the German navy and "Soldiers council formed on lines of Russian Revolution." On the 9th, despite "Revolution in Germany," the Kaiser refused to abdicate, nor had his plenipotentiaries been able to sway Foch, for more lenient terms. There were no papers on Sunday, 10 November 1918, so Canadians did not read the terms of the Armistice until the day it took effect, 11 November.

Lawson did not discuss the terms of the Armistice, which were published in Germany. Amid the chaos that followed the Kaiser's abdication and self-exile to Holland, including running street battles in Berlin, Germans read that their armies were to withdraw behind the Rhine, they were to pay reparations, their navy was to surrender and they were to lose the lands they had gained in the Treaty of Brest-Litovsk. The violence in Berlin was mirrored across the country; a late bit of news to reach Lawson's ear being that Bavaria had declared itself a republic. Lawson did not know, though Canadians reading newspapers did, that the

Council of Workers and Peasants in Munich had reconstituted itself as a diet and declared the Democratic and Socialist Republic of Bavaria, one of a number of German kingdoms to become short-lived socialist republics.

14 November 1918: Near the Dutch Border

While he was less clear on the details, O'Brien knew that the German home front was cracking and that there were running street battles between German soldiers, who tended to be on the right of the political spectrum (many would soon join the *Freikorps*, forerunners of Hitler's SA and SS), and the left-leaning sailors. O'Brien paid a man who worked in the camp ten pieces of soap to spirit him away from the camp in a truckload of sawdust. A few minutes after they were underway, O'Brien pointed to a good place to drop him off, but the German said, "Stay where you are and keep quiet."[15]

To O'Brien's surprise, the driver stopped the cart in his own yard. There, O'Brien gave the man's wife two pieces of soap and RM 20. She gave him some hot food and a cap. O'Brien hid in the couple's shed until nightfall. Before leaving, they gave him a raincoat. O'Brien was worried that he might get caught up in a riot, but he passed through the town unchallenged.

The heavy cloud cover the following night prevented O'Brien from navigating by the stars, and he did not have a compass, which meant that he was often confused about which way he was heading. He spent precious hours walking "many useless miles," even as, unknown to him, the Canadian Corps were suffering their last casualties in the two minutes before the Armistice.

Through the darkness of a mid-November night, O'Brien was worried about the absence of German guards. Had he erred or was he near the Dutch border? Perhaps more confusing was the sight of hundreds of prisoners, their different uniforms telling him they were from a number of different armies. Thinking that perhaps the crowd was a working party, though unlike any he had seen before, O'Brien crawled forward. When he was close to a soldier in a Belgian uniform, he asked him in French if it was a working party.

"Don't you know?" asked the soldier. "Where have you been? Come on up and out of there and join the crowd. The war has been over three days and we are just waiting for a Dutch train to take us into Holland."[16]

Epilogue

Interned Prisoners of War are a species of animal usually found in a neutral country. The word "interned" comes from the Latin word meaning "fed" and ternus, meaning "up." They are used in the winter for moving large quantities of snow from one place to another, and in the summer for doing the same thing with rocks and gravel.

They are amusing creatures to watch. They live in large communities like the bees. These communities or establishments, as they are scientifically called, are presided over by what is known as a Chief of the Establishment, something similar to the "Queen Bee." Unlike the latter, the Chief of the Establishment does not lay the eggs which produce other Prisoners of War. These are hatched out of the mud of France and elsewhere, usually in a hollow in the ground called a shell hole.

—from Harvey Douglas's memoir *Sixteen Months as a Prisoner of War*

1916–1918: Holland and Switzerland

When they escaped into Holland in 1916, neither Mervyn Simmons and Edward Edwards, nor privates Gerry Burk and Herbert Tustin, knew the faux definition of an "internee" (p. 303) that described the word as coming from the Latin for "fed up." Nor did Frank MacDonald and Jack O'Brien, who crossed into Holland in mid-1917. They were ignorant of the circumstances that a year later would lead Captain Harvey Douglas, who was interned in Switzerland in December 1916, to copy into his diary the line about being "used in the winter for moving large quantities of snow from one place to another, and in the summer for doing the same thing with rocks and gravel." However, the escapers intuited that internment "was still a form of captivity," as one historian has put it.[1]

The POWs were grateful to the Dutch. Indeed, given the Netherlanders' kissing cousin relationship with Germany, they were surprised at the warmth of their welcome. Edwards recalled the moment when, after telling a Dutchman in whatever foreign words he could come up with that they were "English *soldats prisonniers*", the man threw his arms around each one of the escapers as he boomed out "*Engels!*"[2] After a luxurious breakfast that included fresh white bread, they were taken for a tour of the town, where one white-haired old lady insisted on kissing their cheeks. Burk and Tustin, who had escaped from Germany the same day as Edwards and Simmons, may have spent their first night in the police station in Enschede. But the officer who woke them the next morning apologized for his officiousness before asking the soldiers standing before him a predictably military question: "But the frontier! How did you pass our guards?"[3]

The official arranged for Burk and Tustin to bathe and eat breakfast, and had Tustin's infected fingers attended to. Because Enschede was a border town, where both Germans and some Dutch who sympathized with them lived, the escapers agreed to stay indoors. Already thinking of how they would tell their story once back home, they asked a guard to buy them picture postcards of the picturesque town.

By mid-1917, when Frank MacDonald and Jack O'Brien crossed the border, Holland was in the grip of a near-famine. As part of its blockade of Germany, the Royal Navy plugged what at the beginning of the war Helmuth von Moltke, chief of the German General Staff, called the Reich's trade "windpipe," and was letting only enough food through to Holland to keep the Dutch from starving. Food scarcity and high prices led to the *Aardappeloproer* (Potato Rebellion), during which MacDonald saw mounted police ride into rioting civilians at a market. And yet MacDonald and O'Brien were warmly welcomed and fed. So, too, were Jack Evans and William Masters when they reached Winterswijk in late 1917, where their first meal consisted of "two big slices of bread and a big hunk of headcheese."[4]

But these men, who had reached freedom by their own guile and under their own steam, refused the offer of internment. They were soon given clean civilian clothes and passports, which Evans noted made him and Masters (as well as three other Canadians who had escaped Auguste Victoria POW camp around the same time, including Private Frederick Boyd) "feel like honest citizens again."[5] But they ached to go back to Britain and hoped to continue their careers as fighting men.

For Simmons and Edwards as well as Burk and Tustin, return to Britain was relatively quick. Two days after entering Holland, these men were in Rotterdam awaiting a ship to take them to Blighty. Dressed in blue civilian suits provided by the American consul, they were lodged at the Sailor's Rest (a sailor's hostel). "We were shaved, clean and could eat everything in sight, at any time of the day or night. And did so," recalled Edwards.[6] When a boy selling cigars realized Burk and Tustin were English soldiers, he said, "English? Ach, then have a cigar."[7] The prohibitionists that had triumphed in most of Canada would have been pleased that that same evening, Burk and Tustin found themselves in the middle of a mission meeting, where they were urged to save themselves "from the ensnaring charms of wine and women." The prohibitionists would have been much less pleased that, after extricating themselves from this meeting, the soldiers went to a little inn, where they sat "over a large glass, quaffing the excellent lager-beer."[8] On the 16th, the four Canadians boarded the tramp steamer SS *Grenadier* for a harrowing trip to Newcastle.

On their first night in Holland after their escape in 1917, O'Brien and MacDonald were so conscious of their filthy state that they turned down the farmer's offer of a clean bed in favour of sleeping in his barn. Once in Rotterdam, they were brought to the British ambassador. He arranged for them to stay with a Mrs. Francis, but provided them an allowance of only one guilder or 35 Canadian cents ($5.90) a day, which was not enough to purchase food. Realizing their precarious financial situation, Mrs. Francis offered them money. When the embarrassed MacDonald pointed out they would not be able to pay her back, she responded with the words of someone well-practised in dealing with bureaucrats: "Never mind that. When you are leaving just go to Mr. —— (the Ambassador) and tell him you owe Mrs. Francis so much money; he will have to pay."[9]

The experience these escapers had immediately upon their return to England differed greatly from that of Arthur Gibbons, who, because of his wounds, had been repatriated from Switzerland in September 1915. The crowd that had gathered at the Tilbury Docks in London had intended to cheer Gibbons and the men with him. However, as in Eric Bogle's song "Waltzing Matilda," as soon as the crowd saw men in tattered uniforms, some armless, some blind, some lame, some so wounded they had to be carried in stretchers down the gangway, the mood changed. "Women sobbed aloud." The "men blew their noses with great vigour" (Gibbons's Victorian way of saying men also cried).[10] He met King George V while he was in London and then, while convalescing in Shorncliffe, survived a number of Zeppelin raids. Upon returning to Canada and undergoing a number of operations, the limping Gibbons became a draw on the recruiting circuit, taking credit for signing up some 1,200 men and selling $7 million ($138 million) of War Bonds.[11]

Edwards, by contrast, was even less pleased with the Canadian officials in London than Major Peter Anderson had been in October 1915. At least Anderson had been able to find a sympathetic clerk in the paymaster's office. Edwards, by contrast, faced a seemingly insurmountable obstacle. For the previous fifteen months his wife had been receiving her separation allowance, and the Red Cross had been sending Edwards parcels, yet according to the army's records, he had been killed in action. Edwards's letters from London evince a justifiable sense of frustration and despondency absent from the letters he wrote while a POW. It took three months and the intervention of Sir George Perley, the Canadian high commissioner to Britain, to establish that Edwards was, indeed, alive and deserving of his back pay, much of which he owed to members of the mess he had been eating at before he was returned to Canada.

Evans and Masters found the people of London welcoming. One man, on seeing how thin Evans was, handed him two crowns while saying, "Have a good feed on me. You need it."[12] London's papers also made a fuss over the fact that the two men were the fourth and fifth POWs to escape in a month. Because of the Halifax Explosion, the SS *Justicia* had landed in New York instead of Halifax. While waiting in an immigration shed on Manhattan's west side, Evans and Masters used their hard-won skills one last time and disappeared up several flights of stairs, at the top of which was an American soldier whom they easily got past. A short taxi ride took them to Broadway.

Later that day, while they were sitting in a restaurant wondering how they were going to pay the bill and find a place to sleep, a well-dressed man came up to them and asked, "Are you Canadian soldiers?"[13] Before they had got partway into their story, the man invited them to a party at Rector's, which turned out to be one of the city's best restaurants, where they were fêted. Late that night, their benefactor took the two very full men to a hotel and paid for their room. The next day, the still broke ex-POWs reported to British authorities, who bought them train tickets for Toronto. They spent their second night in North America in a Pullman car, rumbling toward the Whirlpool Rapids Bridge that links the United States and Canada within sight of Niagara Falls.

When MacDonald and O'Brien reached Britain, MacDonald felt that people were looking at them as though they were deserters. The pair arrived in London on 1 July 1917 and found that both the Canadian pay office and the Overseas Ministry were closed in celebration of Dominion Day. Since the holiday fell on a Sunday, the offices remained closed on Monday as well, which explains the delay in the two men receiving new kit and money. It also goes some distance toward explaining MacDonald's feeling of having been let down with their initial reception in "the Smoke," as London was known because of the combination of fog and soot from coal fires.

The following week was different. After being outfitted, the soldiers were interviewed by a number of intelligence officers. MacDonald was especially proud of being able to identify "the positions of several ammunition factories and military depots." To tell his comrades back in Germany that he and O'Brien had successfully reached England, MacDonald wrote a letter to Wallace Nicholson, who had also been captured at Mount Sorrell, telling them about a hunting trip "up north." In their interview with General Sir Richard Turner, who commanded Canadian soldiers in Britain, MacDonald and O'Brien said they wanted to rejoin their regiments so as to continue the fight against the Germans. Turner, however, ordered the two men home, just as Simmons and scores of other men had been.[14] Turner was concerned that if escaped POWs were captured after fighting again, they would be charged with mutiny and would face the death penalty.

* * *

INTERNEES IN HOLLAND AND SWITZERLAND came under a different legal regimen than escapers; they could be sent back to Britain (or Canada) only for medical reasons authorized by the Red Cross.

In early September 1916, when he crossed into Switzerland, Harvey Douglas joined more than 137 Canadians in the country. Perhaps not surprisingly, the Swiss wanted internees to work. Those in Lady Duff's bakery in Berne baked three thousand loaves of bread each day to be despatched to POWs. Switzerland's decision to host internees had more to do with business than neutral goodwill. Britain, Germany, and later the United States and Canada paid the Swiss to house their nationals, who replaced the Germans and other tourists who would normally have filled Swiss hotels. The Swiss interned German POWs in German-speaking parts of the country while British, Canadian and French POWs were housed in French-speaking cantons. To avoid fights in the streets in those cities that housed both German and Allied internees, each group was allowed out on alternate days.

The internees knew that spies operated in both Holland and Switzerland. According to Douglas, "one hardly dare[d] make a new acquaintance [at a café] without first ascertaining the life history of the person in question."[15] At about the same time in Holland, member of Parliament Henri Béland realized when the congenial "Englishman" he had been speaking to asked him what hour he was leaving Rotterdam for England that he was speaking to a spy. Béland did his bit for misinformation by saying, "Exactly one week from to-day at six o'clock a.m."[16]

Unlike Holland, Switzerland did not suffer serious food shortages. Indeed, a few hours after the train took them into Switzerland, Harry Laird and his group of internees were given sandwiches, chocolate and candy, as well as cigarettes, flowers and postcards to write home on. There were, however, concerns that the money they received (£2 10s. or $75 a month) would contribute to excessive drinking.

In Switzerland, the internment camps were under the command of Swiss officers. Laird and Douglas were interned in hotels in Mürren, which was reachable only by a funicular. Laird was especially struck by the dazzling beauty of the glistening white peak of Jungfrau mountain. A Swiss doctor used electrical instruments to determine that the German surgeon had, in fact, reconnected the nerves of Laird's leg successfully. Over the course of Laird's nine months in Switzerland, another physician, using electrical treatments and massage therapy, helped him make an almost total recovery. Laird was repatriated via England to Canada, where he arrived in Halifax a week before the great explosion.

The biggest problem in the Swiss internment camps was boredom. Though Laird warmly recalled the hockey games, especially the contest in which the Canadian squad defeated a local one 5–1, the games were not enough to either take up the soldiers' idle time or replace their esprit de corps. Some mothers and wives arranged to visit. Douglas enjoyed Christmas dinner 1917 in a chalet in the village with an officer and his wife, who had travelled from Sault Ste. Marie, Ontario, to be near him. In early December 1917, internees in Switzerland voted in the "Khaki Election," which means they had a fair knowledge of how Prime Minister Borden had skewed the election toward his government.

The Wartime Election Act (1917) disenfranchised tens of thousands of immigrants who had not been naturalized before 1902, except for those who had a husband, son or grandson serving overseas. It took the vote away from Mennonites and other conscientious objectors. The Act enfranchised wives, widows, mothers and sisters of all (living or dead) soldiers or nursing sisters. Newspapers ran advertisements that made no bones about the purpose of giving votes to women: "If your husband or father is on the firing line, he will have less chance of being killed or injured if we send more men to help them . . . Vote to save your kin."

How much the men voting in Holland or Switzerland knew of the cleavage that Borden's jiggery-pokery caused between English and French Canada is not certain, but the results of the election made it clear. Borden's "Union Government" (which included many former Liberals) had only three members from Quebec, while sixty-two Quebec MPs sat with Laurier in opposition. Supported by the majority of newly enfranchised women, khaki voters and voters outside Quebec (and some traditional Liberal strongholds in the Maritime provinces), Sir Robert claimed a mandate to prosecute the war to the fullest and to implement conscription.

The Canadian papers that arrived in Holland and Switzerland left no doubt as to English Canada's view of the election. From almost Biblical hyperbole, "Monday was the DAY of DAYS," the *Winnipeg Tribune* slipped into crass jingoism, "because it would reveal to the world the real heart and soul of the people of Canada, . . . their reliability as Empire partners . . . their fidelity to a noble cause and their self-respect as component parts of a nation over which the Old Flag [the Union Jack] has flown since the memorable British victory on the Plains of Abraham." The *Vancouver World* quoted one Vancouver MP saying simply: "The Anglo-Saxon rules in Canada."

Even though the Canadians had not been part of the British army since September of 1916, Britain continued to represent the Canadians for the purposes of POW negotiations. Accordingly, in June 1917, Britain and Germany agreed that officers who had been prisoners for more than eighteen months could be interned in Holland. Among those who were quickly interned were Private John Finnimore, who had received kindness on the battlefield at Ypres when his wounded body was lifted into a wheelbarrow, and Lieutenant-Colonel Percy Byng-Hall, who had been captured in the same battle. Internees were fed the same as the Dutch, which meant that by late 1917 they would have gone hungry had they not been able to purchase more food, though even this was a problem because of inflation. By 1918, however, the situation had worsened considerably, prompting an article in the 14 June edition of the *Toronto Daily Star* entitled "Canadians in Holland Starving for Food." The article quoted a corporal as saying, "The grub here is awful. It is not only none too good but by no means enough."[17] Prime Minster Borden might have been an active participant in the Imperial War Cabinet, but in the councils of the Admiralty his voice would have counted for little had he argued to loosen the blockade that included Holland. As well, in fear of creating tensions between the straitened daily Dutch and what could have appeared as flush Canadians, Ottawa did not increase the internees' allowance. Ottawa's reluctance to increase the allowance was of a piece with its decision not to increase Canadian soldiers' pay rates, even though inflation at home had severely cut soldiers' purchasing power.

Lieutenant John Thorn's memoir of his time in Holland mentions rationing and food riots, but not that he went hungry. Indeed, given that food was rationed, it is all the more striking that when Thorn entered Holland on the night of 23 March 1918, he heard cheers at the first Dutch train station and then another rousing reception at Scheveningen, even though it was already 11 p.m. After two weeks, Thorn was allowed to visit Rotterdam, where he stayed in a hotel. He was especially thankful for recent copies of the *British War News*.

Two months after arriving in Holland, Thorn was permitted to move to Amsterdam. There he learned that Dutch opinion leaders worried that if Germany won the war, Holland "would eventually become a state of Germany." The authorities in Amsterdam did not follow the Swiss example of giving German and Allied internees access to the city's streets on alternate days, with the inevitable consequence of uniforms acting "like a red flag to a bull."[18]

After three months of inactivity, Thorn became desperate to return to Canada. His chance came when a commission charged with repatriating those unfit for further service arrived. Though in perfect health, Thorn decided that his slight deafness was becoming worse, so much so, in fact, that it began affecting his entire nervous system. A specialist in Amsterdam agreed that Thorn's growing deafness was due to being gassed at Ypres and that he would soon be completely deaf. The doctor wrote a letter to that effect for Thorn to give to a specialist in nervous diseases; he, in turn, wrote a second letter saying that Thorn was a nervous wreck and needed rest back in Canada. A few days after presenting the letters to the commission, he received a telegram telling him he was to leave the next day for England.

If Thorn expected the elation at returning to Britain in March 1918 to begin once he boarded the hospital ship, he was mistaken. The German soldiers being exchanged from England were "fat and healthy, and their bandages and slings as white as snow." But even their smiles faded when they saw the condition of the men who had been in German prisons. Instead of clean, their clothes "were hanging in tatters . . . They were gaunt and hungry looking." On board ship, Thorn learned that the POWs "had not had a wash for weeks, and that their bodies were covered with vermin."

These men, who had just come from a country that prided itself on its *Kultur*, were wrapped in "bandages were black and green with age." Worse, at "the sight of food their eyes glistened like those of wild animals, and it took the help of all of us to restrain them from eating too much."[19]

11 November to Late December 1918

THE TELEGRAM ANNOUNCING the Armistice, 11 November 1918, changed everything at Chemnitz POW Camp. Shouts of glee followed Canadian and British POWs' singing "God Save the King" or "The Maple Leaf Forever," not rifle butts or kicks. The guards did not even try to enforce the curfew.

In the weeks since the war had ended, Frank Lawson witnessed part of the revolution in Freiburg, heard about the bloody riots in Berlin and learned that hungry mobs had attacked landowners in Hamburg. He found the sight of trains filled with German troops leaving the front deeply satisfying, as he paid a visit to the Freiburger Münster, the city's seven-hundred-year-old cathedral. On 26 November, the freed men boarded a train that took them to Switzerland, where they boarded another that took them through Paris to Calais and then on to Britain. On 6 December, as he walked up the gangplank of the ship that would bring him to Halifax, Lawson carried the wicker basket that Major McKessock had given him so many months earlier, now half-full of food tins, a change of clothes and a few books. He had it with him on Christmas night while on a train bound for Toronto.

As more than sixty thousand German POWs in Britain waited for the negotiations that would establish the regimen for their repatriation and struggled to come to grips with the Reich's defeat and the Kaiser's abdication, a number of Canadians continued to be held in bondage. Three appear to have been shot and killed for refusing to work, while another was beaten. Private John Carsnew, who had been reported killed in action at Mount Sorrel, was at Giessen when the war ended and at least managed to land a few blows in a donnybrook when he and a few other men refused to continue to work in a hat factory. The men at Giessen were released on 27 November.

Others had to wait significantly longer, including Corporal Peter S. Thornton, who had been captured on 2 May 1916 after being wounded by shrapnel in his head, an ear, his chest and his right leg and suffering a smashed jaw. The German who had found the bleeding soldier by the side of the road thought he walked too slowly and shot him in the back; the bullet exited through Thornton's shoulder. At POW camps in Germany and a punishment camp in occupied Poland, he received poor medical care and was beaten numerous times for refusing to work. At a rural *Arbeitskommando* in November 1918, the farmer responded to news of the Armistice by locking Thornton, his wounds still discharging, in a shed until late December.

Harry Howland and the Fannigans learned that the "*Krieg ist kaputt*" three weeks after the Armistice was signed in Compiègne when the train carrying them to Soltau stopped instead at Baden-Etelsen, where there was only one German in charge.[20] Though there were some tensions with the French former POWs, Howland, his comrades and the other British POWs waited patiently for a week or so, helped by the discovery of a piano that provided the accompaniment to choruses of "It's a Long Way to Tipperary" and

"Pack Up Your Troubles," and endless rounds of poker played with depreciated camp scrip. Then, with no sign of their formal liberation in the offing, one Fannigan suggested that since the German guard had only blanks and the border was just forty miles away, they should set out on their own.

It is unclear whether the German caught wind of their plans, but the following morning, a telegram from the Revolutionary Committee in Hamburg arrived saying that they would be moved to Soltau in three days. Three days later, just about the time the 1st and 2nd Canadian Divisions crossed the Rhine as part of the Army of Occupation, Howland and the others were welcomed by many Tommies whom they knew, but they were no closer to liberation than before. Conditions at Soltau, where the huts were overfilled, were actually worse than at Baden-Etelsen. And the Fannigans were not particularly receptive to the political education the now friendly German guards proffered. Howland's mocking of their efforts displayed near perfect pitch: "You will never educate the British working plug to understand his proper position in society, or get him to act with his pals for their mutual benefit. It is a hopeless task, comrade, so forget about it."[21]

Parcels, two for each man, ensured that they were well fed. And the games of Crowns and Anchors, boxing and wrestling matches, and football passed the time. But they were still in a German POW camp. As the cold weather settled in, huts were warmed with boards taken from the latrines, which made attending to natural functions a balancing act. The slow breakdown in discipline meant that garbage piled up, which inevitably attracted rats. Each day saw more men come to the camp. One man brought the tale of three German soldiers who had come to a farm. When they discovered that a British and a Canadian soldier were still being forced to *arbeit*, they called the farmer over and cracked him over the head with his rifle's butt before booting him in the ribs as they said, "That's for making a slave of a prisoner of war."[22]

As Christmas neared, the men in Soltau became more and more anxious. Their mood was hardly improved when a couple of young officers from England arrived. When they saw how lax the military chain of command had become, they were bent on straightening it out. "It's nice of the dear chaps to come and look after us privates! But believe me," said one Fannigan, "they are making a hell of a mistake with all this regimental stuff, sergeant-majors and orderly and a bugle blowing for us to parade. That sort of bunk's too late in the day for most of us, after bucking Fritz for four years." These same sentiments, it is worth noting, were shared by many of the Canadian soldiers who took part in parades in front of senior Canadian command before taking up occupation duties in Germany. When one of the young officers climbed up on a soapbox in Soltau and began lecturing the men on their slovenly demeanour, he was told, "Your job, Percy, is to get us out of here. Go and tell the squareheads that." ("Percy" being an insult for an effete British officer, while "squarehead" had previously been reserved for mettlesome Germans but now was being applied to one of their senior commanders.) "Tell them we will give them twenty-four hours to find a train," yelled a number of men.[23]

Several days passed before a telegram arrived from Hamburg, saying that a boat was ready (it had been delayed by a storm) and a lengthy train with two locomotives chugged into the Soltau train station. Soon it was loaded with some 1,800 men, whose eyes moistened when they saw the Union Jack fluttering from the SS

City of Poona, and whose cheers were silenced by British marines who ordered, "No noise, boys, please! Quietly there! Line up, four deep, that's the way."[24] Howland credited the Royal Navy's knowledge of what could happen to an officious officer on the deck of a ship at night as the reason the sergeant who had lectured them was transported back to Britain on the destroyer and not on the troop ship.

1918 to 1931: Canada

The freed prisoners of war did not wait in Britain and rejoin their battalions, which meant that any who took part in final parades in cities such as Toronto, Winnipeg, Vancouver or Montreal made arrangements on their own. In accordance with regulations, while interviewing POWs about war crimes, officials took note of the situations in which they had been captured. The sheer number of men meant that the single day assigned to process each batch of returned prisoners—during which they were outfitted with new kit, underwent medical examinations and collected their back pay—was rather too full to gather much information about the circumstances of most men's capture. Technically, their pay could not be issued if there were doubts, as there were for a number of men, about whether their capture had resulted from cowardice or neglect. In the end, there were so many POWs that no committee was struck to examine these questions.

Once back in Canada, the former POWs were registered with the Department of Soldiers' Civil Re-establishment, whose policies appeared to have been designed by mandarins who shared Sir Sam's view that soldiers were "bar room loafers." The bureaucrats ignored the fact that since mid-1916, the Canadian army had worked hard developing initiative among the troops, and fixated instead on the fact that soldiers were clothed and fed. As historian Desmond Morton notes, many in Canada felt the "cure for too many years of military discipline and dependence was brisk immersion in the responsibilities of civilian life" and not generous military pensions.[25] The bureaucrats utterly failed to recognize the initiative shown by POWs to survive behind the wire.

While Lloyd George promised (though he did not deliver) "a country fit for heroes to live in," officials along the Rideau worried about the "pension evil" that had bedevilled the United States after the Civil War. Veterans of General Ulysses S. Grant's army had successfully pressed for higher and higher pensions, which by 1914 consumed one-fifth of the federal government's budget. On paper, Canada had the most generous provisions for veterans in the British Empire. A private who merited full pension received $480, about $60 more a year than a farm labourer and about a thousand dollars less than a steamway conductor. Following the "Table of Incapacities," however, most veterans received significantly less. Whatever veterans like Arthur Corker, Thorn, Nathan Rice, Fred McMullen or David O'Brien thought about their niggardly government, in this case the Liberal rump in Parliament agreed with the government. "I would rather trust the manhood of the man," said Sir Wilfrid, "if he comes back sound in limb and body, than depend upon the existence of . . . a paternal government."[26]

Early in the war, responsibility to reintegrate men invalided out of the army or repatriated POWs fell on local governments and NGOs. By 18 November 1915, for example, the job notice "Employ Returned Soldiers" had run dozens of times in the

Winnipeg papers, indicating that despite the best efforts of the local Returned Soldiers' Association, soldiers who had been invalided out of the CEF were having a difficult time finding work in Winnipeg. Chaired by Mayor Richard D. Waugh, the committee charged with helping those who had "Done Their Bit" for the Empire was supported by the city's great and good (one of these contributed a house that could hold eighteen men).[27] It was, however, a complex task, as Waugh discovered when he learned that the city's two controllers refused to rehire a veteran, Mr. J. McKinley. Waugh called them "on the carpet" and publicly stated that the "city must set a good example to other employers."[28] Equally difficult was dealing with regulations that came down from Ottawa in December that prevented the association from supplying "very expensive wooden legs," overcoats and gloves to the men arriving in wintery Winnipeg; this last regulation was quickly rescinded.[29]

By the end of 1915, the newly restyled Military Hospital and Convalescent Commission was up and running. Its mandate was to return wounded soldiers (and returned POWs) to civilian life as quickly as possible. Thus, the commission provided technical education and "wise council" designed to direct men who, for example, had lost an arm and thus could not return to be carpenters, to become cabinet makers.[30] A public relations campaign by the commission that included a poster showing a man with a prosthetic arm operating a drill press drove home the government's message. In convalescent homes, men were taught to embroider, weave baskets and even make needlepoint pictures in order to "combat idleness and revive workplace discipline," thought to have been lost in the army in which kit and three squares a day were provided and men did not have to think for themselves.[31] On

7 December, the day after the government announced that parts of the civil service exam would be waived for veterans, and despite Sir Sam's promise to supply his boys with the best medical care, complaints about the care being given to men invalided out of the army pushed the government to create that most common of Ottawa species: an advisory committee that would interview the men to determine what policy changes were necessary.

* * *

The complicated story of war reparations that involved civilians, soldiers, several Canadian government officials, the British government and the Treaty of Versailles need not be related here. What mattered for 862 former prisoners of war who filed for reparations in 1931 was Commissioner Errol M. McDougall's attitude toward their stories of suffering and his ham-handed emphasis on paperwork. McDougall held hearings across Canada and in the United States where former POWs could state their cases in person (in addition, of course, to their written submissions). McDougall was less than assiduous in adhering to the rules of due process that he would have studied at McGill law school, not to mention learned at the knees of his father and grandfather, as both men were judges. In McDougall's domain, the rules of evidence were "relative," and former prisoners who believed that a doctor's note detailing their disability would have weight found him expecting legal arguments and extensive medical records.[32]

McDougall's decisions can charitably be described as capricious, though not class-based. He rejected the claim of Thomas Scudamore as well as those of McMullen, whom he accused of greatly exaggerating his mistreatment in Germany. Even though John O'Brien presented corroboration that he had been made to stand at attention in front of a red-hot coke oven, McDougall denied his claim because O'Brien had not said anything about this when interviewed in Britain. Furthermore, McDougall wrote, "Great strain is placed upon one's credulity by the statement that he knew the soup they received was made from dogs because they saved the bones and eventually pieced together a small German dachshund."[33] McDougall rejected Edward P. McQuade's claim because the man, who had been captured on the Somme, told his story of being in a shell hole for four days and then of brutal treatment in a hospital in a "humorous vein."[34] Claims of gastrointestinal problems or infirmities caused by malnutrition were denied because Germany as a whole was suffering from food shortages; McDougall ignored the evidence that Germany had systematically refused to abide by the Hague Treaty's requirement that prisoners be fed the same rations a nearby garrisoned troops.

Ottawa's commissioner had a special animus for Harry Howland. No doubt the former Fannigan was a difficult man, but McDougall went further by writing that the "claimant's demeanor before this Commission was truculent and defiant and was not such as to arouse sympathy." Indeed, he almost seems to excuse the Germans by stating that Howland "created the impression that he was not only capable of inciting hostility but did arouse the active enmity of his captors."[35] Surprisingly, McDougall found for Howland, awarding him $500 ($7,500) with interest of 5 percent per year from 1920 until the date of payment. McDougall also found for Private William Lickers, a Mohawk who travelled from Brantford, Ontario, to enlist in the 15th Battalion. The one-time "strong powerful man" was "now a physical wreck" as a result not of the flesh wound suffered at Ypres, but also because he was beaten, knocked down and kicked in the POW camp. Moved by their racial thinking, guards had tied him to a post for four days and hit him over the face and mouth. In the salt mines, he was repeatedly beaten unconsciousness. Lickers, who was already receiving his full private's pension, was awarded $3,000 ($45,000) plus interest. McDougall also awarded $500 with interest to Private Herman Robinson for the privations he suffered working behind the German front in Libau.

On 29 January 1931, the *Winnipeg Tribune* reported that Commissioner McDougall was in town to hear the cases concerning three former privates: Carman L. Jackson, who had been captured in August 1917 and forced to work in a coal mine in Essen, where he was beaten; Walter Dollard, who claimed his health had been damaged by near-starvation rations; and Harold E. Bennett, who argued that his health had been broken by the inadequate medical care he was given after being captured, badly wounded, on 3 June 1917. Neither Winnipeg paper reported that McDougall disallowed each claim.

* * *

WHAT EXPLAINS THE country's lack of interest in war reparation claims? The most obvious explanation—that in 1931 the country was in the grips of the Great Depression and Canadians simply had other concerns—will not suffice. On 17 March 1931, the *Ottawa Journal* detailed payment of $1,700 ($25,600) to an Ottawa policeman for the loss of his wife, who died aboard a torpedoed ship, and several other small payments to individuals. Unfortunately, the paper does not say why McDougall awarded $12,000 ($180,000) to W. G. Barager of Noranda, Quebec. A day later, the *Globe* reported that McDougall had awarded $561,000 to civilian survivors and families of those who died on torpedoed ships, including the *Lusitania*.

The reason Canada showed little interest in reparation has to do with the nation's attention span. After four long years of war and the tumult of reintegrating the veterans, the depression of 1921, the Roaring Twenties and then the onset of the Great Depression, a few hundred war-related claims of abuse were not of any interest to editors or their readers. The men who had been taken off the chessboard of battle but remained men at war were, if not quite a national embarrassment, judged to be something less than the building blocks upon which the mythos of the Victory at Vimy was built.

Acknowledgements

Noted historians Tim Cook and Desmond Morton have steered me away from error. For this I thank them and, of course, take responsibility for any errors that survived their blue pencils. Jim Gifford, my editor, and Tilman Lewis, my copy editor, ground down more than a few blue pencils helping me shape the whole of the foregoing and more than a few sentences, which, like this one, were simply too long; for this, I am grateful. The staff at HarperCollins, including Maria Golikova, and proofreader Allegra Robinson were, as always, a pleasure to work with.

As they did with my other books, Carole Reid and Maggie Arbour-Doucette worked magic in the archives of the Canadian War Museum. Each found files without which this book would be all the poorer.

Andrew Coxhead and Peter Larock, my chairs at Algonquin College, deserve more than my thanks. They, and my dean, Robyn Heaton, not only support my teaching and welcome my ideas, they enjoy watching me toil in the historical grove beyond the fence of where we work. I would also like to thank my former colleagues Lee McCoy and Kurt Esperson-Peters, who spent years listening to me tell them of the latest piece of news from the past that I'd uncovered. Lisa Kawaguchi's door (next to mine) has always been open—for us to chat, to reminisce about when our kids were in school together, and to hear the answer to the question, "How's the book going?"

As well, I would like to thank the Canada Council for its generous travel grant, which allowed me to tour many of the battlefields on which these men were captured.

Endnotes

PROLOGUE

1. *Manitoba Free Press*, 24 April 1915, 1.
2. Though published in the *Globe* on 28 April 1915, 6, this despatch was issued on 27 April.

INTRODUCTION

1. For discussions of Winnipeg before the First World War, see J. Blanchard, *Winnipeg's Great War: A City Comes of Age* (Winnipeg: University of Manitoba Press, 2010); Charles Emmerson, *1913: In Search of the World before the Great War* (New York: PublicAffairs, 2013), 230–52.
2. Charles W. Gordon, *Postscript to Adventure: The Autobiography of Ralph Connor* (New York: Farrar and Rinehart, 1938), 202.
3. Quoted in Michael S. Neiberg, *Dance of the Furies: Europe and the Outbreak of World War I* (Cambridge, MA: Belknap Press of Harvard University Press, 2011), 92.
4. Quoted in ibid., 120.

5. For a discussion of the cant of manliness in pre-war Canada, see Mark Howard Moss, *Manliness and Militarism: Educating Young Boys in Ontario for War* (Don Mills, ON: Oxford University Press, 2001.)
6. This changed in 1931 with the Statute of Westminster, which explains why Canada's official entry into the Second World War required a vote from the Canadian Parliament.
7. Quoted in Gerald William Lingen Nicholson, *Official History of the Canadian Army in the First World War: Canadian Expeditionary Force, 1914–1919, by Colonel G. W. L. Nicholson,* published by authority of the Minister of National Defence (Ottawa: Queen's Printer and Controller of Stationery, 1962), 5.
8. For a discussion of Bourassa's attack on conscription, see Béatrice Richard, "Henri Bourassa and Conscription: Traitor or Saviour?" *Canadian Military Journal*, www.journal.forces.gc.ca.
9. For discussions of how small-town Canada responded to the war, see John Herd Thompson, *The Harvests of War: The Prairie West, 1914–1918* (Toronto: McClelland and Stewart, 1978); Robert Allen Rutherdale, *Hometown Horizons: Local Responses to Canada's Great War* (Vancouver: UBC Press, 2004).
10. For discussions of French Quebecers' response to the war, see Jean-Yves Gravel, *Le Québec et la guerre* (Montréal: Editions Du Boréal Express, 1974).
11. Arthur Grenke, *The German Community in Winnipeg: 1872 to 1919* (New York: AMS Press, 1991), 164.
12. Nellie McClung, told by Mervyn Simmons, *Three Times and Out* (Toronto: Thomas Allan, 1918), Project Gutenberg: Ebook #12880, 4.
13. Jack O'Brien, *Into the Jaws of Death* (New York: Dodd, Mead and Company, 1919), 4.

14. Tim Cook, *No Place to Run: The Canadian Corps and Gas Warfare in the First World War* (Vancouver: UBC Press, 1999), 11.
15. Quoted in J. L. Granatstein, *Canada's Army: Waging War and Keeping the Peace* (Toronto: University of Toronto Press, 2002), 78.
16. Desmond Morton, *When Your Number's Up: The Canadian Soldier in the First World War* (Toronto: Random House of Canada, 1993), 15. In a letter to his wife, Lieutenant John Creelman went on to characterize the mercurial Hughes as a Canadian Baron Munchausen. The reference to the fictional, overly boastful baron who claimed, among other outrageous things, to have ridden a cannonball to the moon, is an interesting marker for how literate some men in the CEF and their wives were.
17. Ibid., 6.
18. Andrew Iarocci, *Shoestring Soldiers: The 1st Canadian Division at War, 1914–1915* (Toronto: University of Toronto Press, 2008), 34.
19. David Carnegie, *The History of Munitions and Supply in Canada, 1914–1918* (London: Longman's, 1925), 127.
20. For a discussion of how Canada financed the war, see J. J. Deutsch, "War Finance and the Canadian Economy, 1914–20," *The Canadian Journal of Economics and Political Science* 6, no. 4 (1940): 525.
21. Quoted in Desmond Morton, *Fight or Pay: Soldiers' Families in the Great War* (Vancouver: UBC Press, 2004), 123, 100.
22. *Vancouver World*, 26 August 1916.
23. *Manitoba Free Press*, 11 April 1917, 4.
24. *Globe*, 26 May 1916, 1.
25. Cook, *No Place to Run*, 42.
26. On 29 December 1915, 1, the *Winnipeg Tribune* reported a "Wave of

Prosperity Is Sweeping over Canada."

27. Ernest Robert Zimmerman, *The Little Reich on Lake Superior: A History of Canadian Internment Camp R* (Calgary: University of Alberta Press, 2015), xxii and 226.
28. Both the militia minister and the prohibitionists would, presumably, have been even more shocked to learn the words of the song "D'ye Ken Sam Hughes" was sung to "D'ye Ken John Peel," which included the words: "D'ye Ken John Peel / Yes, I know him very well / Sleeps with his wife / But he never gets a feel / Sleeps at her side / But he never gets a ride / So he revels in the joys of masturbation."
29. Robert S. Prince, "The Mythology of War: How the Canadian Daily Newspaper Depicted the Great War," master's thesis, University of Toronto, 1998, 423.
30. Carnegie, *The History of Munitions and Supply,* xix.
31. *Manitoba Free Press*, 1 November 1916, 1.
32. *Winnipeg Tribune*, 9 January 1915, 6.
33. Quoted in Blanchard, *Winnipeg's Great War,* 99.
34. For a complete discussion of the politics behind the Conscription Crisis, see J. L. Granatstein, and J. M. Hitsman, *Broken Promises: A History of Conscription in Canada* (Toronto: Oxford University Press, 1977), 5–104.
35. *Winnipeg Tribune*, 31 January 1917, 8.
36. See Martin F. Auger, "On the Brink of Civil War: The Canadian Government and the Suppression of the 1918 Quebec Easter Riots," *Canadian Historical Review* 89, no. 4 (2008): 503–540.
37. War pedagogy was also present in Prussian grade schools. See Carolyn Kay, "War Pedagogy in the German Primary School Classroom during the First World War," *War and Society* 33, no. 1 (2014): 3–11. We will see below that it was also part of Canadian popular culture for children.

38. For discussion of the link between manliness and militarism, see Moss, *Manliness and Militarism.*
39. Frank MacDonald, *The Kaiser's Guest* (Country Life Press, 1918), 103.
40. Quoted in Herbert W. Tustin, *Escaping from the Kaiser* (Barnsley, U.K.: Pen and Sword Books, 2014), 25, 82.
41. George Pearson [and Edward Edwards], *The Escape of a Princess Pat: Being the Full Account of the Capture and Fifteen Months' Imprisonment of Corporal Edward Edwards of the Princess Patricia's Canadian Light Infantry and his Final Escape from Germany into Holland* (New York: George Doran, 1918), 45.

PRELUDE

1. Nathan M. Greenfield, *Baptism of Fire: The Second Battle of Ypres and the Forging of Canada, April 1915* (Toronto: HarperCollins, 2007), 33.
2. Quoted in Jeremy Paxman, *Great Britain's Great War* (Toronto: Penguin Books, 2013), 120.

CHAPTER ONE

1. *Convention (IV) Respecting the Laws and Customs of War on Land and Its Annex: Regulations Concerning the Laws and Customs of War on Land, The Hague, 18 October 1907* [The Hague Treaty]—*Section I: On Belligerents—Chapter ii: Prisoners of War—Regulations: Art. 4,* The Hague, 18 October 1907, International Committee of the Red Cross, www.icri.org.

2. Ernst Jünger, *Storm of Steel*, quoted in Niall Ferguson, *The Pity of War* (New York, NY: Basic Books, 1999), 381.
3. Thomas V. Scudamore, *Lighter Episodes in the Life of a Prisoner of War* (Aldershot, England: Gale and Polden, 1933), 8.
4. John Lewis-Stempel, *The War behind the Wire* (London: Weidenfeld & Nicolson, 2014), 14.
5. Simmons/McClung, *Three Times and Out*, 8; George Scott, "Three Years and Eight Months in a German Prison," Library and Archives Canada, Manuscript Group 30 E. 28, 3.
6. Lt-Col. Peter Anderson, *I, That's Me: Escape from German Prison Camp and Other Adventures* (Ottawa: Bradburn Printers, n.d.), 82.
7. Quoted in Simmons/McClung, *Three Times and Out*, 8.
8. Morton claims he was sixteen. The only John (Jack) Finnimore (9785) to have been captured during the war was a 3rd Battalion private who was just shy of his twenty-fifth birthday. He was wounded so badly that he was interned in Holland in May 1915.
9. Quoted in Simmons/McClung, *Three Times and Out*, 9.
10. Quoted in Greenfield, *Baptism of Fire,* 241.
11. G. Scott, "Three Years and Eight Months," G. 4.
12. J. C. Thorn, *Three Years a Prisoner in Germany: The Story of Major J. C. Thorn, a First Canadian Contingent Officer Who Was Captured at Ypres on April 24th, Relating His Many Attempts to Escape (Once Disguised as a Widow) and Various Camps and Fortresses with Illustrations* (Vancouver: Cowan and Brockhouse, 1919), 1–2.
13. Scudamore, *Lighter Episodes,* 15.
14. Simmons/McClung, *Three Times and Out,* 11.
15. Anderson, *I, That's Me,* 85.
16. Scudamore, *Lighter Episodes,* 17.

17. Harry Howland, "The Dauntless Fannigans," manuscript, Library and Archives Canada, Manuscript Group 30 E 204 1, 104.
18. Arthur Gibbons, *A Guest of the Kaiser: The Plain Story of a Lucky Soldier* (Toronto: J. M. Dent & Sons, 1919), 121.
19. Ibid., 122.
20. Ibid., 123–24.
21. *Manitoba Free Press*, 30 April 1915, 5.
22. Quoted in Philip Jenkins, *The Great and Holy War: How World War I Became a Religious Crusade* (New York: Harper Collins, 2014), 71.
23. British Prime Minister Herbert Asquith, who considered Winnington-Ingram as "an intensely silly bishop," was appalled at his shallow jingoism.
24. G. Scott, "Three Years and Eight Months," 37–38.
25. Paul Fussell, *The Great War and Modern Memory* (Oxford: Oxford UP, 1975), 13.
26. Conn Smythe and Scott Young, *Conn Smythe: If You Can't Beat 'Em in the Alley* (Toronto: McClelland and Stewart, 1981). Smythe was shot down and captured on 14 October 1917. In 1918, he and another prisoner escaped but were recaptured. Smythe was at Schweidnitz POW camp when the war ended.
27. Alexander Watson, *Enduring the Great War: Combat, Morale and Collapse in the German and British Armies, 1914–1918* (Cambridge, UK: Cambridge University Press, 2008), 27.
28. Quoted in Brian K. Feltman, *The Stigma of Surrender: German Prisoners, British Captors, and Manhood in the Great War and Beyond* (Chapel Hill, NC: University of North Carolina Press, 2015), 83.
29. Quoted in Greenfield, *Baptism of Fire,* 213.
30. *Globe,* 8 May 1915, 8.

CHAPTER TWO

1. Edwards/Pearson, *The Escape of a Princess Pat*, 15.
2. Ibid., 35.
3. Frederick George Scott, *The Great War as I Saw It* (Ottawa: CEF Books, 2000), 48.
4. Edwards/Pearson, *The Escape of a Princess Pat*, 35.
5. Ibid., 43.
6. Shakespeare, *Henry V*, Act III, Scene I. King Henry gives this speech to his men immediately before the attack on the French town of Honfleur.
7. Thorn, *Three Years a Prisoner*, 8.
8. Quoted in Ferguson, *The Pity of War*, 366.
9. Edwards/Pearson, *The Escape of a Princess Pat*, 64.
10. Ibid., 73–74.
11. *Globe,* 9 February 1915, 1.
12. Gibbons, *A Guest of the Kaiser*, 129. To disparage his British opponents, Napoleon is reputed to have said "*L'Angleterre est une nation de boutiquiers*."
13. Ibid., 130.
14. Neiberg, *Dance of the Furies,* 127.
15. Greenfield, *Baptism of Fire,* 362.
16. The version Edwards reports is the only one I have seen of three soldiers being crucified.
17. *Vancouver World*, 5 May 1915.
18. *Globe*, 6 May 1915, 2.
19. Quoted in Ian Hugh Maclean Miller, *Our Glory and Our Grief: Torontonians and the Great War* (Toronto: University of Toronto Press, 2002), 47–48.

20. G. Scott, "Three Years and Eight Months," 7.
21. The Hague Treaty.
22. Anderson, *I, That's Me,* 101.
23. The Hague Treaty.
24. Simmons/McClung, *Three Times and Out*, 21.
25. Robert d'Harcourt, *Souvenirs de captivité et d'évasions, 1915–1918* (Paris: Payot, 1922), 229.
26. Simmons/McClung, *Three Times and Out*, 23.
27. *Globe*, 29 July 1915, 5.
28. Edwards/Pearson, *The Escape of a Princess Pat*, 92.
29. Gibbons, *A Guest of the Kaiser,* 141.
30. Ibid.
31. Given the religious makeup of the German army, it is almost certain that this chaplain was a Lutheran and thus did not believe in St. Patrick. Lutheranism was especially closely linked to the *Kaiserreich*. The chaplain's rabid nationalism, it is worth noting, would have mirrored exactly that of most Canadian churchmen.
32. Gibbons, *A Guest of the Kaiser,* 148.
33. *Ottawa Evening Journal*, 4 August 1915, 5.
34. Edwards/Pearson, *The Escape of a Princess Pat*, 91.
35. *Manitoba Free Press*, 28 July 1915, 14.
36. The Hague Treaty.
37. Whether conditions had deteriorated since Mervyn Simmons was in this hospital or Gibbons was in a different hospital hut is unclear.
38. Olivier Razac, *Barbed Wire: A Political History* (New York: New Press, 2002), 89.
39. Quoted in Feltman, *The Stigma of Surrender*, 47.
40. Watson, *Enduring the Great War,* 88.
41. Gibbons, *A Guest of the Kaiser,* 172.

42. J. Harvey Douglas, *Sixteen Months as a Prisoner of War* (New York: George H. Doran Company, 1918), 38.
43. Jonathan Franklin William Vance, *Objects of Concern: Canadian Prisoners of War through the Twentieth Century* (Vancouver: UBC Press, 1994), 30.
44. Sir Andrew McPhail, *Official History of the Canadian Forces in the Great War, 1914–1919: The Medical Services* (Ottawa: F. A. Acland, 1925), 273. Distinguishing mental breakdown due to the stress of battle from the age-old scourge of malingering was difficult, though by mid-1916, when thousands of men broke down during the Battle of the Somme, psychologists and even the army high command had recognized that casualty clearing stations were dealing with a new phenomenon. At the centre of the debate about how to treat "shell shock" was a young Canadian doctor, Lewis Yelland, the son of a Toronto newspaper editor. Despite his evangelical Christian beliefs, Yelland had no compunction against administering electrical current that was of such high voltage as to cause his patients great pain. He had one patient who shook all over and was unable to speak, "strapped in a chair for twenty minutes at a time while strong electricity was applied to his neck and throat." Additionally, Yelland put the lit end of cigarettes on the man's tongue and "hot plates" at the back of his mouth. (Ben Shephard, *A War of Nerves: Soldiers and Psychiatrists in the Twentieth Century* [Cambridge, MA: Harvard UP, 2001], 77.) Yelland's aim was to replace the patient's shattered will with his own. In another case, after bouts of electroshock therapy, when the patient said "Ah," Yelland complimented him. According to Yelland's records, another half-hour of painful current saw the man repeating vowels. More compliments and more current produced (in a total of four hours) a "cure" as the man was

declared to be "re-educated." Yelland's cure rate of 100 percent is questionable. Another Canadian, Dr. Frederick Dillon, claimed that he could return 62 percent of neurasthenic patients to service using a combination of bed rest, hypnosis and "seclusion or fadism," which, as historian Bill Rawling notes, were code words for electroshock therapy. (*Death Thine Enemy* [Ottawa, 2001], 93.) Those patients Dillon could not restore to the line were sent to Granville Hospital in Ramsgate, where they were again subjected to wire brushes, which Lieutenant-Colonel Colin Russel claimed cured 71.4 percent of the men sent to this special Canadian hospital. Interestingly, the only scholarly study of this and the other two Canadian hospitals devoted to psychiatric patients concluded that while electroshock therapy was used for the most difficult patients, much more common were "'spa' treatments like massage and hydrotherapy," which suggests that when filing their reports, Yelland and Dillon were concerned about looking too soft. (Mark Osborne Humphries, "The Treatment of Evacuated War Neuroses Casualties in the Canadian Expeditionary Force, 1914–1919," 2005, theses and dissertations [comprehensive], paper 44, http://scholars.wlu.ca.)
45. Edwards/Pearson, *The Escape of a Princess Pat*, 107.
46. Gibbons, *A Guest of the Kaiser*, 183.
47. Simmons/McClung, *Three Times and Out*, 28.

CHAPTER THREE

1. Anderson, *I, That's Me*, 124.
2. Ibid., 131.
3. Simmons/McClung, *Three Times and Out*, 29.
4. Ibid., 30.

5. Ibid., 31.
6. Anderson, *I, That's Me,* 132.
7. Ibid., 133.
8. Fred Bagnall, *Not Mentioned in Despatches: The Memoir of Fred Bagnall, 14th Battalion, C.E.F. 1914–1917* (Ottawa: CEF Books, 2005), 45.
9. Simmons/McClung, *Three Times and Out*, 33.
10. Ibid., 34.
11. Ibid., 36.
12. Anderson, *I, That's Me,* 141.
13. Simmons/McClung, *Three Times and Out*, 39.
14. Ibid., 40.
15. Watson, *Enduring the Great War,* 82.
16. Quoted in Morton, *When Your Number's Up*, 90.
17. Anderson, *I, That's Me,* 149.
18. For a discussion of the "spy mania" that gripped Canada in the early years of the war and its link to minorities, see Brock Millman, *Polarity, Patriotism, and Dissent in Great War Canada, 1914–1919* (Toronto: University of Toronto Press, 2016), 75–81.
19. For a discussion of German plans for terrorism in Canada, see Martin Kitchen, "The German Invasion of Canada in the First World War," *The International History Review*, VII, no. 2 (May 1989): 175–346.
20. Anderson, *I, That's Me*, 164–65.
21. Edwards/Pearson, *The Escape of a Princess Pat*, 108.
22. Ibid., 109.
23. Simmons/McClung, *Three Times and Out*, 44. A recent study co-authored by the late Nicolas Katzenbach, who served as U.S. attorney general after Robert Kennedy, shows that Simmons's intuition was correct; after only ten days in solitary confinement prisoners

suffered from measurable mental deterioration. (John J. Gibbons and Nicholas de B. Katzenbach, *Confronting Confinement: A Report of The Commission on Safety and Abuse in America's Prisons*, June 2006, www.vera.org.)

24. Simmons/McClung, *Three Times and Out*, 45–46.
25. Ibid., 47.
26. Ibid., 48.
27. Ibid., 49.
28. Edmund King, "'Books are More to Me than Food': British Prisoners as Readers, 1914–1918," *Book History* (2013), 257.
29. According to neuroscientist Raymond Mar of York University, the POWs' descriptions of the act and effect of reading are not romanticized. Drawing on his discovery (using an MRI) that hearing the word "kick" illuminates both the brain's language centre and the part of the brain associated with leg muscles that create a kick, he believes that in "a very real sense, especially given the extreme situation they were in, when prisoners read letters from home, they were transported into a familiar zone created by their minds that was in an emotional sense tied to being 'home.'" (Personal interview with the author and e-mail, 13 April 2013.)
30. Simmons/McClung, *Three Times and Out*, 45.
31. Tustin, *Escaping from the Kaiser*, 39.
32. G. Scott, "Three Years and Eight Months," G. 9.
33. Edwards/Pearson, *The Escape of a Princess Pat*, 83.
34. *Globe*, 22 November 1915, 1.
35. *Winnipeg Tribune*, 9 December 1915, 11.
36. Tustin, *Escaping from the Kaiser*, 65.
37. Watson, *Enduring the Great War*, 26.

CHAPTER FOUR

1. Tustin, *Escaping from the Kaiser,* 8.
2. Scudamore, *Lighter Episodes,* 42–43.
3. Thorn, *Three Years a Prisoner,* 14.
4. Simmons/McClung, *Three Times and Out*, 55.
5. Ibid., 61.
6. Ibid., 65.
7. Ibid., 66.
8. Ibid., 76.
9. Thorn, *Three Years a Prisoner,* 15.
10. Ibid., 17.
11. Howland, "The Dauntless Fannigans," 169.
12. Ibid., 174.
13. Scudamore, *Lighter Episodes,* 45.
14. Michel Foucault, *Discipline & Punish: The Birth of the Prison* (New York: Vintage, 1995), 205–206.
15. Scudamore, *Lighter Episodes,* 51.
16. Ibid.
17. Donald Fraser and Reginald Herbert Roy, *The Journal of Private Fraser: 1914–1918, Canadian Expeditionary Force* (Ottawa: CEF Books, 1998), 113.
18. Quoted in Tim Cook, "The Blind Leading the Blind: The Battle of the St. Eloi Craters," *Canadian Military History* 5, no. 2 (Autumn 1996): 24–36.
19. Estimates vary, but according to one, of the 1.6 million POWs in Germany in 1916, 1.2 million (75%) were working. See John Yarnall, *Barbed Wire Disease: British and German Prisoners of War, 1914–19* (Stroud: History Press, 2011), 136. On 8 August 1916, the *Ottawa*

Journal published a story under the title "German Prisoners of War Work on the Docks in Busy French Ports," which eluded the question of whether unloading such cargo as heavy timbers that were used to shore up trenches violated the Hague Treaty. Instead, the article, which never mentioned the treaty, subtly invoked it by emphasizing how well the POW labourers were being treated by the French Republic. In contrast to the stories of how Canadian, British and French POWs were starved and mistreated, Canadians read that the Germans "are given eight cents a day pocket money, plenty of soap and water and four meals a day" cooked by German chefs. Repatriated POWs told of sleeping on vermin-infested straw on the floor; the French, by contrast, billeted the POWs in Marseilles on an ocean liner. So as not to weaken the Allies' complaint that the Germans were violating the Hague Treaty by using POW labour close to the front (Private Peter R. Herman, who had been captured at Ypres, was at that very moment forced to labour behind the Russian Front near Libau), the article does not mention that Britain and France used German forced labourers near the front. Indeed, on 16 July Lieutenant Colonel Belford, who commanded the Department of Prisoners of War in London, agreed to allow the use of German POWs "on roads in army areas in question and in quarries on lines of communication, as necessity for this work is urgent." (Quoted in Heather Jones, *Violence against Prisoners of War in the First World War: Britain, France, and Germany, 1914–1920* [Cambridge: Cambridge University Press, 2011], 139.)

20. Edward H. Wigney and N. M. Christie, *Guests of the Kaiser: Prisoners-of-War of the Canadian Expeditionary Force, 1915–1918* (Ottawa: CEF Books, 2008), 169.
21. Ibid., 170.

CHAPTER FIVE

1. Quoted in Nicholson, *Official History,* 149.
2. Douglas, *Sixteen Months,* 35, 39.
3. Fred McMullen in Jack Evans and Fred McMullen, *Out of the Jaws of Hunland: The Stories of Corporal Fred McMullen, Sniper, and Private Jack Evans, Bomber, Canadian Soldiers Three Times Captured and Finally Escaped from German Prisoner Camps* (Toronto: William Briggs, 1918), 45–46.
4. Ibid., 49.
5. Douglas, *Sixteen Months,* 42.
6. MacDonald, *The Kaiser's Guest,* 82.
7. McMullen in Evans and McMullen, *Out of the Jaws of Hunland,* 53.
8. Evans in Evans and McMullen, *Out of the Jaws of Hunland*, 28–29.
9. Douglas, *Sixteen Months,* 20.
10. Evans in Evans and McMullen, *Out of the Jaws of Hunland*, 35, 38.
11. Douglas, *Sixteen Months,* 54.
12. Evans in Evans and McMullen, *Out of the Jaws of Hunland*, 40. Coincidentally, three months earlier the Kingston Trades and Labour Council had objected to the fact that some of the German POWs being held at Fort Henry (817 were transferred to Canada from the Caribbean in late 1915) were going to be paid 75 cents a day to work for a contractor refurbishing the fort. The council wanted preference given to Canadian tradesmen.
13. Simmons/McClung, *Three Times and Out*, 81.
14. J. O'Brien, *Into the Jaws of Death*, 35.
15. Ibid., 36.
16. Ibid.

17. Ibid.
18. Ibid., 37.
19. Ibid., 41.
20. David S. O'Brien, Library and Archives Canada, papers, Manuscript Group 30 E 426, 4.
21. Ibid.
22. Donald Harry Laird, *Prisoner 5-1-11: The Memoir of Harry Laird, 4th Canadian Mounted Rifles, Canadian Expeditionary Force, 1915–1918* (Ottawa: CEF Books, 2006), 48.
23. Ibid., 59.
24. McMullen in Evans and McMullen, *Out of the Jaws of Hunland*, 62.
25. Douglas, *Sixteen Months*, 38.
26. Tim Cook, *Shock Troops: Canadians Fighting the Great War, 1917–1918* (Toronto: Viking Canada, 2008), 206.
27. Quoted in Watson, *Enduring the Great War*, 66.
28. Quoted in ibid., 66.
29. S. L. A. Marshall, *Men against Fire: The Problem of Battle Command* (Norman: University of Oklahoma Press, 2000), 44.
30. Morton, *When Your Number's Up*, 215.
31. Laird, *Prisoner 5-1-11*, 65.
32. Ibid., 65–66.
33. Tustin, *Escaping from the Kaiser*, 103.
34. Ibid., 101. (I have inserted "fucking" based on the number of asterisks in Tustin's book and what Tustin tells about Burk's cursing.)
35. Douglas, *Sixteen Months*, 44.
36. Ibid., 45.
37. MacDonald, *The Kaiser's Guest*, 100–101.

CHAPTER SIX

1. MacDonald, *The Kaiser's Guest,* 109.
2. Ibid.
3. Quoted in Neil Hanson, *Escape from Germany: The Greatest POW Break-Out of the First World War* (Toronto: Doubleday, 2011), 136.
4. Thorn, *Three Years a Prisoner,* 24.
5. MacDonald, *The Kaiser's Guest,* 111.
6. Ibid., 118.
7. D. O'Brien, papers, 11.
8. Edwards/Pearson, *The Escape of a Princess Pat*, 165.
9. Simmons/McClung, *Three Times and Out*, 94.
10. Vance, *Objects of Concern,* 45.
11. Douglas, *Sixteen Months,* 49.
12. Edwards/Pearson, *The Escape of a Princess Pat*, 179.
13. Ibid., 180.
14. Ibid., 181.
15. Simmons/McClung, *Three Times and Out*, 97.
16. Ibid, 98.
17. Edwards/Pearson, *The Escape of a Princess Pat*, 185.
18. Ibid., 184–85.
19. Tustin, *Escaping from the Kaiser,* 123.
20. Simmons/McClung, *Three Times and Out*, 101.
21. Tustin, *Escaping from the Kaiser,* 125.
22. Ibid., 125, 128.
23. Ibid., 131–32.
24. Ibid., 133.
25. Ibid., 109.

26. Ibid., 152.
27. Ibid., 155.
28. Ibid.
29. Ibid., 165.
30. Quoted in Jack Sheldon, *German Army on the Somme: 1914–1916* (Barnsley: Pen and Sword, 2005), 292.
31. *Winnipeg Tribune*, 27 September 1916.
32. John Keegan, *The Illustrated Face of Battle: A Study of Agincourt, Waterloo, and the Somme* (New York: Viking, 1989), 50.
33. Quoted in Tim Cook, *At the Sharp End: Canadians Fighting the Great War, 1914–1916* (Toronto: Viking Canada, 2007), 450.
34. Quoted in Bill Rawling, *Surviving Trench Warfare: Technology and the Canadian Corps, 1914–1918* (Toronto: University of Toronto Press, 1992), 73.
35. Quoted in Sheldon, *German Army on the Somme*, 292.
36. Laird, *Prisoner 5-1-11*, 81.
37. Ibid., 86.
38. Ibid., 83.
39. MacDonald, *The Kaiser's Guest*, 131.
40. Ibid., 133.

CHAPTER SEVEN

1. Sheldon, *German Army on the Somme*.
2. *Vancouver Province*, 7 October 1916, 16.
3. Quoted in Sheldon, *German Army on the Somme*, 326.
4. Errol M. McDougall, Commissioner, *Royal Commission for the Investigation of Illegal Warfare Claims and for the Return of Sequestered Property* (Ottawa: King's Printer, 1931), 180.

5. Douglas, *Sixteen Months,* 55.
6. Ibid.
7. D. O'Brien, papers, 13.
8. Laird, *Prisoner 5-1-11,* 97.
9. McMullen in Evans and McMullen, *Out of the Jaws of Hunland,* 102. See also Tim Cook, "The Singing War: Canadian Soldiers' Songs of the Great War," *American Review of Canadian Studies* 39, no. 3 (2009): 224–41.
10. Martin Pegler, *Soldiers' Songs and Slang of the Great War* (Oxford: Osprey Publishing, 2014), 266–67. Famous for the line "Among these dark Satanic Mills," the poem, which is really a hymn to the "holy Lamb of God," contains the martial words, "Bring me my bow of burning gold! . . . Bring me my chariot of fire!" that had great appeal to the men in the trenches and POW camps. During the early days of the Co-operative Commonwealth Federation (CCF), Tommy Douglas ended political rallies by quoting the poem.
11. MacDonald, *The Kaiser's Guest,* 137.
12. Ibid., 139.
13. Thorn, *Three Years a Prisoner,* 34.
14. MacDonald, *The Kaiser's Guest,* 145.
15. Ibid.
16. Sheldon, *German Army on the Somme*, 314.
17. Ibid., 315.
18. Ibid., 316.
19. Ibid., 317.
20. MacDonald, *The Kaiser's Guest,* 155.
21. Ibid., 156–57.
22. Thorn, *Three Years a Prisoner,* 39.
23. Douglas, *Sixteen Months,* 153.

24. Laird, *Prisoner 5-1-11,* 114–15.
25. Evans in Evans and McMullen, *Out of the Jaws of Hunland*, 93.
26. Ibid.
27. Thorn, *Three Years a Prisoner,* 43.
28. Ibid.
29. *Ottawa Evening Journal*, 21 December 1916, 15.
30. MacDonald, *The Kaiser's Guest,* 168.

CHAPTER EIGHT

1. *Globe*, 1 January 1917, 7.
2. *Globe*, 5 January 1917, 5.
3. *Globe*, 1 January 1917, 21.
4. McMullen in Evans and McMullen, *Out of the Jaws of Hunland,* 117. Field Punishment No. 1 was carried out more than 60,000 times during the war.
5. MacDonald, *The Kaiser's Guest,* 178.
6. Ibid., 188.
7. Ibid., 189.
8. Ibid., 190.
9. Ibid., 191.
10. Ibid., 193.
11. Thorn, *Three Years a Prisoner,* 47.
12. Ibid., 51.
13. Evans in Evans and McMullen, *Out of the Jaws of Hunland*, 170.
14. McMullen in Evans and McMullen, *Out of the Jaws of Hunland,* 120.
15. Ibid., 121.
16. *Vancouver World*, 3 March 1917, 5.
17. *Globe,* 5 March 1917, 9.

18. Jones, *Violence against Prisoners of War,* 147.
19. Ibid., 157.
20. *Globe*, 9 March 1917, 1.
21. Howland, "The Dauntless Fannigans," 218–19.
22. For discussions of conditions at Ruhleben, see Israel Cohen, *The Ruhleben Prison Camp: A Record of Nineteen Months' Internment* (New York: Dodd, Mead and Company, 1917); Joseph Powell and Francis Henry Gribble, *The History of Ruhleben: A Record of British Organisation in a Prison Camp in Germany* (London: W. Collins, 1919).
23. Hon. Henri Béland, M.D., M.P., *My Three Years in a German Prison* (Toronto: William Biggs, 1919), 129.
24. McMullen in Evans and McMullen, *Out of the Jaws of Hunland,* 129.

CHAPTER NINE

1. G. Scott, "Three Years and Eight Months," 18.
2. Ibid., 19.
3. *Manitoba Free Press*, 10 April 1917, 1.
4. Cook, *Shock Troops*, 154.
5. *Manitoba Free Press*, 11 April 1917, 8.
6. Ibid. I have seen no other example of such an account.
7. Ibid.
8. Evans in Evans and McMullen, *Out of the Jaws of Hunland,* 173.
9. It should be noted that the POWs may not have seen these shows as being as erotically charged as we do today. The Freudian frisson must be balanced against the fact that in both vaudeville, which would have been familiar to the Canadians, and music hall shows, which would have been familiar to the British, cross-dressing was common. No Canadian wrote of slipping into an erotically charged reverie and

discreetly reaching into his pocket and "spilling his seed," as ministers of the day put it, though of course, human nature tells us that not all soldiers avoided "self-abuse." The POWs maintained a discreet silence about how what they saw in the theatre influenced their sexuality, as they maintained silence on sexuality in general, save for worrying that the Germans were doctoring their rations so as to lower their libidos.

10. MacDonald, *The Kaiser's Guest*, 208–209.
11. Ibid., 211.
12. Ibid., 212.
13. Ibid., 219.
14. McMullen in Evans and McMullen, *Out of the Jaws of Hunland*, 132.
15. Evans in Evans and McMullen, *Out of the Jaws of Hunland*, 178.
16. Ibid., 182.
17. Ibid.
18. D. O'Brien, papers, 59.
19. Ibid., 58.
20. Evans in Evans and McMullen, *Out of the Jaws of Hunland*, 187.
21. G. Scott, "Three Years and Eight Months," 20.
22. Ibid.
23. Evans in Evans and McMullen, *Out of the Jaws of Hunland*, 190.
24. Ibid., 193.
25. McMullen in Evans and McMullen, *Out of the Jaws of Hunland*, 136.

CHAPTER TEN

1. D. O'Brien, papers, 21.
2. McMullen in Evans and McMullen, *Out of the Jaws of Hunland*, 138.
3. J. O'Brien, *Into the Jaws of Death*, 64.

4. Ibid.
5. Ibid., 65.
6. Cook, *Shock Troops*, 186.
7. Fussell, *The Great War,* 123.
8. *Globe*, 28 July 1917, 1.
9. J. O'Brien, *Into the Jaws of Death*, 67.
10. MacDonald, *The Kaiser's Guest*, 237.
11. *Manitoba Free Press*, 13 August 1917, 3.
12. Derek Grout, *Thunder in the Skies: A Canadian Gunner in the Great War* (Toronto: Dundurn, 2015), 273.
13. *Ottawa Journal*, 15 August 1917, 1.
14. Christopher Westhorp, ed., *The Wipers Times: The Famous First World War Trench Newspaper* (London: Conway, 2013), 205.
15. Alec Waugh, *The Prisoners of Mainz* (London: Chapman and Hall, 1919), 53–54.
16. It is worth noting in passing the difference between Waugh's and Lawson's views of reading and the view of another veteran of the Great War. Adolf Hitler said that he read to confirm his thoughts.
17. Frank Lawson, Diary, Canadian War Museum Archives, Textual Records 58A 1 212.3, 7.
18. Walter Fuller appears to have been sent to Limburg POW camp.
19. Howland, "The Dauntless Fannigans," 252–53.
20. Thorn, *Three Years a Prisoner,* 67.
21. Ibid.
22. Ibid., 68.
23. Evans in Evans and McMullen, *Out of the Jaws of Hunland*, 216.
24. Ibid., 217.
25. Ibid., 218.
26. Thorn, *Three Years a Prisoner,* 72.

27. Ibid., 75.
28. For a discussion of Canadian soldiers and baseball, see Andrew Horall, "'Keep-a-Fighting! Play the Game!': Baseball and the Canadian Forces during the First World War," *Canadian Military History* 10, Issue 2 (2001), Article 3.
29. Lawson, Diary, 18
30. Thorn, *Three Years a Prisoner,* 75.
31. Ibid., 77.
32. Ibid., 77, 79.

CHAPTER ELEVEN

1. McMullen in Evans and McMullen, *Out of the Jaws of Hunland,* 143.
2. Ibid., 148–49.
3. Ibid., 151.
4. Ibid., 154.
5. Thorn, *Three Years a Prisoner,* 80.
6. Ibid., 81.
7. McMullen in Evans and McMullen, *Out of the Jaws of Hunland,* 156–57.
8. Ibid., 158.
9. Ibid., 160.
10. Ibid., 160–63.
11. Ibid., 164.
12. Quoted in Gordon L. Heath, *Canadian Churches and the First World War* (Eugene, OR: Pickwick Publications, 2014), 143.
13. Quoted in Cook, *Shock Troops*, 221.
14. Lawson, Diary, 19–22.
15. Ibid., 30.

16. Morton, *When Your Number's Up*, 219–20. After the text of this book had been set, I learned that Sergeant Alldritt, who had been recaptured after each of his four escapes, successfully sent home several coded letters. To signal to his family his intention to escape, he wrote of "Jack Krafchenko from Rupert Street," who had escaped from Winnipeg's Rupert Street police station in 1914. In at least one letter, his code was signaled by what his grandson, Robert Alldritt, calls "subtle shifts in handwriting style (slanting left instead of right)." One paragraph, written in a letter in 1916, contained the hidden message: "Cutting paper come all right packed in Quaker Oats boxes. Send me a good German Automobile Roads of Hannover (sic) and Westphalia map." Because there was no prune factory in downtown Winnipeg, according to Robert Alldritt, one message continues to stymie his family: "By the way there is a prune factory on Hargrove or Carlton Street managed by Billy Findlay who packed a good size box for export. If you will buy some of them and pack them carefully in the next parcel you send me I am sure they will be appreciated when they reach me." (Robert Alldritt, "Hidden Messages and Code Words: Bill Alldritt's Letters as a Prisoner in First World War Germany, http://activehistory.ca.)
17. Jack Sheldon, *The German Army at Passchendaele* (Barnsley, South Yorkshire: Pen & Sword Military, 2007), 295.
18. Ibid.
19. Quoted in Cook, *Shock Troops*, 333.
20. Rawling, *Surviving Trench Warfare*, 153.
21. D. O'Brien, papers, 21.
22. Ibid.
23. Thorn, *Three Years a Prisoner*, 103.

24. G. Scott, "Three Years and Eight Months," 22.
25. Ibid., 23.
26. Ibid.
27. Quoted in *Globe*, 4 January 1918, 2.
28. *Ottawa Evening Journal*, 12 October 1917, 2.
29. Thorn, *Three Years a Prisoner, 108.*
30. Ibid., 111.
31. Howland, "The Dauntless Fannigans," 257.
32. Thorn, *Three Years a Prisoner,* 114.
33. Ibid.

CHAPTER TWELVE

1. *Vancouver World*, 5 January 1918, 7.
2. Lawson, Diary, 50.
3. Thorn, *Three Years a Prisoner,* 119.
4. Letter from British Columbia Archives, in possession of the author.
5. Tim Cook, *Warlords: Borden, Mackenzie King, and Canada's World Wars* (Toronto: Allen Lane, 2012), 137.
6. Thorn, *Three Years a Prisoner,* 125.
7. Ibid., 126.
8. Ibid., 128
9. D. O'Brien, papers, 24.
10. Ibid., 25.
11. Ibid.
12. Béland, *My Three Years in a German Prison,* 197.
13. Ibid., 201.
14. Ibid., 210.

15. D. O'Brien, papers, 26.
16. For a full discussion of German racial theories, see Andrew D. Evans, *Anthropology at War: World War I and the Science of Race in Germany* (Chicago: University of Chicago Press, 2010).
17. D. O'Brien, papers, 28.

CHAPTER THIRTEEN

1. Howland, "The Dauntless Fannigans," 281, 285.
2. Ibid., 287.
3. Quoted in Hanson, *Escape from Germany,* 136.
4. Vance, *Objects of Concern,* 60.
5. "Arthur Corker Describes His Escape," A City Goes to War: Canadian Cities during the Great War, 1914–1918, http://acitygoestowar.ca.
6. G. Scott, "Three Years and Eight Months," 25.
7. Quoted in Cook, *Shock Troops*, 411.
8. Daniel G. Dancocks, *Gallant Canadians: The Story of the Tenth Canadian Infantry Battalion, 1914–1919* (Calgary: Calgary Highlanders Regimental Funds Foundation, 1990), 172.
9. Granatstein, *Canada's Army,* 13.
10. Quoted in Rawling, *Surviving Trench Warfare,* 195–96.
11. F. G. Scott, *The Great War as I Saw It*, 199.
12. *Vancouver World*, 5 September, 1918.
13. Quoted in Cook, *Shock Troops*, 514.
14. D. O'Brien, papers, 29.
15. Ibid., 30.
16. Ibid.

EPILOGUE

1. Desmond Morton, *Silent Battle: Canadian Prisoners of War in Germany, 1914–1919* (Toronto: Key Porter Books, 1992), 123.
2. Edwards/Pearson, *The Escape of a Princess Pat*, 195.
3. Quoted in Tustin, *Escaping from the Kaiser*, 166.
4. Evans in Evans and McMullen, *Out of the Jaws of Hunland*, 219.
5. Ibid., 220.
6. Gibbons, *A Guest of the Kaiser*, 191.
7. Quoted in Tustin, *Escaping from the Kaiser*, 168.
8. Quoted in ibid., 169.
9. MacDonald, *The Kaiser's Guest*, 241.
10. Gibbons, *A Guest of the Kaiser*, 191.
11. Gibbons's numbers seem high and are probably the totals for the various bond drives he took part in.
12. Evans in Evans and McMullen, *Out of the Jaws of Hunland*, 224.
13. Ibid., 226.
14. MacDonald, *The Kaiser's Guest*, 244–45.
15. Douglas, *Sixteen Months*, 70.
16. Béland, *My Three Years in a German Prison*, 260.
17. Quoted in Morton, *Silent Battle*, 131.
18. Thorn, *Three Years a Prisoner*, 143.
19. Ibid., 145.
20. Harry Howland, *The Dauntless Fannigans* (New York: Vantage Press, 1970), 321.
21. Ibid., 329.
22. Ibid., 333.
23. Ibid., 335.
24. Ibid., 337.

25. Morton, *Silent Battle*, 141.

26. Quoted in ibid.

27. *Tribune*, 22 November 1915, 5.

28. *Tribune*, 29 October 1915, 1.

29. *Free Press*, 17 December 1915, 5.

30. Morton and Wright, *Winning the Second Battle*, 17.

31. Ibid., xx and xxiv.

32. Morton, *Silent Battle*, 150.

33. McDougall, *Royal Commission*, 282.

34. Ibid., 181.

35. Ibid., 261.

Photograph Sources

I sourced the photographs in this book from various books in the public domain. The photographs of wounded Canadian receiving medical treatment in the trenches and the four photos of Arthur Gibbons are from Arthur Gibbons' *A Guest of the Kaiser: The Plain Story of a Lucky Soldier*, published by J. M. Dent & Sons, 1919. The photograph of Major Peter Anderson came from Lt-Col. Peter Anderson's *I, That's Me: Escape from a German Prison Camp and Other Adventures*, published by J. M. Dent & Sons, 1919. The photographs of Thomas Bromley, Mervyn Simmons, the officers' quarters where Simmons was held, and the Friedrichsfeld POW camp, as well as the map of Simmons and Bromley's first escape attempt, are from Mervyn Simmons with Nellie McClung's *Three Times and Out*, published by Houghton Mifflin (distributed by Thomas Allen in Canada), 1918. The photographs of Lance Corporal Edward Edwards, the page from Edwards's diary, and the POW cemetery at Celle Lager are from Edward Edwards with George Pearson's *The Escape of a Princess Pat: Being the Full Account of the Capture and Fifteen Months' Imprisonment of Corporal Edwards, of the Princess Patricia's Canadian Light Infantry, and His Final Escape from Germany into Holland*, published by George Doran, 1918. The photographs of Jack Evans, the postcard Evans wrote to his mother, the map showing where Corporal Fred McMullen was apprehended, and the class picture of four escaped POWs are from Jack McMullen and Fred McMullen's *Out of the Jaws of Hunland: The Stories of Corporal Fred McMullen, Sniper, and Private Jack Evans, Bomber, Canadian Soldiers Three Times Captured and Finally Escaped from German Prisoner Camps*, published by William Briggs, 1918. The photographs of Private Frank MacDonald, Lance Corporal Jack O'Brien, the play put on at a POW camp, and the postcards from Friedrichsfeld POW camp are from Frank MacDonald's *The Kaiser's Guest*, published by Country Life Press, 1918.

Index

C

Y

Z